THE ANGEL MAKERS

THE ANGEL MAKERS

Arsenic, a Midwife, and Modern
History's Most Astonishing Murder Ring

PATTI McCRACKEN

WM

WILLIAM MORROW
An Imprint of HarperCollins*Publishers*

HarperCollins books may be purchased for educational, business, or sales promotional use. For information, please email the Special Markets Department at SPsales@harpercollins.com.

FIRST EDITION

Designed by Bonni Leon-Berman
Photos on pages x and xi from the collection of Attila Tokai

Library of Congress Cataloging-in-Publication Data has been applied for.

ISBN 978-0-06-327503-4

23 24 25 26 27 LBC 5 4 3 2 1

In memory of my father, J. Everett McCracken

CONTENTS

AUTHOR'S NOTE

Most first names have been anglicized, and some surnames have been, as well. Some first names have been changed for clarity, as many of the people portrayed had the same name. Some street names have also been anglicized. The names of historical and political figures who do not figure prominently have been left in their original Hungarian form.

This is a true story. All events happened as recorded here, or as I believe them to have happened, based on years of research, interviews, trial transcripts, and piecing together the volumes of archival data.

However, to fill in gaps, I have had to imagine or assume certain scenarios. I've done this with deep respect for the integrity of this case.

Any dialogue in quotes was taken directly from archival materials.

Kis Hírlap, a Budapest newspaper, ran a photo spread of the investigation. From top left: Curious onlookers, who flocked in from other Plains villages, peer into the graveyard caretaker's hut in Nagyrév to watch an autopsy being performed; prosecuting attorney John Kronberg; portrait of Auntie Suzy, date unknown; gendarmes in the graveyard; Auntie Suzy's pantry; gendarmes round up suspects in Nagyrév.

The family of M. W. "Mike" Fodor and Elizabeth de Pünkösti owned the *Pesti Napló* newspaper in Budapest, which ran this photo spread of what came to be known as "The Arsenic Trials." The women exercise in the prison yard while guards keep watch.

If your husband has you seething

Belladonna you must feed him

Add some pepper, make it pleasing

He'll be laid out by the evening.

—*lyrics to a Hungarian folk song*

Nagyrév lies in an angle formed by the bending of the Tisza River, therefore in a little valley about fourteen miles square. It looks a quaint, Old World village where it sprawls by the river side, its low white cottages encircled by gardens. It is twenty-five miles from the nearest railway station.

Budapest, which is puzzled and shamed by the discovery of this plague spot in the midst of a smiling countryside not sixty miles from its own doors, has sent many newspapermen and other investigators to discover the conditions which produced it. They found [a village] inhabited by poor farmers, dependent for existence on farms and vineyards already small and ever newly divided as sons succeeded fathers; the whole ringed round as by an iron girdle with huge estates. Growth has been impossible, young people have been denied both land and opportunity, and by the same vicious process children have been transformed from a blessing into a curse. . . . But this field which culture had allowed to lie fallow proved fruitful for [Auntie Suzy].

The name [Nagyrév] has spread through the whole world. The notoriety has made all Hungary uncomfortable. It has been bad propaganda abroad. It has been a shock at home to find, within sixty miles of the capital, a neighborhood which might better belong to the darkest period of the Middle Ages.

It makes a strange tale in 1930.

—JOHN "JACK" MACCORMAC,
VIENNA BUREAU CHIEF, *NEW YORK TIMES*, MARCH 1930

PART I:

THE MURDERS 1916–1925

TWO GRAVES AND
A GIRL TO MARRY

The boldness and utter callousness with which they carried on
their criminal activities seems to have been equaled only by the
stupidity of the men who were their victims, the husbands and
fathers who saw friend after friend die in the same sudden agonies
without ever divining a secret which seems to have been known
or suspected by nearly every woman in [Nagyrév].

—JACK MACCORMAC, *NEW YORK TIMES*

Wednesday, August 16, 1916

Anna Cser lay on the floor of her living room.

Her back was red and crawling with an itch. She had been lying for hours on the sackcloth the midwife had laid out for her, and the burlap had left a platoon of faint crosshatches imprinted on her skin. Maddening bits of the flax were clinging to her. She was cloaked in a thick hide of summer sweat, and all the impossible bits of filth she had failed to clean from the room had floated to her, freckling her with speckles of dirt and dust.

Her stringy brown hair hung wet around her neck and shoulders. She took quick swipes at her forehead to push the strands from her brow, but they soon found their place again and plunked big stinging droplets of sweat into her eyes, which rolled down her face as tears.

Anna gasped. She gripped the sackcloth with both hands and pulled herself up on her haunches. Pain ripped through her. She could hear herself shrieking at it, and she could hear the midwife shouting hoarse instructions over her.

She guided a breath up slowly, carefully, around the edges of the pain, and concentrated hard on the midwife's words. She had done this before, Anna reminded herself, and she could do it again.

She soon felt the midwife's hands on her belly. Auntie Suzy had placed a warm, wet cloth across her abdomen, and now pressed it to her gently. A faint smell of cooking oil rose off the compress, part of an elixir that the midwife used to soothe muscles.

The pain slowly dissolved. Anna lay back breathless on the sackcloth. Her legs shook with exhaustion. The palms of her hands burned where she had clenched the burlap too tightly.

Anna was small for a Plains woman. Had she been beautiful, others might have viewed her as petite, but Anna was all knobby bones and reedy muscles, a haphazard geometry of hard angles that had her moving through the world as if bumping into it.

Her skin was nearly translucent. Her thin blue veins were like stained glass, as she had not a lick of fat on her. She was as spindly and rawboned now as she'd always been, except for her pregnant belly.

Auntie Suzy had been with Anna for most of the afternoon. She circled around her, padding heavily in bare feet across the cool, earthen floor. She had left her boots on the porch when she had arrived earlier in the day with Anna's husband, Lewis, whom she had not seen since. She wondered and worried where he had gone.

Auntie Suzy wore, as ever, a black dress with an apron fastened over it. In her apron pockets, she kept her essentials. One held her corncob pipe and a small pouch of her favorite tobacco, along with a case of striking matches. In the other was a glass vial filled with her solution, capped with a wooden stopper and concealed in white paper.

She considered her solution one of her greatest magics.

The midwife ferreted in her pocket and withdrew her pipe. She lit it and took a long, studied draw as she considered the possibilities. Lewis never went far. She thought he could be in the shed, or perhaps he was still at the bar. The midwife exhaled a small, ghostly cloud of white smoke, which curled out of her mouth and hung briefly in the air in front of her before dissolving. Where was Lewis? That was the question.

The living room depressed Auntie Suzy. It was small and the ceiling was so low she could nearly touch it with her chubby hand. The walls were bare, except for a few Catholic icons fitted inside homemade frames. They hung loosely from pegs with the rough twine Anna had taken from the shed. The Catholics were an unenviable lot in Nagyrév, the midwife thought, the poorest of the poor, and landless, like Anna.

A battered credenza leaned crookedly against the far wall. A ragged towel hung from a peg, as did a calendar, given out free by the village council. There was a mishmash of items arranged on the floor and table: an old wooden pail that Anna used to fetch water from the well, a step stool, a few bowls, some of them cracked and chipped, and a paraffin lamp, for which Anna never seemed to have oil. There was a single wooden bench to sit on—nothing more. In the evening, Anna slept in the room with the children on straw mats they rolled out. Sometimes Lewis came in from the bar and passed out there, filling the room with his rasping snores.

It was a room filled with poverty's clutter, a heartbreaking mix of threadbare essentials scattered among the few tattered keepsakes of an unfulfilled life. Auntie Suzy felt cheated by it. Everything together had about as much value as the dirt she swept from her own walkway, but Auntie Suzy was also unnerved by the sight, as it brought to mind her own scarcity and hardship of long ago, which she hated to think of.

A door led to the kitchen, the only other room in the house. It was without a latch. Nagyrév was a village of doors without latches or locks. Normally, this suited Auntie Suzy quite well, but not this day.

She cast her eye on the door now. It was marred with scrapes and deep gashes and looked to her as if it had been salvaged from an even more decrepit house. It hung crooked in the frame, with weak slivers of light passing through the uneven seams into the living room.

Throughout the afternoon, Auntie Suzy had wandered to the window to stare out onto the hodgepodge of whitewashed cottages. They were laid as randomly as fallen twigs on a forest floor. The houses were tiny, most had no more than four rooms, the rest only two, and they were packed tightly on narrow side streets. The village was a spaghetti of dirt roads and paths strewn with such homes. The midwife could see the old Plains proverb was true, that a peasant built a house wherever a brick happened to fall out of his cart.

Auntie Suzy took another slow draw from her pipe, keeping her gaze at the window. She could see Anna's toddler daughter. Anna had fashioned a doll for her out of corn husks and twine. The little girl often liked to play with it on the thin patch of grass out front by the ditch, but the midwife could see her now in the small yard, plopped down right among the chickens.

The midwife had also seen Anna's son coming and going from the yard. He had earlier ambled out of the gate with a long, hardy stick and a wooden bucket. He was six and a half years old and had spent much of the summer down by the Tisza, fishing with his homemade rod and reel. But he was back now, tasked with keeping an eye on his little sister.

Even with the door closed, Auntie Suzy could hear chairs and benches scraping across the barroom floor. The pub was attached like a third arm to the Csers' tiny cottage, and Auntie Suzy listened to the timbre of voices rise and fall as the pub began to fill again with its afternoon crowd.

A loud racket jolted the midwife from her reverie. She turned toward the door. She could see the door handle jerking up and down.

There was no way for Auntie Suzy to bar the door shut. The bench was too short to jam under the handle and she could find nothing else in her sparse surroundings that would do the trick. The room had become a trap.

What the midwife had been dreading all morning was happening.

The door was flung open wide. It banged against the wall and ricocheted back.

The afternoon sun blazed in from the kitchen. For a moment, Auntie

Suzy could see only Lewis's hulking silhouette in the doorway, but his odor announced him best. He reeked of brandy and urine, and of the stale tobacco odor that clung to his shirt and trousers. That these same clothes had hung on him for days made him a devil's bouquet of fetor.

Beads of perspiration pimpled his face and neck. Lewis was as filthy as the mongrels that roamed the village streets, and nearly as flea ridden. His weekly bath in the oak tub outside had little effect, since he rarely could focus well enough or long enough to soap up properly. Layers of dirt and grime had lodged deep in his skin, providing shelter for the bloodsucking lice that nestled there.

Lewis was even drunker now than when he had awoken that morning. Most men in the village enjoyed their first nip of brandy after breakfast, possibly as late as lunch, but everyone knew Lewis liked to take a long guzzle before the first light of day reached his eyes. The brandy was a local blend of fermented plum and beetroot (and sometimes apricots and potatoes that had gone bad), but when that couldn't be had, he reached for the wine, of which there was always plenty.

Lewis lurched toward his wife. His legs seemed foreign to him, as stiff and heavy as oak logs. He jockeyed them with great effort. Each clumsy, thundering footfall abetted his fury. By the time he landed his dirty boots on the burlap, he was a boiling pot of rage. He pitched forward over Anna, grasping at the air to steady himself. He blew the stench of alcohol and rotting teeth into her face.

"Stupid woman," he shouted, scowling.

He closed his lips into a pucker. His face grew a look of deep concentration as he corralled all of his attention to the task of working up a large wad of saliva inside his sour mouth. He threw his head forward and spat the wad onto his wife.

"If you weren't such a stupid bitch, you wouldn't get pregnant every year."

Anna had squeezed her eyes shut when Lewis had burst into the room. She closed them tighter now. The rough fibers of the burlap sack cut into her palms as she gripped it. A contraction that had begun had withered, and now moved through her as nausea. She didn't dare sneak a breath.

Lewis drew back his leg to kick her. He grasped again at the air, but it gave him nothing. He flailed. His arms spun like cart wheels as he tried to relocate his center of gravity. Finally, he reeled backward, as if punched by some unseen attacker.

Auntie Suzy seized her chance. Her bare feet smacked on the floor as she charged toward him, her skirt rustling in the grip of her fat thighs. She thrust her arms out as she lunged at Lewis with all of her weight. Her pipe flew from her hands. Feeling the grunge of his sweat-soaked shirt on her palms, she shoved him as hard as she had ever shoved anyone. The old midwife was hardly a match for a man of Lewis's size, yet she felt him slacken. She grunted as she heaved him back across the room and through the door, where he fell back into the brightness of the kitchen. He made a tremendous clatter as he collided with the table.

The midwife slammed the door shut. She pressed her body against it as the barricade she had so badly needed moments before.

Earlier in the day, when Lewis had been less inebriated, he had managed to fetch the midwife from her house to come deliver his wife's baby. Auntie Suzy didn't live far from the Csers. She was just up the road at 1 Orphan Street.

Her house was one of the nicest in Nagyrév. It was situated on an ample lot and her high wooden fence largely hid her prized garden from view. In the spring and summer, she tended a magnificent array of flowers, which blanketed the yard like a patchwork quilt.

Auntie Suzy normally kept a small fire going in a pit in the yard no matter what the weather, and it was there that her favorite old dog liked to bed down for the night.

She had lived there for more than fifteen years. The village council had given her the home when she was appointed the official village midwife. She also received a healthy salary, though she could still exact fees from her patients when she wanted to. Her agreement with the council forbade her from charging the poorest among the populace, but Auntie Suzy always found a way to be comfortably reimbursed.

Her duties were wide ranging, as she was also the de facto village doctor. The real physician was based in Cibakháza, a five-mile journey that took an hour and a half on the jutted, wagon-track roads. Old Dr. Szegedy had an examining room in Nagyrév, and he came every Tuesday, providing the roads weren't washed out or frozen over— which they were about half the year. As a result, it was Auntie Suzy the villagers relied on day to day.

In the pantry off her kitchen, she had a supply of glass vials filled with her solution, and a larger stockpile secreted elsewhere.

She brewed up batches regularly. She would pour a quart of distilled vinegar into a ceramic pot and heat it on the stove, or over the firepit in her yard. She kept the fire burning low, and once the vinegar was sufficiently warm, she tossed in several sheets of hexagon-shaped "million-fly" flypaper, which she bought in large bundles from Feldmayr's General Store on Árpád Street. The shop was not far from the Cser tavern.

The vinegar evaporated slowly. It was a painstaking process that took several hours, but when it was finished, a concentrated solution of "white arsenic" lay liquid in the bottom of her pot. The midwife carefully poured it into the vials. The fluid had a milky color from the glue extract in the flypaper. The toxin itself was colorless, odorless, nearly undetectable. Auntie Suzy liked to say that "not even a hundred doctors could notice" the presence of her deadly elixir in the bodies of the villagers who fell victim to her deeds.

ANNA LIFTED HERSELF again from the burlap sack and squatted once more on her haunches. Her knees now smarted from the pressure, and her scrawny legs once again shook with fatigue. A stream of sweat raced down her back and another trickle snaked a crooked path down her chest between her two small breasts.

More than an hour had passed since Lewis had bolted into the room. The harsh smell of old urine and his horrid breath had continued to waft over Anna even after he had gone. Only when it had disappeared did she begin to unknot.

Another contraction came. She drew a full breath and bore down hard. She bared her teeth. She clenched so hard she felt a sharp pain cut through her jaw. Her eyes had begun to burn with tears. She let forth an immense and prolonged grunt that rolled from her as if down from a mountain. The sound seemed monstrous to her.

Auntie Suzy was kneeling in front of Anna. She had cinched her dress up and her bare knees pressed into the floor. Her hands were flat against it and she could feel the coolness rise up through her hot palms. As the day had turned to dusk, the light in the room had grown dim. She drew her hand lantern closer to her and picked up the small mirror she had at her side. She drove her head low to the ground and held the mirror under Anna. In its reflection, the midwife could already see the crown of the baby's head, shiny tufts of matted brown hair, all in whorls. The baby was positioned on its side.

The midwife knew it wouldn't be long now.

Anna drew in another breath and with a loud groan pushed down hard again. Auntie Suzy watched through her mirror as the infant's head receded and came forth again, this time revealing more of itself.

Another mighty grunt and another long push, and the infant's head emerged. The wet tousle of hair was framed by the rims of the baby's tiny ears.

Slowly, the infant shifted its head to the left, followed by the whole of its body in the same direction. The baby was now positioned on its other side.

Another great push and the shoulders were born. Auntie Suzy bent down as close as she could get. She held her hands out, palms up.

Anna rested, panting. She gulped at the air, as if trying to drink it. She bellowed and gave another prolonged and powerful shove, until the baby came slithering all the way out, like a snake from its skin, and slipped swiftly into the hands of the midwife. The small room filled with the musky aroma of the newborn.

Auntie Suzy cradled the baby with one hand, tenderly gripping the belly. With her other hand, she gently rubbed the baby's back, cueing the infant to breathe. One tiny gulp filled its lungs with village air.

Auntie Suzy laid the baby girl on Anna's belly, where she began to squirm toward her mother's breast. She opened her rosebud lips and shaped her mouth into a tiny O, anticipating the nipple and nourishment. Anna cupped her infant, pulling her closer. The baby latched on and Anna could see the depressions in her little cheeks as she worked to suckle milk. When none came, she sucked harder, then harder still. She scrunched up her tiny forehead, the mound of wrinkles turning into little seams of determination. When it became clear there was nothing for her, that the well of her mother's bosom was dry, the baby unlatched from Anna's breast and exhaled angry cries of hunger and contempt.

This wasn't the first time Anna had let down one of her babies. Had she lived in Szolnok, she could have gotten milk from the free nursing market, but Nagyrév had no such program in place for mothers. She had prayed it would be different this time. She had watched and waited for her breasts to become engorged with milk. When they had not, she had felt nothing but the fear of this moment. She looked at her baby, who was as red as a cherry and shuddering with rage.

Plainly and impassively came the midwife's words.

"Do you want me to do something about the baby?"

ORPHAN STREET WAS near a forest, where at night the reed wolves could be heard, and where at times nightingales courted mates, their melodies drifting out onto the quiet Nagyrév lanes. On this night, the evening air had been blessed with a breeze. The moon was nearly full, lighting Petra Joljart's way in the dark.

She stepped through the fence gate. She lifted up her long dress and crossed over the ditch. A host of fireflies flickered their lights on and off all around her. The air was still, and she stopped for a moment to listen. Even this far out from the house, she could hear her husband. She reached back across the ditch to close the gate, then moved along in the scruffy grass and let herself into the gate next door at Auntie Suzy's house.

She saw the glow of a lamp burning inside the midwife's home. She walked up the trim path to the door and passed by the firepit, where the dog was sleeping. At the porch, she rapped at the window. She couldn't peer in, as the midwife always kept her curtains drawn.

Auntie Suzy's daughter was at home. Mari was a few years older than Petra and married with two young children. Mari's young family shared the house with the midwife, "lived off the same bread," as people in the village liked to say, and the midwife was quite content with the arrangement. Auntie Suzy was happiest when her family was near. In fact, one of her greatest fears, next to poverty, was that her children would leave her. She did everything in her power to ensure that would not happen. Her husband, on the other hand, was another matter. Auntie Suzy had married what the Romany called a *gadjo*, a white person, a non-Romany, who had left the home years earlier and never returned. This fact had bothered the midwife not at all.

Mari was Auntie Suzy's eldest, followed by her two sons. The older of her sons was married and the younger was divorced. The midwife had made it well known in the village that this was a position to fill.

Petra had lived next door to Auntie Suzy for two years, in the home of Mr. and Mrs. Ambrusz, her husband's grandparents. Petra and her newborn baby had moved in with the elderly couple when the Great War had broken out and her husband had been called to fight. Stephen had spent five months on the battlefield before the Russians had stormed his trench, throwing grenades. He had lost one eye in the attack, was blinded in the other, and was taken prisoner for half a year before being released back to Hungary.

It was her husband's suffering that brought Petra to her neighbor's house on this evening. Stephen had been racked with illness for months, but it was his relentless insomnia that pushed him to the brink of madness. Petra hoped the midwife could give her something to calm him.

She rapped again at the window. She looked down at her wooden shoes, all wet with dew. A few blades of grass clung to the heel. Petra looked over at the dog. She watched his chest rise and fall with the steady rhythm of a clock. She rapped at the window again. Another breeze blew past, rustling the leaves and creaking the limbs of the older trees. She could still hear Stephen's shouting, even from the midwife's porch.

The curtain suddenly peeled back and Petra saw Mari in the window, lit from behind by a lantern, which hung over the table. She watched as Mari shook her head *no* and pointed to the sign near the front gate. The handcrafted sign painted with the image of a baby had been unhooked from its post and lay on the ground, a signal that the midwife was out on duty. Petra had missed it when she came in. She turned and walked back down the path, careful not to disturb the hound from his sleep.

THE BABY GAVE up trying to suckle. She curled her toes and pulled her tiny hands into fists. She arched her back with fury. Anna pulled her closer, but the little one could not be comforted. She filled the room with fraught, piercing screams.

Anna looked down at the curls that adorned her newborn's head. Her babies always had beautiful locks, which she loved to stroke. The infant looked so much like her two other children—it was as if she were holding one of them again, and in this moment she realized that no matter how hard her baby tried, she would never be able to extract a drop of milk from her mother's empty bosom.

The answer to the midwife's pointed question came to her.

"I don't care," she said.

Anna lay back on the sackcloth, while Auntie Suzy busied herself. The midwife waddled to the kitchen and found a sugar cube and a *findzsa*, a small cup the villagers used to drink their strong Turkish-style coffee. Auntie Suzy poured in a bit of water from a standing pitcher she found on the table. She plopped in the cube of sugar, then reached into her apron pocket and pulled out her glass vial. She pulled away the white paper and plucked the wooden stopper from the vial. She dropped a tiny amount of the potion into a teaspoon and mixed it in with the sugar water. She padded back into the living room. Auntie Suzy dunked her finger into the mixture and swirled it around, then lifted her finger out and dabbed the potion onto the newborn's tongue and lips.

THE NIGHT WATCHMAN strolled up Orphan Street. His dark, musty cape was draped across his bony shoulders, hiding both the bread and the flask he kept secreted underneath. His duty lasted from sundown to sunup, and he walked the jumble of side streets sometimes three or four times before his shift was over.

He ambled past the midwife's house. It was dark at this hour, but lanterns burned in the house next door. The windows had been pulled shut against the cool night air of the Plains, but he could still hear all the ruckus coming from old Mr. Ambrusz's house. Such a racket was usually cause for a watchman to let himself into the home and investigate, but he knew about the troubles the old couple had been having with their grandson since Stephen Joljart had returned from the front. The tragedy was on the lips of nearly every villager. The watchman kept walking.

Inside the house, Stephen lay in his bed. His head was a mottle of confusion. Not a clear thought had entered in nearly a year. He often went three, four, five days without sleep, and his only defense against the insomnia was rage. He polluted the bedroom with expletives. He told his wife to go to hell. He told his grandparents the same thing. His tongue was a venomous serpent that only uncoiled to hiss a curse of damnation at everyone.

His tirades lasted for hours. It was a nightly spout of hate and anguish fueled by a cocktail of exhaustion, pain, panic, and self-pity.

Petra and the grandparents had tried to set a schedule among themselves that would allow them to sleep—or at least rest—in shifts, but there was nowhere in the house Petra could go without the tumult finding her. She had tried taking her daughter outside for the two of them to sleep in the stable, as Mr. Ambrusz often did anyway. It was the habit of farmers to treat the stable like a private sanctum. Yet even out there, the noise still found them, just as it had found the watchman.

Stephen's outbursts were punctuated by periods of determined silence, when he tried to force sleep to come. He laid a trap for it by being very still. If he did not move at all, he thought, the portal to unconsciousness would appear and he could slip through to the other side. Yet, it was never long before a theater of images paraded into view, grotesque and disturbing faces and sounds that leered and mocked him—the product of a dream-starved brain. He was sure he was going mad.

On the nightstand next to Stephen's bed was a pair of wire-rimmed glasses. Stiff, black canvas had been expertly fastened under the lenses. The spectacles had been issued months earlier by the Hospital for the Blind in Budapest, where he had been fitted with a glass eye. Stephen had also been blinded in the eye that remained and had spent much of the past year there, or at the Zita Hospital, which was also in Budapest. He went to the Hospital for the Blind to learn new skills so he could still work. He learned to make brooms and weave baskets. But at Zita the doctors were trying to treat his many ills, which ranged from lung infections to severe intestinal pain. The country's hospitals had rooms full of young war vets like Stephen, but because of the Blockade of Europe, medical supplies had dried up. There were no sheets for the beds, no medicine for the sick, no bandages for the wounded. Doctors had to tape paper over wounds and hope that would be enough to guard against infection.

He had only recently arrived back in Nagyrév, twenty-five years old and broken. He kept telling Petra that he wished he had been shot dead on the battlefield.

Just before 3:00 a.m., Petra padded into the kitchen. She lit the lamp on the table. She climbed the ladder into the open loft above the pantry, grabbed a handful of straw from a basket, and climbed back down. She lifted the latch of the firebox on the stove, tossed in the fistful of straw, and lit it. She placed a pitcher of water on the stove to warm, which Mrs. Ambrusz would use later in the morning for cleaning. Petra went out to the stable to milk the cows. Just before dawn, she would leave for the fields.

The Great War had nearly emptied Nagyrév of its men (although Auntie Suzy's sons had managed to escape conscription). Petra and the other wives had taken over the farmwork and they all joined the four o'clock caravan each morning. A long line of rickety wagons with flickering lamps lit the darkened village. The clank and clatter of jostling tools rattled in the night air. The patter of horse hooves sounded a drumbeat for the replacement farmers exiting the village. They passed by the long line of poplars, which stood arow and erect like dispassionate guardsmen, and trundled out onto the vast openness of the Plains, the silhouettes of sweep poles dotting the horizon as the sun rose over the fields.

THE MIDWIFE TIDIED up before she left Anna's house. She peeled the sackcloth off the floor to take back to her own house to clean. She poured the bit of water still standing in the pitcher onto a cloth and helped Anna bathe. She put Anna's straw sleeping mat back on the floor where the sackcloth had been and laid out the sleeping mats for the children. On her way out, she paid herself. There was scant food in the cupboards, so she scooped up a few kitchen items and deposited them into her baskets—Auntie Suzy almost always carried a basket on each arm—then let herself into the now darkened pub to grab a flask or two of brandy before lighting her lamp and heading home. She could still hear the baby shrieking as she headed up the road.

Anna lay on her mat in the dark, cradling the baby. Her two other children lay near her, struggling to sleep amid the crying. She could bet Lewis was passed out in the shed.

Most mothers she knew didn't sleep on the floor after giving birth. They slept in the *first bed,* a showpiece bed piled high with fluffy eiderdown pillows and quilts, which Anna had always coveted whenever she saw them. Nursing mothers would stay in the bed for six weeks, under a canopy of netting to ward off the "evil eye." But Anna had no such netting, or any bed at all. She had always had to manage with just a straw mat.

The baby, she had decided, would be named Justina. She caressed her now in the dark.

She had not wanted to marry Lewis. She had always felt afraid of him, and whenever she spotted him coming her way she had tried to dodge him. Sometimes she would cross to the other side of the street, or slip into a shop and wait for him to pass. That she didn't shout at him and smack at him like the other women he hunted seemed, to him, an invitation. Anna never felt able to fend off anyone, so when she found herself alone with him, she hadn't known what to do. Suddenly, there was his mouth pressed hard on hers, prying open her lips so his sour tongue could roam around hungrily inside. Before long, he pushed himself against her. He was so heavy on her she felt she couldn't breathe. She only wanted it all to be over with. She floated up out of her body into the clouds, drifted like a balloon into the atmosphere, when she was quite suddenly and violently yanked back by the sharp pain she felt as he plunged into her.

Her first son had been born the following January. For months, Lewis refused to claim the baby as his own. Many women would have gone to the midwife to abort the pregnancy, but Anna, either by faith or fear, let him live.

Lewis had been married when he had impregnated Anna. When his wife fled and there was no one to look after him—nor his pub or his ailing, elderly parents—he decided it was time to marry Anna.

Now her husband was her captor. Some months would go by in which she could barely recall leaving the grounds of the house and pub, except to get pails of water from the well on the square. She dreaded inching her way through the clacking group of *crows,* what Catholics called the Calvinist women, since they always dressed in black. The crows would huddle to gossip there each morning. "Look at her," they would jeer, pointing at any woman they saw whom they knew had more than two children. "She's whelping like a dog."

Anna knew they mocked her, too, and their silent stares each time she approached the well made her nerves shatter even more. She was a broken hummingbird, flitting and skittish, unable to eat more than a nibble, unable to rest more than a minute, and nearly always fighting back tears. She was an easy target for their taunts.

Joy always surprised her, peeking as it did through the cracks in her life. She didn't know pleasure well enough to call it by name. She would find herself suddenly moved by the sight of her son's fingers as he reached out to take a piece of bread from her, or her daughter's winged shoulders, wet and gleaming with soap in the sunlight, or the gentle hollows of their necks. These moments were thin filaments of bliss stitched through the coat of frenzy that seemed always to be fitted around her. When she recognized them, she chided herself for her foolishness and pulled at the threads to break them free.

Thursday, August 17, 1916

By breakfast, the sun was already sweltering. Old Mr. Ambrusz had been at work since dawn, tending the animals, sharpening his tools, tidying his stable. He was too old to go to the fields every day, but he meticulously looked after his grounds and the small number of livestock he kept.

The heat made the job more difficult, but he persisted until midmorning, when he took a break to head over to Auntie Suzy's house. He was hoping for better luck than Petra had the evening before. This time, Auntie Suzy was home. She gathered her baskets and followed the old farmer back over to his place.

The Ambruszes and Auntie Suzy had been neighbors for as long as she had lived there. She and the elderly couple spent many late summer nights on their porch drinking wine and shucking corn. The midwife's sister, Lidia, lived up the street and often joined them, shuffling over before sunset with some brandy.

The midwife had come to Mr. Ambrusz's rescue on the many occasions his back went out, applying special creams and ointments, which she concocted from plant extracts. Sometimes he paid her in cash, which she stashed in a money box she kept walled up behind the stove. She kept most of her money there, but she also had sewn bills into the hems of her petticoats, as well as into the linings of some of her pillowcases. She also had a few jars of cash buried in her yard. As far as old Mr. Ambrusz, she was usually just as eager to arrange a barter for him, although nearly always on her terms. On this day, he had offered her fresh pails of milk, which the midwife gladly accepted.

The Ambrusz living room was plush. Down pillows cushioned the chairs and delicately hand-painted pitchers and bowls brightened the shelves. Many of the finer furnishings had been brought by Petra when she had moved in, and Auntie Suzy couldn't help but admire them all.

Sun splashed brilliantly onto the newly whitewashed walls. Fitted between two windows was a lithograph of a gallant soldier with a tiny ferrotype of Stephen's face affixed to the illustrated body. It had been given to the family as a keepsake to commemorate Stephen's service in the Austro-Hungarian Army. Next to the lithograph was a picture of Kaiser Wilhelm II.

Petra was sitting below the two pictures. Since the crisis with Stephen, she had at times left the fields early to relieve the grandparents. Family members often brought lunch out to the workers, and she would flag one of them down for a ride back to the village.

Auntie Suzy seated herself amid the lavishness. She withdrew her pipe from her apron pocket, careful to avoid the bulk in the other for now.

Clouds of her smoke fogged the air. Her *putsi* hung on a cord around her neck, the Romany gris-gris bag, within which she kept her treasured talismans: an amulet for protection, a twig of rowan for magic and wealth. Her grandmother had taught her how to carve the twig to increase the power. She fingered the putsi now as she listened, attentive and impassive, to Petra open up about her husband's troubles.

Auntie Suzy had always been the kind of woman in whom others confided. She would meet a stranger, perhaps on a ferry or a train, and after giving them one or two insignificant details about herself, they would immediately set to prattling about problems they were having with spouses and bosses and children. Some walked away wondering how it was they had shared secrets with a person they had only just met, while she had revealed so little of herself.

The midwife surveyed Petra as she spoke. The young woman was neither tall nor short, fat nor thin, though she leaned toward heavy, and Auntie Suzy could imagine her becoming plump like herself in a few more years. Auntie Suzy had never considered herself a beauty. She had narrow, deeply inset eyes set too close to her nose, and her thin lips were stitched like a zipper across the two wide planes of her cheeks. She often fashioned her brown, flyaway hair into a tight bun, rather than cover it with a scarf like the other women did.

When she was a girl, she had patted flour on her face to relieve her skin of its dark Romany color. Now all it took was a pinch of her toxic elixir to lighten her complexion.

Petra was attractive enough, the midwife thought. She was also well regarded in the village. She was polite and reserved and had finished five grades of school, as much as the most well-educated men in Nagyrév. Best of all, as far as the midwife was concerned, she came from a wealthy Plains family. Her father owned enviable amounts of land, including the large, well-stocked fishing lakes that surrounded the whole western rim of Nagyrév.

The list of complaints Petra had about Stephen was long, and none of it shocked Auntie Suzy, who had been monitoring the situation awhile. She could remember being drawn to her window by the clatter and squeak of cart wheels as a horse came to a stop in front of the Ambrusz gate one afternoon. With her thick hands she had pulled back her lace curtains to catch sight of Stephen climbing down awkwardly from the cart, guided by his brother. He was coming back from the hospital the first time. The midwife had eyed him ever since.

Petra asked the midwife if she could give her husband something to calm him down.

"I have a way," said Auntie Suzy.

Petra ushered Auntie Suzy back into the bedroom, where Stephen was waiting.

Saturday, August 19, 1916

Justina's skin was blue. Her tiny lips, briefly crimson, were now the color of midnight. For three days she had screamed her siren of ire, but no mews or whimpers had escaped her little moon of a mouth in the last hour. Since the moment of her arrival, she had kept her half-pint body clenched so tight it quivered, as if electrified by indignation. She had knotted her hands into wee balls of red fury and held them to her cheeks like a boxer in retreat. Now in defeat, her body lay drained, and when her hands unfurled, Anna could see the faint lines of the infant's life traced across her palms.

Lewis had made a kind remark about his new daughter when he had met her. He had said that she had the most beautiful brown hair, and Anna could see it was true. Her hair was downy and lay on her head like a snug cap, tousled rows of happy ringlets.

Outside, aromas of dinner drifted on village breezes. Anna heard the tinny chime of the church bells announcing the time.

As the hour moved past six o'clock, Justina's heart stopped beating.

THE MOON LIT the potter's field as if by lamplight, and Auntie Suzy worked by its glow. She squatted on her knees in the wet dirt. She leaned forward and hacked at the ground with a spade, sometimes stopping to pull large clumps away with her bare hands. She had employed Lidia and Mari as lookouts, as her sister and daughter often assisted her, but Auntie Suzy felt confident the task was safe from watchful eyes. The field was nearly a mile from the center of the village, and the caretaker, who lived in an adobe hut on the field, was known to spend most of his summer evenings on the small vineyard he had outside the village.

The women dug until their shovels clanked against the hard surface they were looking for. Auntie Suzy leaned into the shallow hole and brushed away as many worms and as much soil as she could from the grimy wooden planks buried there.

The midwife had kept her ear tuned to alert her to the presence of passersby, but heard no one. Certain they were alone, she reached into one of her wicker baskets and withdrew a tightly wrapped bundle. In her other basket was a freshly made, unsealed wooden casket. It was so small that it looked like it had been made for a doll. The midwife had arranged for it to be made. She placed the bundle inside the casket and hastily nailed it shut.

Each woman grabbed a side of the tiny coffin. They lowered it into the hole until it rested evenly atop the wooden planks. They held their breath against the stink of mold and rotting pine that rose up between the slats, for underneath the rotting plank was another tiny casket, which held the remains of Justina's brother.

The boy had been born three years earlier, premature and "half-alive," according to Anna. She had not had a drop of milk to feed him, either, and had watched as he withered to bone. After three weeks, he went to sleep and never again awoke, which is when Auntie Suzy had come to take him away.

The grounds of the potter's field were fertile with the flesh of Nagyrév's secret babies. Auntie Suzy could look around and see graves marked only by her memory. In the times she had come in the night to dig a new resting place, she had thought of her own secret buried on the grounds. She had named him Henry.

The three women quickly refilled the hole. When they were finished, they stomped on the grave to pat down the dirt.

NEARLY THREE WEEKS had passed since Stephen's family had first called on the midwife for help. After the first treatment, Stephen's insomnia was nearly cured, which Auntie Suzy credited to some tablets she had fed him. But she had continued to treat him, waddling back into his bedroom in her apron and carrying her baskets. There, she worked with him in private.

She had told Petra that the elixir she poured into her husband's water—Stephen kept a small glass of water on his nightstand—was nothing more than stomach drops.

His symptoms had stayed relatively consistent with the ones he had been suffering from his wartime maladies, and that included mostly coughing and diarrhea. The dose Auntie Suzy administered on this particular day, which she believed would be the last, had been much stronger. Had she timed it right, and she was confident she had, by the time Petra got a notion to schedule an appointment with the doctor, it would be too late for Stephen.

As Auntie Suzy stepped out of Mr. Ambrusz's gate, she could hear a tinkling bell and a soft patter of hooves. She stood at the edge of the ditch, clutching the skirt of her dress. She watched as the vehicle approached. It drew nearer to her. It was a stunning, two-horse carriage painted in a dazzling coat of maroon, with a soft black leather hood atop. Both horses appeared well-fed. Their coats glimmered with star-tling health.

The carriage was among the most exquisite she had ever seen. The sight of it made her feel as though she were on the grand boulevards of Budapest, not the dusty, wagon-track village roads filled with broken, rotting carts.

Auntie Suzy usually preferred to walk everywhere she needed to go. Being on foot afforded her the chance to easily step into a home and collect a payment. But when she saw who was driving the carriage, she could not resist the opportunity it presented to her. She raised her fat arm in the air and flagged the driver down.

Lawrence Czaszi saw the midwife waving and pulled on the reins, bringing his horses to a halt. Auntie Suzy hurried to the carriage with her baskets. She yanked on the door and heaved herself up into the back seat and flopped onto the fine brown leather. It sighed with her weight. Lawrence, his wife seated next to him, gave the reins a shake. The horses continued onward.

The roominess inside impressed the midwife. She could envision her whole family fitting in next to her. The fineness of it all made her feel splendid indeed, as if she were suddenly draped in jewels and furs.

Lawrence was Petra's cousin, part of the same rich clan that domi-nated Nagyrév, and Auntie Suzy could not help but imagine the fortu-itous possibilities that were at hand.

She asked Lawrence to bring her to the village square. As they trotted along toward Árpád Street, the couple struck up a conversa-tion with Auntie Suzy. They asked how Stephen was faring.

The poor war vet was sick and getting sicker, the midwife reported. She let out a sad, exasperated sigh, eyeing Lawrence, then his wife.

"Who knows how long he'll be able to hold out?"

Lawrence was surprised to hear this. He had visited Stephen not two weeks earlier and witnessed nothing to suggest his cousin's hus-band was gravely ill.

Seizing the chance to lay some groundwork, Auntie Suzy proceeded.

"I feel sorry for Stephen," she said, "but the real victim is Petra, who has had to take care of him."

The midwife paused while her words sunk in, then pressed on.

"If Stephen dies, I hope you will accept my son as a new member of your extended family. Petra would make a good wife for him."

Lawrence was stunned. He looked over at his wife, as if she had an answer for the midwife's forward and shocking words. But she, too, was speechless. She stared back at her husband, openmouthed.

He returned his gaze to the road.

"Who Petra marries is her decision," he said. "It takes two to make a deal."

Thursday, September 21, 1916

The rain had been coming down in torrents since morning. The wetness in the air had prevented the paint from fully drying on the coffin. In keeping with tradition, the coffin maker had a system, in which he painted the coffins of older folks a dark shade of brown, the coffins of little children white, and those of adolescents and young adults royal blue. It was this hue that now tinted the palms of Stephen's pallbearers.

Petra stood in her sodden yard. Her boots sunk into the wet ground. She pulled her cloak up over her head to shield herself from the pelting rain. She looked into the coffin one last time. She had dressed her husband in his favorite dark gray shirt. She had fixed his black canvas spectacles to his eyes and taken his wool army kepi, now scrubbed clean, and placed it in his left hand. She stepped back as a white cloth was placed over Stephen's face. The casket was promptly nailed shut.

Stephen had stopped breathing just past noon the previous day, and it was the midwife who had been called immediately to assist the family. Since there wasn't a doctor in Nagyrév, Auntie Suzy was always the first person summoned when there was a death in the village. She organized the undertaker, prepared the body for burial, and sent for the bell ringer, who not only announced the death to the village by tolling the church bells, but came to the house to cite an official cause of death, whispered to him by Auntie Suzy.

The pallbearers hoisted the coffin into the Ambruszes' wagon. The driver shook the reins, commanding the horses into a slow gait. A line of mourners trailed behind on foot for the long, wet procession to the graveyard. Petra was at the front. The young widow carried her baby on her hip, trying to avoid the wagon's juddering wheels, which spat thick mud back onto her. She had pulled her daughter's coat up over the child's head to shield her from the worst of the assault.

Auntie Suzy kept an eye on Petra from a few paces back. Nothing was standing in her way now. She would make her move at the funeral. She would pull Petra aside, propose her plan, and before long, the young widow would be her new daughter-in-law. It was all she had been able to think about for the last few weeks, and it thrilled her.

She had not yet considered that Petra would refuse her. Or worse, turn against her.

HOMECOMING

A wise man knows how to be scared when necessary.

—OLD ROMANY SAYING

Wednesday, May 2, 1917

The railcar bench was full of splinters and not too sturdy. Maria knew it could split in two under the right circumstances. A fat man plopping down in the middle, where it sagged. A heavy farmer's crate hoisted upon it. A wild child with a gift for destruction.

When she looked around, she could see the compartment walls were made of the same pinchbeck wood as the bench. They had been painted over with an artist's brush to give the illusion of fine timber, but Maria wasn't fooled. The cracks zigging up from the floorboards gave away the cheap truth, as did the hollow sound the wood made every time her back hammered against it.

She had been jostled about on the train for hours, knocked back and forth like a pebble in a miner's sieve, and she could feel every mile of the journey in her small body. It had settled in her like a virus.

The taste of metal was in her mouth, its inky traces painted on her tongue and on her breath. The taste had been with her since she had arrived at Keleti Rail Station in Budapest that morning.

When she had gotten there, she had not seen any fires burning in the station stoves, despite the dawn chill. The days of endless scuttles of coal were gone. Fuel was not wasted on keeping travelers warm while they waited for their trains. There were far fewer locomotives in use, anyway. Nearly half of them had been taken out of service. Some had been commandeered by the military, but thousands more needed mechanical work and parts, and those trains had just been piled into the rail yard. Many were still operational, but they weren't in service because there wasn't any fuel to run them. But even with fewer trains in service, and fewer fires burning in the station stoves, the air on the platform had still managed to be choked with coal, and Maria had been covered in a fine mist of soot by the time she boarded the train.

Maria had wanted to depart Budapest the previous day. Her old friend Suzy Fazekas, perhaps her only friend, had often reminded her that the first day of May was the true birth of spring and a fortunate day for a new beginning. Maria took Auntie Suzy's magical guidance seriously. The two women had hardly seen one another over the years, except for the odd occasion when the midwife had business to tend to in Budapest, or a cousin to visit there. But Maria still relied heavily on the old Romany witch. She used her like a dowsing rod to uncover invisible clues about her future, or to craft a gambit to get out of a tricky situation in which she happened to find herself. Maria consulted Auntie Suzy for nearly all of her decisions, sending off telegrams for the urgent ones and letters for the less urgent.

Deciding which day would be the most auspicious for this journey back to Nagyrév seemed quite possibly to Maria the most critical choice she had ever had to make. She was filled with excitement about what she imagined lay ahead for her. Yet Maria could feel the loose underpinning of her joy, a foundation that had worn thin, and she knew this was her last chance. She had run out of options. This time, she had to get it right.

But her plans for leaving Budapest on May Day had been foiled. From her apartment window, she had seen the mobs on the streets below. Factories and shops had shut down for International Workers Day, and the city had been overrun with protesters. They were mothers, laborers, militants, and returned prisoners of war who shouted Marxist slogans the POWs had learned from their Russian captors in Moscow. The protesters demanded everything from more bread in the markets to an end to the empire. All day, Maria had listened to the unsettling roar of the hostile crowds outside her window. It was unlike anything she had ever experienced. Down on the streets, the only peace to be found was in the narrow alleys and crooked back lanes, where the quiet shops of the cobblers and tailors were ensconced, and where the tenements blocked the noise, leaving only the musical hum of stitching awls and sewing machines.

With the city overcome, there had been nothing Maria could do, except wait alone in the safety of her apartment and leave the following day.

The crowds might have provided a perfect cover for Maria's getaway. With all focus on the protests, she might have been able to slip out of the apartment building unnoticed. She could have shouldered her way to the rail station on foot, a tiny beauty laced in jewels, pushing her way through the peopled streets. But Maria was traveling with a heavy trunk, as this was a trip from which she would not be returning.

She had hailed a fiacre in the morning to take her to the station. She hoped that no one in the building had seen her leave. If they had, it made little difference now.

Maria was glad to be rid of Budapest. It was no longer the city she had once known. Stink rose up from clogged sewers. Theaters were boarded up. Coffeehouses, once teeming with chess players in heated matches, and reporters and playwrights scribbling notes at marble-topped tables better suited to empresses sipping tea, had been taken over by wartime racketeers. The big markets, once fat with pleasing aromas, were nearly barren. No food could get in from the countryside, where there was a bounty of it. There weren't enough trains to transport the goods.

The city was bloated with more people than it had ever known, everyone crammed into apartments like commuters into streetcars. It smelled like an unwashed body. Water was as precious and as pricey as gold, so no one seemed to bathe with more than a few drops of it and a dab of ill-gotten soap. Many were sick or starving, and when they died, their bodies were rolled into the gutters of the once-glorious avenues and left for days. There was no one to haul them away.

The occasional old count could still be spotted, a well-waxed mustache perched atop his lip like a stage curtain, and a hairy eyebrow holding tight a monocle to survey his failing environs like a one-eyed owl. But Budapest, the Grand Dame, was ruined—and Maria had convinced herself that was the reason she was leaving, and none other.

If she should have felt regret, or perhaps even a scintilla of failure, she did not. The rhythm of the train, the steady slap of wheels on the tracks, told her Budapest was retreating from her, and with it, her little kettle of troubles that had begun to boil there. Once she had stepped onto the train, she hadn't given any of it another thought.

She sat up higher in her seat and smiled to herself.

She could feel now all the possibilities whirring inside her. She was charged with energy, a bolt of power and promise coursing through her. Maria was on the cusp of a great new adventure, and there was no one who could persuade her otherwise. After nearly twenty years, Maria was coming home.

Deep inside the fruit of this great new adventure was a dark little seed, within which lived her greatest catastrophe, the disaster that had sent her running from Nagyrév. Maria was only faintly aware of it now as a silent, dead space that occupied the center of her glee. She could not yet detect its rot.

Her baby was crying. She could hear him throughout the house, even from back in the bedroom where she had been all morning, the door closed to his wails. She had left Alex Junior alone in the living room.

Her bed was soaked in sweat. Her legs entwined in his. The heavy weight of him pressed against her. She could feel the heat of his breath in her ear, on her neck. Every morning for the last several days she had met with him like this, the two of them slipping back into her bedroom after the sun had come up, and long after Alex Senior had left for the fields.

The roosters crowed in the side yard. She couldn't hear the mild clatter of hooves as the wagon pulled slowly up to the gate, or the click of the front door as it gently opened, or the soft footfalls in the hall. She hadn't heard her husband at all until she heard him gasp. Then she heard the heavy rattle and thud that rocked the door as he collapsed against it.

The railcar jolted as the train switched tracks. Maria was thrust forward. Her skirt and petticoats rustled, as if aggrieved by the mayhem. The suitcases thumped on the rack above her. Maria knew it wouldn't be long now.

She had thought Alex Senior was in the fields that morning. Why had he decided to sneak back to the house? Had it been a trap?

Maria had set on the messy drama with her knife of correction, paring from it only the details that served her. She was left with a heap of loose facts unhinged from the truth, like a spine removed from a body, and all the slivers of her blame had slipped away.

Indignation had stayed with Maria, even after her hasty divorce from Alex Senior. If her husband had been where he had said he was going to be, no trouble would have come. She was tireless on this point. It was the chief fact of her gospel. Maria had carved her truth from this trivial detail and it had pitted the village against her. Only Auntie Suzy had remained her steadfast friend.

Maria was sure she had been forced to flee the village for what had amounted to little more than poor timing, but she was triumphant now. By a very timely twist of fate, she had landed a much bigger fish than Alexander Kovacs Sr. And right in Nagyrév, too. She was returning from exile to be enthroned as the de facto queen of the village. Nothing could have pleased her more.

As the train ambled across the Plains, she kept her hands busy, tending herself. She patted her face with her lace handkerchief. She gently rubbed the flat of her palms up and down her dress, the bodice, the sleeves, the skirt, enjoying the feel of the fine silk. She picked at invisible fibers, disdainfully plucking them away, watching as they fell invisibly to the floor. She stroked her long, sleek hair, which was still starkly raven, with only a strand or two of gray. She fingered her necklaces and bracelets, remembering as she did the men who had given each of them to her. Maria kept a running count of all the men she had ever had and the treasures she had gotten out of them. Like a bank robber, tallying heists. The men she had entertained in Budapest made her most proud. They weren't cheap coins, the lowly peasants of her youth. They were gold bars. Members of Parliament. Provincial governors. Bankers. Over the years, they had granted many favors to her, and best of all, they were discreet. Yet still, not all of them had slipped past the notice of her Budapest neighbors. She had known when it was time to leave.

By afternoon, Maria's voice had grown hoarse. The coal-choked air had dried her throat, but she had also been talking without end all day, hardly at a loss for something to say. When passengers got up to disembark, or to find an available seat in another compartment, she continued on, unfazed by the interruption. When someone new entered the railcar, she rattled off her tales to that point, to catch them up on all they had missed. There was no topic at which Maria could not find herself at the center. With a second or two to focus, disguised as a breath, she could link nearly anything back to the subject of herself. Most of what she said was pointless prattle, but she also talked about her grand adventure, and the sudden invitation that had sent her hurrying back to her native village. Of Budapest, she said little.

The locomotive slowed to a chug. The railcar rocked gently side to side, like a rowboat caught in a lazy wake. Maria dabbed her face with her handkerchief one last time. She tried to catch her reflection in the window as she bobbed to and fro. The raggedy appearance of the women around her had been a source of private amusement for her during her journey. Hobnailed shoes resoled with scraps of wood. Stockings with gaping holes. Threadbare shawls. She felt gratified to be reminded by her reflection that she had not allowed herself to be stained by the war as they had.

A long deep blast of the whistle sounded as the train made its approach to the station. The depot was nearly in view.

A surge of adrenaline rushed through Maria, quickly followed by a flash of panic.

What if he isn't there?

Maria realized only now that she had chanced her fate on the strength of a single letter.

What if he's changed his mind?

She poked now at the snake of self-doubt. What if she had been wrong about him? What if she had made a mistake? A frantic calculation had her back in Budapest by the following evening. But where would she go? Surely not back to the apartment. Could she go to Szolnok? To Kecskemét?

The steady screech of brakes brought the locomotive to a halt with a modest jolt, punctuated by a roaring hiss of steam. Maria lurched back against the hard seat one final time.

The cold, gray noise of departure began to fill the car. Shadows came over her as passengers reached above for their traveling bags. The wooden shelf creaked and groaned each time it was relieved of another portmanteau. Maria had no belongings with her in the railcar. She had insured her trunk against wartime looters before she left Budapest and stored it in a separate luggage compartment before boarding the train.

Maria peered out the window. The white glare of the afternoon sun had nearly erased the scene, but if she pitched her hand to her forehead to block the sun, discernible shapes began to emerge. She could only then see in full the whistle-stop of Újbög. The station was in Tiszaföldvár, just a hop across the Tisza by ferry, but a full twenty-five miles from Nagyrév by wagon-track road.

Nothing had changed since the last time she had seen it. The small, boxy depot was still in need of a whitewash, as if it hadn't been painted in all the years she had been gone. The letters on the sign were still cracked and faded. There was still a meadow across the way where cows grazed. Everything seemed untouched, just like her memory of her departure years earlier. She had hardly forgotten a moment of that dreadful time. Her father's grim face. Her mother holding fourteen-month-old Alex Junior, who hadn't seemed sick back then.

Maria had been anxious to get on the train and escape. To see her baby recede from view, and with him, the ruin of her old life. Maria had been as eager to make a fresh start then as she was now.

She squinted out the railcar window and scanned the platform. There were some crows with their children. They had come to greet their husbands and fathers coming back from the market in Szolnok, where Maria had switched trains. There were a couple of dogs nosing around the outer edges of the platform, a safe distance from the jarring sounds of the locomotive. A soot-covered railman raced back and forth along the edges of the tracks in front of her. Small groups of men were huddled together, smoking cigarettes. The soft, gray silt of the Plains had blown in off the road, and she watched it swirl in the air.

In the midst of it all stood Michael.

The sun glinted off the streaks of silver in his hair. His face had reddened in the heat. His shirt and trousers needed to be pressed. The brightness of the day had highlighted their many folds and wrinkles. A gold bracelet hung from his wrist and his thick fingers were ringed with cigar stains. The soles of his boots were flecked with wood chips, picked up from both the floor of his favorite tavern and the floor of his wagon. Michael Kardos was a country squire who had a thrown-together look of dashing to catch a streetcar, or a runaway mule. He looked windblown and rakish.

In his hand was a bouquet of flowers, plucked for him by the station agent, who tended a small, tidy garden on the side of the depot.

When Maria spotted Michael, the little bird of panic that had briefly nested in her flew away. She was restored and all the pieces of her were back in order.

She took a breath of vainglory.

There were so many people who should have been there to witness her arrival: Maria Szendi dressed in expensive silk, extending her hand for Michael Kardos to kiss. Maria Szendi accepting Michael Kardos's bouquet.

For nearly twenty years, Maria had fantasized about delivering such a supreme comeuppance to the people of Nagyrév. It was a disappointment to her that the train could not bring her directly into the village center and deposit her straight onto the square. Her moment would have to wait.

It took a minute before Maria noticed who was standing next to Michael. She had to strain to see past the rustle and disorder that now filled her compartment, as passengers had begun to pass their suitcases through the window to relatives who had gathered below. She stared at him through the dirty windowpane, taking stock.

His back was as crooked as a country lane. His pin-thin legs hiccupped with a tremor. He was bent sideways and had to thrust his head up to see, which made him look crazed. He was as bony as a carcass, and it seemed to Maria that he could snap in half with the help of a strong wind.

She might not have recognized him, as she could count on one hand the number of times she had seen him in the last twenty years. But he had the pale blue eyes and sandy blond hair of his father, unmistakable traits of the Kovacs men.

Maria stepped down to the platform. The clear Plains skies had none of the coal clog of the city. A spring breeze floated toward her and eddies of dirt blew around her at the ground. She moved in the dusty air to Michael, who greeted her with a kiss on both cheeks.

Alex Junior stood beside him. His breath was rasping, and every deep breath he tried to take left him coughing and sputtering. His skin looked jaundiced, his hair wispy and dry. He had a faint odor of decay that Maria could not help but sniff at. She leaned in just far enough to give her son a frosty kiss on each cheek, then snapped herself back. She had always regretted that it had been her first child who had died, and not this one.

Maria had not known about Alex Junior's condition when she left Nagyrév, because the more obvious symptoms had not yet appeared. But when he was eight, his grandparents received the diagnosis from a specialist in Budapest: Alex Junior had been born with syphilis, passed to him in utero by Maria, who was an asymptomatic carrier. Since then the disease, progressive and untreatable, had stolen most of his muscles and nerves from him, and had begun to cause an increasing amount of pain.

Alex Junior never should have been born at all, Maria thought. She threaded her arm through Michael's and snatched the bouquet from him when he offered it. Why Michael had brought Alex Junior along to the station, she could not fathom.

Michael retrieved her trunk from the luggage compartment, and the three boarded the ferry to head back to Nagyrév. The Csongrád-Szolnok Ferry Service operated a route back and forth twice daily, spring through autumn. In winter, when the Tisza was frozen, many folks simply crossed the river by foot.

The ferry engine was so loud Maria had to shout to Michael when she spoke. Her voice cracked with the effort, and she choked on the small winds stirred up by the ferry's speed. The engine rumbled as the boat left the Újbög station, nodding around the bend toward Nagyrév. The roar threw off a heavy vibration that numbed Maria's feet until she could barely feel them. Her hands shook wildly, and the soft petals of the flowers in her bouquet were being ravaged by the strong judder. Michael stood near her, unaffected.

Maria had known Michael all her life. She had been only nine when he was nineteen, but she had heard the stories of his love life that had circulated through the village for as long as she could remember. What she knew, what everyone in the village knew, was that Michael wouldn't give up on a girl until she had fallen in love with him, and it never took much.

Her own affair with Michael had started only weeks earlier. His wife had recently died, he wrote in the first letter he sent to her. He was coming to Budapest on business. Could he see her? The letter had come at just the right time.

The boat slowed as it neared the banks. The skipper cut the engine to let the ferry drift its final few yards, where the mates moored it at the dock.

Maria disembarked and struggled up the wet bank, being as careful as she could not to soil her silk dress. When she got to the top, she stood for a moment, unsteady but undaunted, and began to take it all in.

The songs of the river warblers and woodpeckers were as familiar to her as the soft aroma of pine she now inhaled. She could hear children at play on the oxbow. Ahead of her, just beyond view, was the chapel, whose tall steeple commanded the bleak square on which it sat. It was where she had married Alexander Kovacs Sr., in a wedding that was one of the most lavish affairs Nagyrév had ever known. The Szendis were arguably the wealthiest peasants in the province, and the marriage had joined the clan with the rich Kovacses. The revelry had lasted for days.

But it wasn't that husband whom she thought of now. It was her second husband who came to mind. The one in Budapest. She wondered briefly what he would do when he got home and discovered she was gone.

THE FOLLOWING MORNING, Maria awoke to another bright sun. By its light, she could immediately see what work there was to be done. When she and Michael had arrived at the house the evening before—*their* house now—it had already been dusk, and the sooty paraffin lamps had done a poor job of revealing her new home to her. But now she could see it.

There was none of the orderliness that could be expected from a blue blood like Michael. The floors were unswept. The rugs were musty. The windows were smudged and spotted with dirt. Michael's wife had not been dead long, but it was clear to Maria that Michael had neglected to do anything to keep the house up and running since her death. It would need a thorough cleaning, but first, Maria wanted it stripped of the dead woman, so from kettle to counterpane, all would need to be replaced.

Maria grabbed the dead wife's wicker basket to set out shopping. Thursday was market day in the village, a perfect opportunity, Maria knew, for browsing new wares, and more.

As she left the gate, she could hear the din from the Cser tavern. The house was across the street from the pub and already Maria regretted the location. Michael owned several houses, some of which she assumed could even be called villas, and Maria would have preferred to live in any one of those to be farther from the tavern rabble.

But 65 Árpád Street was a quick walk to Auntie Suzy's house, where Maria knew she would be visiting nearly every day.

Her bracelets jangled as she swung the gate shut. She lifted her long skirt and jumped over the narrow ditch to the road. A soft spray of dirt flitted at her feet. Up ahead, children played with corn-husk dolls under the shade of a locust tree.

Some villagers turned to stare at her as they rattled by in their carts, not quite believing who they were seeing. Maria walked airily along her path. She lifted her head high, as if straining to hear a secret whispered to her by the heavens. When mongrels began to trail her, she beat them back with a stern hiss and a threat to strike them with her basket.

She passed by all the familiar merchants and workshops from her childhood. The haberdashery, where her first wedding dress had been made; Feldmayr's, where she had bought sugared candy sticks as a child; the post and telegraph office, where she could hear the jingle of the telegraph machine ringing out onto the street.

When she got to the square, she could see the familiar jumble of wooden stalls wedged every which way onto the village's makeshift marketplace. There was only space for a few cluttered and snaking aisles, but the air was redolent with spices. A dozen or so bony horses and mules were tied to posts, which had been hammered into the ground near the well in the morning. The carts had been unhitched and wheeled close to the vendors. Food had been brought in large bundles and spread on a long table near the whipping bench, and wine-filled demijohns had been set out to sample. A few children darted between the stalls, but most were involved in a game of tag on the church lawn. The fine weather had brought scores of shoppers out, and there was a festive, near carnival atmosphere that Maria remembered well.

Market day was an event the villagers looked forward to each week. There were never any exotic sellers from Constantinople or Sarajevo, like there were in the bigger bazaars in Kecskemét and Szolnok (although the war had put a halt to those). There was usually just a ragtag bunch of peddlers who came by foot across the piping hot roads of the Plains to sell crockery, sewing gadgets, Bibles, and bathing tubs. Sometimes there were Romany selling sheets of music for a penny apiece. There were also villagers selling goods, and these were the people who most interested Maria.

For most of the morning, she perused the stands. She held up ceramic pots to the sunlight for inspection. She peered inside bowls, frowning at the poor quality. She frowned at hand cloths, wooden buckets, ladles, ornamental ewers. She pointed out splinters and frayed ends. Eyes were on her. She crafted questions so she could be heard speaking her Budapest dialect. She had worked hard to wash all the traces of Nagyrév speech from her tongue, and she wanted the effort to show. To no one in particular, she rolled out German phrases, expressions her Budapest husband had taught her, then looked around to see if anyone had noticed.

By the time she left, Maria had made sure that Nagyrév knew she was back.

SPRING WAS PERHAPS the busiest time of year for the midwife. It was not only lambing and calving season, as Auntie Suzy often midwifed the farm animals as well, but it was also planting and threshing time, when injuries to overworked muscles were common. Auntie Suzy had a long list of farmers with aching backs who depended on her for relief. Several women in the village gave massages and leeched for headaches, but big pains like muscle spasms, torn tendons, or even hernias required Auntie Suzy's medicine.

Many mornings she set out for the woods before sunup to gather herbs to make her tinctures. She was often on the hunt for deadly nightshade. She had to get the plant when it flowered, when its buds were richest in atropine and hyoscyamine. Deadly nightshade was one of the most useful medicinal herbs she knew, and she found it effective in treating the farmers' ailments.

On this day, Auntie Suzy returned from herb gathering by breakfast, and was soon off to make her daily rounds. As ever, she started with the Ambrusz house.

The midwife was still on good terms with Mr. and Mrs. Ambrusz. Eight months had passed since their grandson's funeral, and the old couple treated Auntie Suzy as they always had. Mr. Ambrusz still plied her with milk and other goods, and Auntie Suzy and her sister Lidia had joined Mrs. Ambrusz several times at the sewing circle Mrs. Ambrusz hosted in the winter. The group of crows had met and stitched by lamplight in Mrs. Ambrusz's living room, as they had done every year, yet Petra had excused herself from the circle all winter. If Mrs. Ambrusz had noticed her granddaughter-in-law was avoiding the midwife, she said nothing about it to Auntie Suzy.

The midwife pushed open the Ambruszes' gate. She shooed the chickens from her path and made her way to the stable.

Next to the fodder boxes were the milking stools and slop buckets, and Auntie Suzy stepped noisily around them to get to Mr. Ambrusz's workbench. He had left some eggs in a crate there for her. Auntie Suzy put the eggs in her basket, then headed to the house.

Inside, she yanked open the curtains. She stomped into the kitchen and opened a cupboard. She pulled out a tin of dried spices. She pried open the lid and reached in for a fistful. In another cupboard, she sorted through Petra's fine tableware. She plucked out a teacup and placed it in her basket, careful not to disturb the eggs.

Petra's refusal to marry Auntie Suzy's son had at first stunned the midwife. The midwife tried hard not to believe it was true. She had come to Petra again with talk of a wedding. She scouted houses the couple could live in, which her son could purchase with Petra's resources. She had looked around her own house and had seen what could be replaced with a little of Petra's money: a new washbasin, a new sideboard, a new tapestry for the living room. She had seen a peddler once who sold long mirrors, one of which would have fit well in her bedroom.

That Petra had resisted her plan was unconscionable to the midwife. Auntie Suzy had relieved the young woman of a lifetime of misery, and Petra had refused to pay the midwife's price.

Since Petra had denied Auntie Suzy access to her riches, Auntie Suzy would take them, one teacup at a time.

She shuffled out of the Ambrusz place to continue her rounds. Several of her calls were to check on clients, but Auntie Suzy was also collecting payment. Many villagers had become accustomed to coming home and finding the midwife in their attic loft rifling through their supply of beans or lentils, or regarding with a long eye the smoked meat that had been hung from the rafters to dry.

After she had finished her rounds, Auntie Suzy stepped finally onto Árpád Street, heading toward her daily reward. She made her way past the post and telegraph office, where her eldest son worked delivering mail all over the region. Auntie Suzy had many clients farther afield, owing to her Romany connections and the many peddlers who spread the word of her good medicine. Her son's job with the post office made it easier for her to tend to them. She could send potions to them directly, without her mail ever being checked by the postmaster. This was exactly why she had secured the position for him. Auntie Suzy knew several members of the village council, and enjoyed a special friendship with the village clerk, Mr. Ébner, a relationship she had worked hard to cultivate. She had found the friendships useful in placing people where she needed them to be.

The midwife looked across the road to where her son-in-law's barbershop stood. Daniel kept the shop open two days a week in winter, but he had already switched to his Saturday-only summertime hours. He had a plot in the fields and, like many Plains men, he kept a small reed hut there, where he often spent summer nights. But Daniel's absence had been especially notable recently. He had hardly been seen in Nagyrév at all.

By the time the midwife had arrived at the Cser tavern, she had already walked several miles with her baskets. She was huffing with the effort her ample weight forced upon her. In two weeks, the midwife would turn fifty-six, and she felt every day of it.

Auntie Suzy shooed back the mongrels who lingered at the door. She bent over her baskets and with a grunt heaved a thick wad of spit onto the ground. The dogs scattered. With another grunt, she yanked open the tavern door.

It was dark and cool inside. Sunlight struggled to come in from one small window. On the wall, old farmers' hats covered in grime hung from pegs. They smelled like sweat. The tables were scuffed and seemed randomly placed, as if storm tossed. Wood chips were sprinkled on the floor.

She lumbered to a table and plunked her baskets down on top of it. She plopped herself onto the bench, squeezing herself in among the men. The midwife was the only woman in the village, perhaps the only woman in any province of the kingdom, who dared to swing through the doors of a tavern.

The tavern was as familiar and comfortable to her as her own living room, and she often thought of it as just that. She knew all of its secrets, too. She could look at any of the men and know just what kind of troubles were lurking at home, sometimes better than they did. She knew about Mr. Takacs's daughter, for many young girls in Nagyrév had come to the midwife pregnant and scared. She knew about Mr. Nagy's rash, which she had treated. She knew that Mr. Csabai, just back from the front lines, had begun to beat his wife, and she knew that Mr. Virag's wife was often terrified of him. Being the keeper of these secrets made her feel more powerful than any potion she could have concocted in her kitchen.

Auntie Suzy hollered her order to Anna. She fumbled in her apron pocket for her pipe and lit it at her thin lips. She surveyed the room. Lewis was sprawled at the serving bar. Alex Junior was playing cards at his table near the window.

Alex Junior was a good card player. He had mastered several games, which he was sure gave him an edge over his friends. When he won the pot, he bought rounds of drinks at the tavern for all of them and went home with his pockets as empty as when he had arrived.

He was most comfortable when sitting down. He would loll for hours at the table where he played, his rawboned body leaning back into the chair, his legs drooping beneath. He liked to sip coffee and drinks throughout the day. He smoked, too, but he never more than picked at his food.

Over the years, his gait had become more twisted and awkward as the muscles in his legs had become increasingly paralyzed. At times, he felt sharp pains shoot into his abdomen.

Most of the friends Alex Junior had grown up with had been called up to fight, but some older farmers had befriended him, and some teen boys who looked to him as an older cousin were also close to him.

He was unruffled and good-natured. He still had a hint of mischief in him, but his days of fooling around were behind him. The antics he used to pull off as a teenager were only good now for the stories he could tell about them while another deck was shuffled and dealt.

Auntie Suzy was pained by his appearance. It was a pity, she thought, that something had not been done about him long ago. Half a life, like he had, was nothing but a problem to be solved. She knew well what she would do with him, given the chance.

When the midwife saw Michael, there was a slipping down inside her. Michael was not as regular a patron of the pub, as she was. He preferred the reading circle, because it was a place where he could enjoy a glass of sweet Tokay wine while reading the weekly newspapers on hand there. Seeing him at the Cser pub had given the midwife a start, though she quickly recovered. She had learned over the years to appear indifferent toward Michael. What had happened between them had been long ago, she often reminded herself.

Michael was as well-liked as anyone had ever been in Nagyrév. He had been a popular judge years before, and nearly everyone considered him a friend. Michael Kardos was the man every other man wanted to be and every woman wanted to bed. That he had chosen Maria after his wife's death had baffled many, and broken the hopes of many more.

If the midwife begrudged Maria's new relationship with her old lover, she kept her resentment well hidden from her dear friend. She had a high regard for Maria, who reminded her of the Romany women she had known growing up, fresh with life and a far cry from the crows who stood at the well and pointed gossipy fingers (a sin of which Auntie Suzy and her sister were certainly also guilty).

Michael was at the pub to celebrate his name day. He was seated at the head of a table filled with jugs of wine and a bounty of food and gifts. He was surrounded by some of his closest cronies, and Auntie Suzy eyed him as a hawk observes prey. When she was ready to leave, she tapped her fat finger in the bowl of her pipe and tamped it out. She gulped down the last of her brandy and slammed the glass on the table. She eased herself up from the bench and fixed her heavy baskets to her arms.

"Are you paying today?" Anna called out to her.

The midwife didn't bother to look up. She waddled to the door, inching her way around the tables in her path.

"The good Lord will pay for it!" she shouted.

Back out on Árpád Street, she headed home for her daily nap.

MARIA SPENT HER first weeks back in Nagyrév reacquainting herself with the village. She went down to the oxbow, where she had played with her dolls as a child, and out to the Plains to survey her fields. They were weed-filled meadows with dry, browning grass that had grown beyond Maria's waist, but she was still comforted by the sight of them. She was the last surviving member of her family. The entire Szendi fortune belonged to her.

When Maria came back from her afternoon outings, she often passed neighbors out on their porches shucking corn for animal fodder. She would stop to sing a hello at the gate. In return, she would get curt replies, voices as terse and finishing as the sound of the husks being stripped off the cobs. Besides some cousins who felt obligated to be civil to her, Auntie Suzy was still Maria's only friend.

Sometimes when she got home, she found Alex Junior at the house deep in a conversation with Michael. Alex Junior shared a house with his father but had become friendly with Michael in the short time since Maria had returned to the village. Michael and Alex would talk in the living room, or go out to the stable and drink from the flask of brandy Michael kept stashed there. Michael was patient with Alex, and the forbearance he showed him only stirred Maria's ire. It nettled her to see how the village coddled Alex. There was always someone or another stopping to offer him a ride to the pub, to the village hall, down to the river, or wherever he happened to have a need or a whim to go. The baker made sure to make him an extra loaf when he thought of it, never mind that Alex barely had an appetite anymore. Every kindness shown to him came at a cost to her. *Why so much fuss over a crippled boy?* was what she wanted to know.

Maria had found evidence of the trouble in her son in a single incident of mischief three years earlier. On a dare, he had swiped three chickens from a councilman's yard when he was working as a night watchman. Michael had been a judge at the time and had given Alex Junior the lightest sentence possible. But Alex Junior had lost his job as the watchman and hadn't had a proper job since.

As difficult as she found Alex Junior to be, Maria also thought the problem of Alexander Senior was troublesome. She had underestimated how difficult it would be to live together in the same village again. Everywhere she went, the shadow of her sin followed her.

With these burdens pressing on her, Maria had only one thing she could do: go to her friend, Auntie Suzy, who would read her fortune and tell her what to do.

MARIA WALKED OVER to Orphan Street and let herself into Auntie Suzy's gate. She stepped onto the porch and rapped on the window. When the midwife opened the door, Maria was met with the sickly sweet smell of Auntie Suzy's tobacco. The kitchen was where the midwife spent much of her day when she wasn't out and about in the village, and the scent often stayed trapped in there.

Maria took a seat at the midwife's long table. She had on one of her plainer dresses, but it was still a prize to see. She had pressed it with a smoothing iron in the morning and it had yet to sprout a wrinkle. She sat anxiously, waiting for the midwife to join her. These daily visits with Auntie Suzy held something more for her than just companionship. The letters and telegrams the two had exchanged over the years had been a guiding force for Maria during her time in Budapest. Now that she was living so close, she was able to come to Auntie Suzy for counsel at nearly every turn. Maria had come to consider the midwife her personal magician, able to trick the future into bending to her will. There was no grievance Maria had that she couldn't take to Auntie Suzy's kitchen table to solve.

The midwife shuffled to the sideboard to fetch her old deck of playing cards. She moved back over to the table and plopped down onto the bench across from her friend. She didn't have to ask Maria what was on her mind. Auntie Suzy had heard the complaints about Alex Junior often enough. She had already grown quite tired of them.

"Why are you bothering with him?" the midwife often asked.

Auntie Suzy laid the deck on the table in front of her. She pulled several cards out from the stack and fanned them out in her favorite forecasting pattern. Auntie Suzy had several tools at hand she used for fortune-telling, but Maria preferred the cards. Auntie Suzy flipped several of the cards over and gave each a grave look of contemplation. Then she explained to Maria what the cards were telling her.

She reached across the table to retrieve her tobacco. She dropped a pinch into the pipe bowl and tamped it. She plucked her thin pick off the table and poked it down the center of the bowl as she eyed Maria, who was studying the cards.

"I have a way," the midwife told her friend.

Auntie Suzy ferreted in her apron pocket for her matches. She relit her pipe, taking a long, satisfying draw on it.

"It won't last long," Auntie Suzy said. She blew the smoke out of her mouth as she spoke.

The midwife reached across the table and scooped the cards into a pile.

"You won't have to watch your son's torture."

As for the second of Maria's twin troubles, Alexander Kovacs Sr., Auntie Suzy had an idea about that, too. As Maria knew, the midwife had a solution to every problem.

THE SUMMER CROPS brought in a nice bounty for the village. The watermelons and potatoes had been plentiful, and by late September the wheat was being harvested. On one late September day, news reached the fields that Alexander Kovacs Sr. was dead. His death shocked the village. The older Alex was only forty-four years old, and had been working hard in the fields all summer. It was a surprise to all that such a hardy man could fall so fast.

Had Maria been curious, or at least daring, she would have gone to the village hall to peek at the death register. She would have read what had been reported as his cause of death. This time, Auntie Suzy had told the bell ringer to write "apoplexy."

Alex Senior had wanted little to do with Maria since she had come back, but Maria had nonetheless felt her ex-husband's presence everywhere she went. He seemed to loom around every shop aisle, around every corner, around every bend in the road. He was like a heavy fog spread over her, and with his death the fog was lifting. Maria could see clearly what to do next.

She had not been able to bring herself to accept Auntie Suzy's solution for her troublesome son, but she had most certainly devised a way to excise him from her life in Nagyrév. Now, with Alex Senior out of the way, she wasted no time implementing it. She still had useful connections in Budapest. Through them, she arranged a job for Alex Junior with the Budapest Transit Authority.

Finally, her fresh start was unhindered.

DANIEL HAD BEEN living for weeks in his fields and the autumn nights had grown cold. Throughout most of the summer, he had slept in the open, lying on his mat under the dazzle of stars. He did this night after night, sometimes singing to himself as he prepared to bed down for the evening. His voice carried across the Plains like birdsong.

Some nights he slept inside his reed hut, but the peak of it was no higher than the tops of the conical haystacks that were dotted across the fields. He had to duck to get in and out, so if the weather was nice, he was happier to just sleep outside.

Daniel drank just enough to keep warm. He kept his sheepskin coat over himself as a blanket, and by his side was his cross-shaped flask, given to him as a gift years earlier. He held it to his lips and knocked back a gulp, feeling the burn as the brandy streamed down his throat.

He pondered what to do. He had felt the midwife's evil eye.

In the nine years since he had lived under the same roof as Auntie Suzy, he had come to know his mother-in-law as one might know a captor. Daniel had watched her as she moved through her days, waddling in the door with her baskets full of goods and waddling off again for her afternoon guzzle at the Cser pub. He had also seen how she was with his young son and daughter, casting a judicious eye on what they ate, bundling them off to school each day, walking with them around her garden to tutor them about plants and caution against poisonous leaves and berries. She was as tender and attentive with them as his own grandmother had been with him.

Yet the light she cast had shown Daniel the snare of the silk she spun. He had come to understand that what she brewed in her kitchen was not always intended for healing. And he had not so long ago overheard the hushed, late-night discussions the midwife had with his wife and her brothers. They were conversations not meant for his ears.

One afternoon he had skipped the caravan home and had just stayed in the fields. A lot of bachelors lived in the fields for weeks in the summer, and he had, too, when he was single, but for different reasons than he was now.

Daniel knew he couldn't stay out in the fields much longer. With winter coming, he would have to move back into the village. He had spent several nights planning, working out where to live. He had finally decided he could arrange a small space for himself at the back of the barbershop. What he knew he could never do was return to 1 Orphan Street. Like his father-in-law had done years earlier, Daniel knew he had to flee.

A DEADLY FLU, A FALLEN
KINGDOM, A FOILED PLAN

[Auntie Suzy] had keen powers of observation, sharp
understanding and seems to have been a monster of energy
and unscrupulousness. A fat, smiling, Buddha-like figure,
she knew all the cares and troubles of the villagers.

—Jack MacCormac, New York Times

Auntie Suzy's handkerchief was sopping. The midwife had soaked it in her concoction of Marseilles vinegar. She held the hanky over her nose and mouth as a shield against the illness in her midst. It was a malady unlike anything she had ever seen. It was taking down folks like branches in a windstorm. Her lizardlike eyes squinted over the top of the kerchief. They burned from the strong camphor fumes. Yet her herbalist nose could still detect the other herbs she had mixed in with the potion, as well as the wine she had added, all for extra potency.

It was shocking how quickly the virus had come and how much damage it was doing. The country had sent three and a half million men into battle and now, nearing the war's end, had tallied two million casualties. But this plague, called Spanish flu by the American press, was a fierce, final weapon unleashed by an unseen beast. And it had a particular appetite for young adults. The midwife herself had noted this.

The doused hankie was bitterly cold. Holding it made her arthritic hands throb. She bent down to snatch the last blanket from the floor when her putsi, always hanging from a cord around her neck, dropped down and dangled in front of her face. She was sure the amulets inside the small leather pouch were as responsible for her well-being as the Marseilles vinegar. She also attributed her relative good health, in the face of what surrounded her, to the rites she performed at home. They protected her. Auntie Suzy had often thought that if the gadjo respected Romany magic, they wouldn't be so weak in body. She rolled the blanket into a ball and stuffed it into the burlap sack she had brought with her from home. Afterward, she wiped her hands with the soaked handkerchief.

The midwife eased herself down onto her hands and knees. Her black woolen coat was uncomfortably tight around her. It had been made for her by the village furrier years earlier, when she was a tad less plump, but now the seams bulged, and as she crouched on all fours and strained its wool, they bulged even more. Near her was a wooden bucket, which she had filled with vinegar and water. She drew out a rag that had been floating in it and began to scrub the earthen floor. Each time she dipped the rag in the bucket, she slopped more icy water onto the floor in front of her. She could see her breath as she huffed with the effort of cleaning. No fire had yet warmed the drafty, weather-prone cottage on this morning. The little dwelling remained frigid.

When Auntie Suzy was finished scouring the floor, she stood up and wiped down the dingy walls. They were cold, too, and damp, with cracks and slits where the wind blew in. The village crier's battered cottage was to her the saddest, most broken-down little home in the village.

She had spent so much time at the crier's cottage recently that she had come to know every decaying detail of the two-room home by the river: the ill-fitting door, the bare cupboards, the faded tapestry hanging from loose pegs in the front room. It was empty now, and she was anxious to leave it.

For weeks, the crier's cottage had been filled with sick villagers who had been quarantined there. Auntie Suzy had ministered to them throughout the first wave of Spanish flu, and now the second. No medicine had come into the country for two years, but Auntie Suzy was far more confident in her own poultices and tinctures than she had ever been in anything the doctors or hospitals used.

The floors had been scattered with *dikus* on which the sick had lain—straw mats that the farmers normally kept in their stables for napping. Some of the sick had brought their dikus with them when they had come to the cottage. Others had been brought over later by family members when Auntie Suzy had requested them. Relatives also brought bread, soup, and goulash. They stood on the porch and handed the pots to the midwife. Most of her patients were too ill to eat, but Auntie Suzy was keen to help herself to the bounty.

Auntie Suzy had struggled to keep the crier's cottage warm for the sick villagers. She had burned through the firewood, then the hay, then the dried corn husks, then the dung and whatever dry leaves she could find, just to keep the fire lit in the tiny kitchen's wood-burning stove. She had wrapped her patients in the wool blankets they had brought with them from home.

There was an old, scraped-up table in the main room, which she had pushed aside to make room for the infirm. There were stacks of chamber pots in rows along the walls, all recently washed and made sterile with her vinegar concoction. Auntie Suzy had spent much of her time emptying the pots into the privy outside, and she was glad now to at last be free of the duty. The kitchen was situated on one end of the main room, and the only other room in the sparse house functioned as a bedroom. This was where Auntie Suzy went for catnaps.

Like Auntie Suzy's house, the crier's cottage had been provided to him by the village council. When his house had been commandeered for the quarantine, the crier had moved into an anteroom in the village hall, taking with him his clothes and his drum. The space was largely used as a storage closet, but it was also where, from time to time, villagers had to go to serve time for petty crimes. Some got whipped on the whipping bench on the square, some walked the street carrying a sign that read, perhaps, I STOLE MR. TAKACS'S GOAT, and some spent the night in the storeroom of the village hall. It's where Michael had ordered Alex Junior to be confined as punishment for stealing the chickens.

The crier had started out a fisherman. He was the son of a fisherman, and the grandson of one, but ever since the regulation of the Tisza River fifty years prior, most of the fish swam a new course that bypassed Nagyrév. With empty nets and lines, he had been obligated to take the crier position when it was offered to him.

He bellowed bulletins and news at least two days a week, five times each day, starting at dawn at the well on the square and moving on to several other locations in the village. He rolled out his scroll and shouted headlines from the Budapest and Szolnok newspapers that had been sent over the telegraph machine, but he also cried bulletins the village clerk gave him to read.

He would strap his drum to his chest and trill a long beat before reading out:

A NEW TEACHER HAS BEEN HIRED AT THE SCHOOL.

THE SZOLNOK COUNTY FARMING REGULATIONS ARE TO BE IMMEDIATELY IMPOSED.

MR. BERA IS SELLING HIS COW.

MR. TOTH HAS NEW WINE BARRELS FOR SALE.

MR. PAPP'S SON HAS BEEN FREED FROM THE RUSSIAN P.O.W. CAMP.

Everything else the town crier needed for his job—rags to clean the two kerosene streetlamps, a broom to sweep up around the village hall and after market days—was kept in the storeroom in which he now slept.

The crier had another duty assigned to him, which was to maintain the vital records, and to oversee old Dr. Szegedy's weekly appointment book.

Despite the second wave of the pandemic, which had hit the village at least as hard as the first, no one had seen the doddering old doctor in weeks. Heavy rains had washed out the roads to Nagyrév, making them impassable even for the most determined would-be visitor to the village. Auntie Suzy didn't expect to see the old man make his weekly rounds in Nagyrév again until the following spring, when the bad weather had let up and the roads were finally clear.

For now, the worst was over. Nagyrév had already lost villagers to the deadly flu, but not nearly as many as had died elsewhere, and the midwife's last remaining patient had returned home.

Auntie Suzy grabbed the burlap sack with the blanket inside and hoisted it up. She was content that she had cleansed the crier's cottage of the scourge. She picked up the remaining diku and tucked it under her arm. She balanced her baskets on her forearms and wrenched the door open. Rain and frigid wind blasted her. She stood for a moment on the rotting porch. She could hardly see the Tisza, though it was only a few yards in front of her. She tried to shield herself from the river sand that stung her face. She stepped out onto Shoreditch Road, a soggy path that looped from the crier's house at the river to the village square behind it. She was headed back to her own place to boil the blanket.

She lumbered past the church and through the empty square, and before she knew it she was in front of the barbershop. Daniel often kept the door ajar, and the midwife could see straight inside, where she would often train her eyes on him. The pandemic had forced the closure of nearly every shop, but Auntie Suzy waddled over anyway. She peered through the window. She looked beyond the shop floor to the curtained room in the back, where she knew he stayed.

She did not altogether mind that Daniel had left the family home. It was the simpler alternative.

IN NOVEMBER, NEWS came to the village that a truce had been signed. The Great War was over. The Austrian Empire, which had ruled Central Europe since the fall of the Roman Empire—for the last fifty years jointly with Hungary—lay in ruins. The Kingdom of Hungary, which had been intact for one thousand years, was no more. It hastily reemerged as the Hungarian Democratic Republic, but everyone knew Hungary was in grave danger. Enemy Romanians had occupied Transylvania, an eastern region of Hungary, for almost two years. The Allies threatening to carve up much of what was left of Hungary and give the spoils to the other victors. Two-thirds of Hungary's territory was at stake.

At the same time, Hungarian POWs, who had been radicalized in Russian prison camps, were aiming to seize control and put Communist Bolsheviks in power.

Budapest was filled with rioters, revolutionaries, and assassins, and the nation was in tatters. But the only news to come through that mattered at all to Maria was that her lieutenant husband, returned from his duties on the battlefield to find her gone, had granted her a divorce.

All these months back in Nagyrév, she had been living with Michael in a "wild marriage." Still legally married to her husband in Budapest, this was the only kind of union she could have with Michael. But she had been truly disappointed that she was not being treated as if she were Michael's real wife. She had imagined a much different situation for herself than what she had gotten, and it seemed that nothing she did improved it. Nagyrév treated her with the same contempt now as when she had left, and this infuriated her.

There were rare occasions, countable in a few sleepless nights, in which Maria was seized by the hand of regret for having left Budapest. It was true she had been bored there, and lonely, too. Her husband had been away fighting the war for half their marriage. Not to mention the hardships in the city, which beggared description. She had locked away that horror and vowed to herself never to speak of it, one promise she had kept. But being the wife of a prominent man had lifted her high up on the ladder she had been trying to climb since the day she had learned how to crawl. It had taken her a long time, but she had obtained the social standing she knew she deserved.

Now, she was able to wed Michael. There was nothing stopping the two of them. If the villagers would not freely give her their respect, she would soon be able to demand it from them.

Yet, just as one stone was cleared from her path, another was flung onto it. In the sea of telegrams that had begun to swamp the post and telegraph office in the chaotic wake of the war's end—Village Clerk Ébner was receiving hourly updates on the volatile political crisis—came a cable from Alex Junior. The Budapest Transit Authority had declared him "unfit for duty." He was coming home.

"SING, MY DEAR BOY!"

Wherever Gypsies go, there the witches are, we know.

—OLD ROMANY SAYING

When spring came, the farmers caravanned to the fields as they always had, except now with a greater beat of fear in their hearts.

The war had affected the village insomuch as it had sent its sons to battle. But in so many ways, the villagers had been protected from the worst of it. As for medicine, they had always had the midwife. As for food, they had their crops. As for the battlefields, those were hundreds of miles from them. So it was, that after the Great War had ended, the real threat to their lives began.

In late March, a brutal Communist regime took over the country. It commandeered the press, the schools, and the banks, and created a new military force: the Red Army.

The people of Nagyrév most feared a group called the Lenin Boys, who roamed the countryside wantonly killing and torturing those they believed to be against the new regime. Villagers had learned that the "Boys" cut a woman's teeth out with a chisel and sewed another woman's tongue to her nose. They hammered a nail into a man's head. In one afternoon in Szolnok, the leader of the Lenin Boys—the Red Army's commissar for military affairs—executed twenty-four people, including the president of the court.

The horror trapped the villagers in fear, and they longed for the days when the crier read bulletins about who had a cow for sale, instead of the lists of atrocities he now read.

The Red Army, for its part, was fighting back invaders. Since the Great War had ended the previous autumn, much of Hungary had been occupied, mostly by Romanians. For more than four months, the Red Army had held the final front at Szolnok, before surrendering to the Romanians at the end of July.

Friday, August 1, 1919

The bell at the post and telegraph office had not stopped jingling. Most of the dispatches reported the location of the Romanians on their advance toward the capital to declare victory. There were already scattered reports of looting and skirmishes in villages en route.

Only scraps of news were being passed on to the locals, but the villagers were nevertheless on tenterhooks about what was to come. And most of them would have preferred anyone else but Ébner to lead them through a crisis.

Ébner seemed to them like a character straight out of a tale the storytellers wove for them on those magnificent summer nights before the war. Back then, an array of storytellers, minstrels, performers, and peddlers often passed through the village: long-haired prophets selling big Bibles, sword-swallowers, knife grinders, dancing bears, and poets, but the most plentiful and most popular were the storytellers. Those were evenings spent in the stable, where a fire burned in the pit and a jug of brandy made its way around the circle. The children in their nightclothes rested their tender bodies against a slumbering cow hitched to a chain, or snuggled together under a blanket. The adults sat rapt. Some closed their eyes to see the pictures emerge more clearly. In the dancing shadows of the firelight, a storyteller filled the stable with images of kings' feats, of magical ravens, of dogs imbued with godlike powers, and of self-serving, oafish, fat-cat noblemen, who reminded them of Mr. Ébner.

He looked like a foreigner among them, an alpine elder who wore boots ordered from a catalog and a Tyrolean hat with a tuft of goat hair tucked in the band. He often had a large stick in his rheumatic grip that he used to shove away stray dogs.

Ébner had been appointed village clerk in 1900, the same year Auntie Suzy was appointed village midwife. It was the highest office in the village. Ébner was a member of the gentry, and viewed being chief as his birthright. He put himself on various boards and gave himself titles, but otherwise spent his days hunting and gambling.

He considered Auntie Suzy one of the perks of his position. The midwife gave him free treatments for whatever ailed him (as well as for whatever ailed his wife and his two spoiled daughters). But he was also truly fond of her. When she waddled into the Cser tavern and plopped down across the table from him, he was always pleased to see her.

For her part, the midwife knew Ébner was just the man she needed at Nagyrév's helm, a powerful yet indolent nobleman who viewed the villagers as his personal toys. It cheered him to play crude jokes on them. Fill their carts with feathers. Set their pigs loose. In the backwater of Nagyrév, he took no one seriously. Not even the midwife.

Auntie Suzy had tested Ébner once. They had been together drinking at the pub when she reached into her apron pocket and brought out her vial. She unwrapped it from the white paper and handed it to him.

Ébner held it close to the table lantern. He eyed the milky solution. He uncapped the bottle and sniffed it with his large nostrils. The vial, so close to his nose, tickled the coarse hairs of his walrus mustache.

He could smell nothing but a faint hint of metal. It smelled to him like old water.

"What is it?" he asked.

"Arsenic," said the midwife. "There is enough in here to kill one hundred men. No doctor could ever detect it."

Ébner laughed. The midwife and her wild notions always amused him. Auntie Suzy laughed with him and slipped the potion back into her pocket.

But not even Ébner could joke now. In the village hall, he received the news of the advancing army with grave alarm. He urgently ordered the crier into his office. He shoved the telegram into the crier's open hand and told him to hurry. It was imperative the villagers be informed at once. The crier took the crumpled paper and sped out of the hall with his drum. Meanwhile, Ébner dashed out to round up the council for an emergency meeting.

The crier ran first to the square. He pushed his way through a cluster of sheep and mules, which lapped at the water from the well. A few crows were huddled together with their buckets at their feet. The crier positioned himself in front of the whipping bench.

He beat furiously on his drum. The crows stepped back from the noise. When he finished drumming, he shouted as loudly as he could: "TAKE HEED!!! ROMANIAN TROOPS ARE CHARGING TOWARD NAGYRÉV!"

The crows scattered. The women looked like a colony of confused ants as they scurried home in all directions, water sloshing from their wooden buckets. A small crowd had gathered in the churchyard to hear the crier, and they, too, rushed home. Some villagers hurried to unhitch their carts from their horses and galloped off to the fields to spread the word.

At home, people did what they could to batten down their property. Some had makeshift wine cellars in their yards. This was one of the best places they had to hide their valuables. They went through their cottages and gathered their best embroidery, their best pitchers, their prized pocket watches purchased as souvenirs in Budapest, and hauled them into the cellars. They ripped away the creepers that grew on their fences and scattered the vines over the cellars in a poor attempt to camouflage the entrances. And they hid their money wherever they could.

The Romanian forces couldn't garrison at the estates on the outskirts of Nagyrév. The Red Army had destroyed all of the manors. Instead, the troops would billet inside the village. Conscripts would bed down in stables. Officers, who would be taking over village affairs, would house themselves in the finest homes.

With a cavalry charging toward Nagyrév, the council knew there was little the village could do to brace for the invasion. The only action they could take was to protect the most vulnerable among them from the brutal behavior they feared was to come by vicious conscripts. The most helpless, they knew, was Alex Junior.

In the early afternoon, Maria was startled by a sharp rap at her fence gate. It was followed by the crier's drumroll. She and Michael had been working feverishly to prepare. They knew without fail that Romanian officers would billet in their house, given who Michael was.

"Marriiiaaa Szendi! Come out, pleeease!" shouted the crier.

The crier seldom came to village houses. Protocol required him to accompany gendarmes—the arm of the law that policed the provinces—when they came to make an arrest. But no one in the village had seen a gendarme in Nagyrév in more than a generation. Nagyrév hadn't had any kind of police force for more than fifty years. So in Nagyrév, when a crier appeared in front of a cottage, he was most certainly escorting a councilman who had affairs to discuss with a resident.

Maria flitted to the gate and swung it open. The crier stood with his hands on his drum. Standing in the grass behind him, looking as ragged as a windblown weed, was Alex Junior, surrounded by a small group of councilmen.

Maria had become even more frustrated with her son in the months since he had returned from Budapest, a failed driver for the Budapest Transit Authority. He had come back to Nagyrév and picked up the same odious routines. He whiled away his days playing cards at the pub. Just like before, he would limp down to the riverfront in the afternoons, where he would smoke cigarettes and watch the few boats that came and went around the jagged bend in the river. In the evenings, he was back at the pub playing cards. Each day it was the same. Maria clucked about the misfortune with which God had cursed her to anyone who would listen, but that was usually only the midwife. Maria had sat stricken at Auntie Suzy's kitchen table daily since Alex Junior had come back, asking the midwife what she should do. Auntie Suzy's answer was always the same: "Why do you keep bothering with that sick boy?"

Maria took a long look at her son. She saw again how everything about him was misaligned, as if an earthquake had found the fault line in his body. She felt a swell of bitterness rise up, but her attention was soon drawn to what the councilmen were saying. Romanian conscripts would certainly decide to garrison in her son's stable. The councilmen trusted the officers to behave in the homes where they billeted, but they had no such trust in the recruits. They feared for Alex Junior's safety if he stayed at his house.

Maria surveyed the councilmen. They had all known Alex Junior's father, and she sensed that they were doing this in his name as much as they were doing it for his disabled son. Nagyrév had always rallied to support Alex Junior. Many in the village were like parents to him, an important reason why his father had never sent him to live at a hospital in Budapest, something the doctors had encouraged him to do. When Alex Junior returned from his brief stint with the transit authority, he was received home with cheers. This last point raised Maria's disdain another intolerable notch.

But Maria was a gifted fox, and she scented opportunity. She knew that as sure as she had heard the crier's drumbeat, in the bent and diseased bones of her son standing before her was a lucky twist of fate. She would not fully grasp the measure of what was being handed to her until more time had passed. But for now, she knew she had to take it.

Promptly, and to the surprise of the councilmen who had come prepared to argue their case, Maria hustled her son through her gate and into her home. Yes, of course he could stay with her.

THE STREETS OF Nagyrév became as empty as a ghost's grave. The usual hum of workaday traffic had come to a sudden halt. The soft patter of ambling hooves, the clanging from the blacksmith's workshop, the pounding mallet of the cobbler, the hum of the haberdasher's stitching awl, had all ceased.

Hours passed. Breezes rustled through the trees, up where the songbirds chirruped. Dogs trotted back and forth in the middle of the road, happily commanding in daylight what they normally owned only by night.

The villagers huddled at home. Doors normally left open in the

August heat had been shut tight. Chickens had been rounded up and put into their coops. Shutters had been fastened against the windows. Some villagers could be seen skulking to their poorly concealed wine cellars to hide one last treasure. Older children were solemn, following their parents' code. They crept from one room to another. Their homes, until now a second skin to them, felt alien, and they felt the thrill and fear like blood in their veins.

More hours passed.

The first signal came when the songbirds fell silent. A moment later, a rumbling could be felt beneath earthen floors. Windows rattled. A few brave folks slipped out to their yards and peeked between the wooden slats of their fences to eye the cavalry storming in.

Panicked dogs raced from the roadway ahead of the charging horses. They sailed over the ditches and pitched themselves under shrubs. The tiniest ones shimmied under fences. The cavalrymen roared up Árpád Street. Their ridged helmets bounced low against their foreheads. Dusty rucksacks bounced on their backs. Bayonets slapped at their sides. Trailing them was a thick band of dirty foot soldiers.

The horses came to a stop. The officers put their bugles to their lips and blew. The horns screamed up and down the higgledy-piggledy streets and out to the marshy meadows that flanked the riverbanks, where the reclusive black storks slunk among the reeds, waiting for their autumn escape.

BY LATE SEPTEMBER, Nagyrév was unrecognizable. Where before Árpád Street had been filled with a bustle of horses and carts, now it teemed with uniformed armed conscripts. They strode up and down the middle of the road like a menacing pack of wolves. They looted what they pleased from the shops. The haberdasher had been forced to sew new dresses for free so the soldiers could send them back home to their wives. Feldmayr's shelves were all but empty. The conscripts put a hand up to halt any villager who tried to pass by them. They pressed sharp bayonets at their chests and demanded to see a national identity card. While the villager fumbled to produce the document, the armed men pilfered whatever meager goods happened to be in the peasant's basket. Some of the soldiers forced passersby to get down on their knees. There on the sidewalk, they made them take an oath of allegiance to Romanian King Ferdinand.

Ébner had been expelled by the invading forces. The Romanian commander had taken over his position. In the village hall, the commander had set up a customs desk, where he levied massive duties on even the simplest products.

The Thursday market was canceled. Crows no longer gathered at the well on the square. The conscripts, who sweltered in their woolen uniforms during the hot months, had taken over the well and used it to clean themselves.

Not even Auntie Suzy ventured to the Cser pub. The tavern was now the domain of the enemy troops. Lewis had finally been replaced as the most dreaded in the village.

And at night, Nagyrév's caped watchmen, who had never carried anything more than a lantern, had been replaced with troops patrolling with rifles.

A nine o'clock curfew was in effect, although the sun didn't quit the sky until an hour later. Day or night, villagers preferred to be home to guard their houses. More critically, few were willing to leave their wives unprotected.

MARIA TRIMMED THE charred bit of wick in the lamp with an old penknife from the kitchen. She wiped the soot from the glass with a rag. She lit the small lamp, watching as the flame rose steadily through the chimney. The smell of paraffin was strong. She picked up the lamp. The flame flickered as she pulled it closer to her.

The light glinted off the bayonets as she crept like a thief along the edges of her living room. She stole past the band of officers still huddled at the eating table. The air was clouded with their cigarette smoke. Their uniforms hinted of gunpowder and horsehair. She stepped over a pile of drab canvas sacks choked with days of dust, and headed down her narrow hall.

Michael had trailed out of the house sometime after dinner. He usually hid out in the stable. If there was enough straw or dried dung, he would light a fire in the pit when night fell. Maria could see its glow from the window. If there was nothing to burn, he would sit in the dark wrapped in blankets until he fell asleep.

In the first weeks after the invasion, Michael had stayed close to Maria. When she walked outside to feed the chickens, he walked out with her. When she went into the kitchen, he stayed near enough that he could see her. He had been loath to let her out of his sight, but he eventually eased off. The threat of rape or caning was real for the villagers who were billeting conscripts, but officers didn't pose the same threat. They had shown appropriate behavior when it came to Maria, aloof but civil, and Michael had begun to retreat to his stable as often as he could. His house was packed with subjugators, foreigners with a foreign tongue, and it was intolerable to him. Every night he thought about the oppressors gathered in his living room, planning their take while seated at his dinner table, eating his food.

If Michael had any nagging reservations about leaving Maria in the house with the officers, they were put to rest by the presence of Auntie Suzy. The midwife had begun to show up at the house nearly every day, and he knew that Maria was as safe with her as she was with him. The Romanians knew to give a wide berth to a Romany wise woman.

Maria opened the door to Alex's bedroom. In the corner was a single bed where he lay shivering. He had drawn a thin blanket over himself, and Maria could see the rickety outline of his shape underneath. The sharp ridges of his bones poked at the cover.

He had not left his bed in days. He emptied his loose bowels in the chamber pot. The pot was just feet away from his bed, but he still managed to soil himself much of the time.

He twitched and shuddered under the blanket. It had taken a great effort, but he had changed into his nightclothes. He had left the clothes he had been wearing for Maria to collect. She had begun to wash both sets daily.

Earlier in the day, Auntie Suzy had brought Alex a cup of coffee.

He drank it after she had left. Along the wall near his bed was the sill of a window that had long ago been bricked up. He placed the empty *findzsa* there, at the blind window, where it still sat.

In his darker moments, Alex had confided to his mother that he feared the disease that had been chasing him his whole life had finally caught up with him. Alternately, he asked Auntie Suzy, who checked on him daily, if he had contracted Spanish flu.

Maria took the cup from the blind window to bring back to the kitchen. She picked up the clothes. They smelled foul. The whole room smelled like a privy. The stink had started to saturate the air even beyond his bedroom. Maria left Alex and hurried with the clothes outside, where she would air them in the night before washing them in the morning.

THE MIDWIFE PULLED back her curtain. A layer of frost covered her window. She cast a chilled breath on the pane and rubbed the glass with her fist to clear her view.

Her trees and shrubs were decked with ice crystals. Her dog had taken cover in the stable. The fire she normally kept burning in the pit in the yard hadn't been lit in days. Under normal circumstances, Auntie Suzy was well stocked with fuel. But the autumn had already been colder and wetter than most, and she had been unable to replenish her fuel supply. The Romanians requisitioned every cartload that came into Nagyrév, no matter who was towing it or what was inside. She feared that what she had in her stable now would have to last the family until spring.

The midwife had been less affected by the occupiers than most in Nagyrév. They had not billeted in her house or stable, and they didn't taunt or trouble her the way they did others in the village. Even so, this was still among the most difficult times the midwife could recall. The presence of the Romanians had cost her in ways she could not begin to calculate. She had largely given up her daily rounds of collecting, and her son had been ousted from his job delivering mail for the post and telegraph office. A Romanian officer had replaced him.

This meant Auntie Suzy had been unable to get her elixirs to any of her clients outside the village.

She had begun to feel nearly as poor as she had felt growing up. She could clearly remember those days, when she had dashed with a plate of hot embers from the neighbor's hut to light the fire in her own family's shanty. She remembered being hauled by cart to the village hall at Christmas so the gadjo could throw their old clothes into the crowd of Romany children in the name of charity. Little Suzy had reached for the tattered rags in a free-for-all grab.

Auntie Suzy yanked open her door and waddled out onto her porch, where freezing rain had begun to spit. She eased down her steps and trod carefully across the slippery patchwork of autumn leaves. She lifted the fence latch and shoved hard on the gate to dislodge the ice. She spat into the ditch as she crossed over it to totter up the road.

The road was an awful mix of ice and mud. She stayed to the side, where even the wet leaves threatened to pull her down. She walked like a hunter, every step cautious.

She had left her baskets at home. Her national identity card was tucked into her apron pocket, next to her pipe and pouch of tobacco. Her vial, wrapped as ever in white paper, was full. She looked up. She framed her hands around her face to protect it from the sleet coming down. She scanned the road up and down, but it was empty, except for a lonely conscript on patrol. She knew only a soul on a mission would be out in such horrid weather.

The midwife tramped across Maria's yard and heaved herself onto the porch. She let herself in without knocking.

Inside was warmer than her house had been all month. No frost was gathering on any windowpane at the Kardoses' house. Woodsmoke was in the air. Auntie Suzy eyed the bounty of firewood, which the conscripts had purloined from the villagers and given to the officers.

Mixed with the woodsmoke was the spicy aroma of goulash. When Auntie Suzy sniffed it, she felt a low, satisfying rumble in her stomach.

Several officers were seated at the table. Spoons clanked and pots thudded. Benches scraped on the floor. She eyed Michael as he brought his bowl to his mouth to better slurp the stew.

In the kitchen, Auntie Suzy spotted Maria standing near a steaming pot of goulash that simmered on the stove.

"Is Alex still the same?" asked the midwife.

"Yes, of course," said Maria.

Auntie Suzy unfastened her coat. She stood inside the doorway. She made sure her ample body blocked any view to the kitchen by Michael or the officers. She reached into her pocket and ferreted for the vial.

"This, dear Maria," she whispered to her friend, "will also cost six thousand crowns."

This was not the first vial Auntie Suzy had supplied. Maria's sickly boy was not succumbing nearly as quickly as the midwife had imagined he would.

The sum was enormous. Enough to purchase ten tons of wheat. It was nearly all the cash that Maria had left. The bundle of bills was so large, Maria had had trouble hiding it all morning.

Auntie Suzy snatched the roll of bills from Maria and hastily shoved the money deep into her own apron pocket.

The payment was enough for forty additional doses.

Auntie Suzy removed the wooden stopper and poured two tea-spoonfuls of her flypaper elixir into a glass that Maria had filled with water. The solution could be mixed with anything now and go unde-tected: stew, coffee, wine.

The voices in the living room rose and fell like a wave.

"Start giving this to Alex three times a day," Auntie Suzy whis-pered, as she emptied the solution into a bowl of goulash. She stirred the soup with her fat finger until it was fully blended.

She handed the bowl to Maria, who disappeared with it down the hall.

The midwife reached into the cupboard and grabbed a bowl for herself. She ladled a big serving of goulash into it and carried the bowl out to the dining table. She plopped down on the bench, sitting tight against the officer next to her. She sank her spoon into the meaty soup. She knew she would nap better after a hearty meal.

Sunday, November 2, 1919
All Souls' Day

The skies ripped with rain.

Exhausted horses and mules strained to heave carts through mud that was a foot deep. The cart wheels were laden with sludge and spun slowly along the deep, jagged ruts of the wagon tracks, slapping the mire back onto the street or flinging it onto the sodden grass along the ditch.

November was a month as despairing as the Hungarian soul. Every year, a thick, harrumphing fog moved in. It was a heavy, disapproving gray haze that stitched itself into the firmament. This dreary coat thrown over the Plains sky reminded Hungary of her losses, and on no day was this more evident than on the Day of the Dead, a time of personal remembrance that Magyars took more seriously than perhaps any other holy day.

Nagyrév's drenched streets carried a tide of villagers to the cemetery to lay offerings at the grave sites of loved ones. They were gifts to soothe restless souls. Yellow chrysanthemums, brandy, ham (a true scarcity), treasures that on this day only were not subject to the scrutiny or sticky hands of conscripts. Before the Romanian occupation, the baker usually sold plenty of his huge loaves of Seelenbrot, bread that was more than two feet long and nearly a foot wide, and weighed in at ten pounds. The villagers had always purchased the loaves to give to the poor. But the baker had stopped baking them since the start of the occupation.

Auntie Suzy pressed against the current of people and arrived at Maria's house by midday. Michael and Maria had left a candle burning, lit in remembrance of their dead relatives. The flame flickered wildly sometimes, throwing harsh shadows on the midwife as she shuffled about her friend's kitchen.

The tin pot on the stove trembled as it came to a boil. Auntie Suzy shuffled over to the pot with a towel in her hands and lifted it from the stove. She snuffed out the fire. Maria had been trailing nervously behind her, but when the midwife was focused on a task, very little disturbed her.

The midwife and Maria had been together nearly every day in recent weeks and Auntie Suzy had been reminded how peculiar Maria's behavior could be. One afternoon, she had found Maria nearly giddy after witnessing the midwife administer a dose to Alex. And every time Maria and Auntie Suzy spoke about their strategy, she noticed her friend's voice was tinged with excitement.

The midwife lifted the pot lid. The ersatz coffee smelled bitterly of carrots and turnips. Steadily, Auntie Suzy poured the coffee into the findzsa. Next, she measured out two teaspoons of her own solution, since Maria's supply had been used up, and plunked it into the coffee.

"I will give you this for fifty crowns."

Weeks had gone by since the first dose. Both the midwife and Maria found it incredible that the boy had not yet passed.

THE BAD WEATHER eased for a few days and a springlike atmosphere came briefly to the village. Some men took advantage of the warm spell and climbed onto their roofs to patch holes and secure the thatch. Sometimes they sat up there awhile, perched on their haunches and peering silently into their neighbors' yards. Like birds, they watched the movements in the billet next door, tracking the action sidelong. From that vantage point, the men could also look down to the road and see the conscripts out on patrol, strolling the muddle of byways like predators. It was a scarce sight to see a dog roaming now. The mongrels had learned to stay a safe distance from the soldiers.

Maria had been relieved to have the sunshine come. At the first drop of warmth, she moved Alex outside, where she set up a bed in the side yard. She piled extra blankets on him, and he lay under them like an injured animal. She dragged a bench over and sat near him. She put her face to the sun and closed her eyes. She relished the fresh warmth on her skin. She had been forced to spend her days in the dark, smelly room with Alex, and she felt the room had become as much her oppressor as the foreign army bunking in her house. It was the officers' watchful eyes that kept her trapped in there. The sun and the outdoors were a welcome respite.

Maria knew what duty looked like. She had carried trays of food back to Alex's room, and old magazines offered by the reading circle. She had brought back ointments and poultices. She had told his friends when they turned up at the door that Alex was too ill to receive visitors. Auntie Suzy often sat with her in the room and together they scrubbed the walls and floor with vinegar to clean and help cut back the odor.

When Alex slept, it was a restless sleep, but it was then that Maria was most attentive to him. She moved over him like a spirit, observing but never touching. She eyed the pallor of his skin. She drew in close with a lamp to examine his hair, which had become very brittle. She pulled back to watch his breath, waiting for it to stop.

Wednesday, November 19, 1919

Overnight, the temperature dropped severely and the brief streak of warm days came to an abrupt end. At dawn, Maria lit all the fires in the stoves, and by breakfast the Romanians had grown sleepy in the cozy warmth of the living room, where Maria had laid out their food.

Strips of cloth had been packed against the doorsill and along the window edges to keep out the bitter draft. A blanket had been drawn over the entrance to the loft to further seal in the heat. Inside the house, it had quickly become as warm as a summer day. The officers usually headed out straightaway in the morning to their posts. They had offices inside the village hall and the post and telegraph office, and they had set up a makeshift office inside the reading circle, but it was so snug inside the house, they decided to loll for a bit longer. They were all so taken with the luck of their comfort, no one noticed Maria slip out of the house. Not even Michael.

She sprinted across the frozen yard. Icicles had formed on the tree, and as she ducked under it, one or two dropped down on her.

When she got to the stable, she pulled hard on the frozen latch. The door opened with a violent thrust. She let herself in and shoved the big door shut behind her. Maria leaned against it to catch her breath. Michael kept his hand lantern on a peg on a wall near the door. She plucked it off and lit it with one of the matches he kept on the shelf, next to his flask of brandy.

She set the lamp on Michael's workbench and hurried, her heart fluttering wildly now, to Michael's diku. It was situated beside the stable door among the fodder boxes and slop buckets. Alex lay upon it like a fallen fledgling.

Maria leaned over him. He smelled putrid. His skin was gray, like winter. He was drained of fluid, and his face was puckered and sunken. His head looked to Maria like a half-plowed field, as large patches of his hair had fallen out.

She fluffed out the skirt of her dress and gently lowered herself onto the diku. She patted softly at the pile of blankets she had placed over her son. Maria had moved Alex in during the night, a feat she was unsure she could accomplish until it was finished.

When Maria was alone with Alex, she had begun to speak to him as if he were her confidant. He became a repository for all of her private thoughts and secrets, a lockbox of confessions. Alex slipped in and out of consciousness as she spoke to him about his father, the little traits that had drawn her to him and the big flaws that had driven her away. She spoke about her marriage to the lieutenant, and about Michael. She reminisced about her favorite childhood memories and the grievances she still carried against the friends she had when she was young. She talked about the son born before him who had died of typhoid. Maria talked to him like a little girl to her doll.

She patted the blanket once more. She looked at his face. His jaw had slackened. She knew it couldn't possibly be much longer now.

She felt a touch of goodwill toward him, which sent her searching through her bank of memories until she landed upon a pleasing one of him. It was the day of her second wedding. The church was packed with guests. The time had come to sing a hymn and she could hear Alex, who was seated in front with her parents, singing the melody with the voice of a cantor. Her guests had remarked what a lovely voice he had. It was a good memory. The single best memory she had of him.

She reached down and touched her hand to his head.

"Sing, my dear boy," she whispered. "Sing me my favorite song."

MARIA STUMBLED OUT of the stable. A blustery wind caught under her petticoats, blowing them around like pinwheels as she dashed back across the yard.

She shouted into the wind.

ALEX IS DEAD! ALEX IS DEAD!

Bits of straw from the diku that had caught in her long shawl fluttered to the ground as she ran.

ALEX IS DEAD!

She crouched down, looking through the gaps in the fence. The officers' horses, which had been hitched there earlier, were gone.

Maria hurried up the icy steps and into the house. She pushed open the door and shouted for Michael. Before the occupation, he had spent mornings at the reading circle, but now he often retreated to a friend's house, or went for walks in the woods, away from the eyes of prying soldiers.

Dirty dishes and pots still cluttered the eating table. Burning logs still hissed and popped in the stove. There was an innocence preserved in the warmth and stillness.

The ancient rites to protect the living from the souls of the recent dead had to be fulfilled swiftly, before the boy's spirit had any chance of becoming trapped. Maria didn't want Alex to haunt her house. So she hastened to the clock on the far wall. It was situated above her prized phonograph machine. She reached across the phonograph and put her elfin, trembling hand over the clock pendulum. The ticking stopped. It was just after ten thirty.

She grabbed a pitcher of water from the table and slung it into the stove to douse the flame. She tamped out the fire burning in the kitchen stove, too. In a few moments, the house would begin to grow cold, but tradition forbade a fire to be relit for at least a day.

Flecks of ice that had lodged in her boots began to dislodge and melt, forming tiny puddles behind her as she raced down the hall. She could smell Alex more strongly than she could in the front of the house. She dashed past her son's room to her bedroom, where she turned the mirror facedown.

Auntie Suzy was the first to arrive at Maria's house. She summoned Michael, who went off to notify Alex's friends. Afterward, he and the group of friends headed out to the cemetery to dig the grave.

The midwife sent one of the neighbors to fetch the coffin maker to come measure the body for the coffin. She sent another neighbor to fetch the bell ringer.

Auntie Suzy was with the body in the stable when the bell ringer arrived. She shuffled with him over to the chicken coop. She opened the latch and shoved her thick hands in, palms open wide to grab one of the trapped, panicky hens. With the scared bird firmly in her grip, she lifted it out of the coop up to the bell ringer, who plucked out a feather. Auntie Suzy dropped the squawking bird back into the pen and went back over to where Alex's body was still laid out on the diku. She watched as the bell ringer held the feather over Alex's mouth. The feather moved not at all. The bell ringer held the feather under Alex's nose, but the feather did not waver there, either.

The bell ringer pronounced Alex dead.

He asked Auntie Suzy what he should write in the death register.

"Consumption," she said, a malady she had pulled out of the blue. "Pulmonary tuberculosis."

As the bell ringer was leaving, the coffin maker was arriving with his reed to measure the body. He would have a coffin ready by the afternoon, painted blue, the same color Stephen Joljart's coffin had been painted three years earlier.

THE BELL RINGER set about informing the village of Alex Junior's passing. He went first to Pastor Toth's house to notify him of the death. From Toth's house, it was a short walk to the church.

Inside the bell tower, he stood with his feet positioned firmly on the ground. There were two bells, and the rope of the smaller bell, the "soul bell," hung before him. He gripped the sally with both hands and yanked on it. The clapper struck the rim, giving a resounding toll. He grabbed hold of the rope's noose-like tail as it rose above him and tugged down on it again for the next strike, and the next. After 150 tolls, he moved over to the larger bell and struck it 150 times as well.

When he was finished, he opened the church doors and stood at the threshold. A number of people had already gathered in the church-yard. Some merchants on Árpád Street stood in their doorways to listen. The clanging at the blacksmith's workshop had stopped, and the blacksmith, too, stood attentively at his door.

"Alexander Kovacs Jr., the son of the deceased Alexander Kovacs Sr. and Maria Szendi," bellowed the bell ringer, "has died this morning at the age of twenty-three."

IN THE AFTERNOON, Michael came back from the graveyard cov-ered in muck. His hair, his hands, his face, the old coat he wore on the occasions that he hunted, were all caked in it. The two vacant patches the mud hadn't claimed were his eyes, but flecks of mud had knitted into his brows and hardened there. Most of the mud had already dried into brittle chunks that dropped off him every time he took a step.

Michael had tiny, nearly invisible scrapes on his hands, left by the leafy branches he had dragged over the empty grave. It was a custom to cover it that way, to keep evil spirits from getting in overnight and making a snug home. It might also keep out the smaller animals who darted in the graveyard after dark.

He was exhausted. He had just turned fifty-three the week before and was no longer cut out for a young man's work. Digging through the unforgiving ground had been like chopping rocks. He had pulled up the grave marker, a weathered cross a little more than two feet long. "Here lies Charles Kovacs, who lived nine months. Died 1895." On the other side, a new inscription would soon read: "Here lies Al-exander Kovacs Jr., who lived 23 years." Alex Junior would be buried atop his brother in the same grave. It was a simple, plain marker and had several nicks and scrapes that had been gouged into it over the years. Maria had refused the offer to replace it. There was no need to waste money on the dead.

THE OFFICERS EXCUSED themselves from the home to sleep at the village hall overnight. After they left, Auntie Suzy, Lidia, and Mari began to prepare the body. They tied up Alex's chin with twine, so his mouth wouldn't open. His face was shaved clean, which was a more delicate task than it should have been, as the arsenic had left his skin flaky and severely aged. There were folds and wrinkles not normally found on such a young person.

Maria had again thought it a waste of good money to bury coins, so Auntie Suzy tore two pieces from the paper that she kept her solution wrapped in and shaped them into circles to cover his eyes. They would have to do to ward off evil spirits.

The women stripped off his soiled clothes and bathed him with rags dipped in soapy water. Auntie Suzy normally dabbed vinegar on the corpse to give the skin a rosy look, but she saw no reason to bother with Alex. His body was too far gone.

Maria was of no help at all to the women. She flitted to and fro, darting from room to room like an excited child. She fussed with the furniture, moving it an inch this way or that, and nervously fingered her necklace. She absentmindedly began to hum a little tune, as she often did when she was anxious or excited, but stopped when Auntie Suzy scolded her. More than once, Auntie Suzy had to give Maria a stern warning to remind her to behave like a bereaved mother.

Finally, the women dressed Alex. They put him in the same clothes he had worn to his father's funeral two years earlier. They had spent hours preparing the body, yet the midwife was still concerned. It looked desiccated, and the mourners might notice something was amiss.

Auntie Suzy lifted him. He was light, like driftwood, all the essential parts of him washed away. He weighed less than seventy pounds.

She carried him to the living room. The eating table had been moved to the side of the room and two planks had been set up between two chairs to make a "cold bed." Auntie Suzy leaned down and laid the body on it.

By now, the house was bitterly cold. A coat of ice had formed on the insides of the windowpanes. The walls felt wet to the touch. Auntie Suzy could see her breath. She had on several petticoats, but she still felt the cold as if she were lying facedown in the snow. Her joints ached. No one would be allowed to warm the house until after the body was removed.

She could hear Michael outside greeting the mourners.

A large group stepped into the room, forming a larger circle around the tight circle of women surrounding the body. It seemed to be an impenetrable wall around the corpse, which Alex's friends dared not disrupt.

"God console the sad-hearted ones who are left behind, and take the dead into the Kingdom of Heaven," the visitors chimed.

"May God hear you," Maria responded, not lifting her head.

Auntie Suzy, Lidia, and Maria began to keen. The wailing was shrill. Each time a mourner entered uttering the prayer, the crying song grew louder. As the women keened, Maria lamented a chain of sorrowful words.

The mourners were cycled swiftly through the viewing and none were permitted to see Alex up close, nor were they allowed to stay more than a few seconds. Their time with him was disturbingly quick. Feeling spurned and confused, Alex's closest friends retreated to Michael's stable. Some fashioned stools out of empty, upturned buckets. Some sat on the diku, unaware Alex had taken his last breath there. They took down Michael's flask from the shelf and passed it around. They found his jug of brandy stored in a cupboard. They could still hear the keening, though the distance had given the women's cries a more mysterious quality. They could hear some of the older men singing psalms.

They began to heap affection on their friend. No one played tarok as well as he did, no one was a more hapless chicken thief, and nowhere in Nagyrév, or in all of the Plains, would there ever be someone with a quicker wit than Alex Kovacs Jr.

As the brandy jug drained, they posited theories about his death. He had been sicker in recent years, but none among them expected he would die. Maybe, one friend suggested, his failed time in Budapest had hastened it.

They talked about Alex's father's death, and a few other men they knew who had recently passed away. Men who had survived the war had come home and died after a quick illness. Mr. Farkas had surprised everyone when he died in September, as he was only thirty-nine. Mr. Major's grave had been dug just two days earlier.

So many were passing away, Alex's friends were starting to get confused about who had died and who hadn't. They laughed soberly as the story was told about one friend who had headed out to another friend's wake, only to see that friend passing them on the street.

The laughter gave way to fond stories of Alex. His pals stayed on into the night, and left as a new snow began to fall.

Thursday, November 20, 1919

Maria's house was dark, except for the small glow emanating from Auntie Suzy's lantern. The house was still icy and noiseless.

Auntie Suzy had left the funeral early to come back to Maria's house, but she didn't have much time, because the mourners would be back soon for the feast. She waddled into the kitchen and set her baskets down. They were filled with twigs and fruit she had dried especially for the occasion. She reached into the cupboard and took out the same large pot Maria used to prepare the goulash.

The midwife grabbed the twigs and dried fruit from the basket and dumped it all into the pot. She lit a match and set the mixture on fire. She was immediately grateful for the rush of warmth from the small blaze.

Auntie Suzy had rarely been afraid of a gadjo's soul returning. She knew it was only the *mullo*, the Romany spirit, that could come back and wreak torture on the living. But the duration of Alex's suffering had her worried about his restlessness. A safeguard was required.

The midwife watched the flames lick around the twigs and then devour the fruit. A marvelous scent filled the home as Auntie Suzy walked with the flaming pot through the house, cleansing the air of Alexander Kovacs Jr.'s spirit. He belonged to the other world now.

ALEX JUNIOR'S COTTAGE was situated farther out Árpád Street on a sizable plot of land. Auntie Suzy knew the house. From time to time, she had treated Alex Senior there for muscle spasms and sprains, and she considered it a fine house, a perfect house for her youngest son. She felt especially pleased thinking about it now. She felt sated, as if by a good meal. Maria had agreed that her final payment to the midwife, due in six months, would come in the form of Alex's house.

A DOCTOR'S SUSPICIONS

It was an open secret.

—ISTVÁN BURKA, MAYOR OF NAGYRÉV

Maria lifted her basket into the wagon and dropped it onto the leather bench inside. She hitched up her skirt and hoisted herself in. She adjusted her hat. It had a broad brim to keep out the sun and a long ribbon that she had fashioned in a petite bow under her chin. The smell of roasted bacon wafted up from her basket. She had also packed large pieces of white bread, and at the bottom of the basket was some fruit. She was happy to be heading to her fields, where she had begun to show up nearly every day.

The horse plodded up Árpád at a yawning gait and as they got farther from the village center, Maria directed the horse slightly off her course, to where Alex Junior's house was located. Nearly eight months had passed since Maria had promised the house to the midwife. To Maria's great annoyance, Auntie Suzy was beginning to pester her about the deal.

She slowed the horse to a stop in front of the house. It was a large enough home on a large property, as the Kovacs family had their share of wealth, too. It had been too nice for a boy like Alex, who had never really appreciated it, she was sure. She took it in a moment longer, then snapped her gaze away. She leaned back against the seat and, lifting and flapping the reins, motioned the nag onward. Surely there were far better uses for the house than to give it to the old midwife.

The horse trundled on for another half mile or so. Once they were out of the village proper, they passed a few Romany women, who walked with large bundles strapped to their backs, but otherwise the road was nearly empty. It wouldn't fill again until dusk, when the caravans lumbered back to the village.

Maria pushed the brim of her hat up and looked out at the fields. There was a network of footpaths connecting one plot to another, and many farmers had stopped to eat their lunches there. They sat on the ground with their satchels of food beside them.

Maria tugged the reins again, and the horse came to a halt. She squinted her eyes against the sun to search her golden crops.

She saw him look up. He squinted back at her, holding his hand up and waving to her. He lumbered out of the high fields to the path. He loped toward her, short strides on short legs. Franklin had the look of a Plains man; no matter where he was from, she had seen that straightaway.

He walked like other young farmers and farmhands did, barefoot with his boots slung over his shoulder. His linen clothing was encrusted with dirt. His feet had been sunk into the soil all morning. His skin had turned as golden as the wheat. She picked up the basket of food to give to him. In the breeze, she could feel the ribbon of her hat brushing against her face. She looked forward each day to bringing Franklin's lunch to him.

Franklin and his sister, Marcella, had escaped Transylvania on foot in June, just after the region was lost to the Romanians when the Treaty of Versailles went into effect. Other large swaths of the country were broken off to give to existing countries and to form new ones, but Romania by far got most of Hungary and its resources. Hungary's borders had been so drastically reduced that more than half the population was now living outside of the country. Franklin and Marcella were among hundreds of thousands who had fled to set up new lives inside new borders.

They had aimed for Szolnok, but when they arrived there, they had seen right away that the city was overwhelmed with refugees. Thousands of families were living in abandoned boxcars at the rail yard. The unluckier ones took shelter in even worse spaces. Franklin and his sister had continued onward, following some minstrels or peddlers east out of Szolnok to Nagyrév, where the two siblings prepared a bulletin for the crier to read at his drumming:

BROTHER AND SISTER FROM TRANSYLVANIA WILL WORK FOR ROOM AND BOARD.

Maria had seized on them. She had put Marcella to work with her around the house and Franklin she had put to work building up her farm again. Her fields had yielded little in recent years.

Before she put the brother and sister to work, she had given them a tour around the village. She took them down to the riverfront to meet the women there, who were cleaning their scythes or their clothes. She introduced Franklin and Marcella as her "new son and daughter." She took them to the church, to Feldmayr's, to the post office, to the Thursday market, and everywhere it was the same: *Meet my new son, Franklin. Meet my new daughter, Marcella.*

Maria had arranged Alex Junior's old room for Marcella. Lately, Michael had spent fewer nights at home, neither in the house nor in the stable, so she set Franklin up on his diku in the stable.

Franklin took the lunch basket from her. She watched him as he breathed in the aromas. She waited for him to invite her to eat with him. She had packed enough food for two.

THE MIDWIFE REACHED under the table. She put a hand to her fat knee and rubbed at the ache. Both of her knees were tight and swollen, and needle pricks of pain tapped at her calves, too. She had spent a lot of time lately bent over her flowers at home, and the toiling had aggravated her arthritis. She looked around the pub, which was nearly empty. Most of the benches were still slid up under the tables, and the floors had been swept clean. Anna would not spread wood chips until the evening, when the farmers were back in the village. Auntie Suzy cradled the bowl of her pipe in her hand. She sucked the tobacco vapor deep into her lungs and exhaled a long fog of smoke, which floated across the table into Ébner's fat, wrinkled face.

After a moment, she took another long draw. Ébner took a pinch of tobacco from his snuffbox and stuffed the powder into his nostrils. Small bits fell back onto his freshly waxed mustache. On days the barbershop was open, Ébner liked to step in and have Daniel wax his mustache for him, as he didn't have the patience for the tedium himself. Auntie Suzy could see the glistening tips. She watched the mustache move up and down as Ébner spoke.

Their visits together had been interrupted by the occupation, and Auntie Suzy had missed seeing Ébner. When they were finally able to meet again, she saw that he had managed to grow fatter in those months, though she wasn't sure how.

Auntie Suzy had long ago noticed that when Ébner talked, he was a fisherman casting lines. He threw out tidbits and waited to see which ones would get a bite. For the most part, he had learned this practice from his wife and two daughters, who were a well-known trio of gossips in Nagyrév.

While he nattered, he drank wine and ate from the large plate Anna had put in front of him. Between the slurping and the chomping and the wiping of his mouth with his handkerchief, he told Auntie Suzy the news about old Dr. Szegedy, which was that the old man was stepping down from his duties.

There was a small hiccup in time for Auntie Suzy when she heard this. She had relied on old Dr. Szegedy's inebriation and indifference for decades. She had not had to imagine the thorny problems a new doctor might bring.

She eyed Ébner. He was as hearty an eater as Michael was, and she could see he took his food far more seriously than most other matters in his life. Auntie Suzy watched as he lifted a forkful over his lip, where the mustache hovered like a hairy guard. Yet he talked still, forcing his words through the heavy terrain of meat on his tongue. A new doctor was to be appointed in November, he told the midwife. He speared more meat onto his fork and sent it into the chamber of his mouth again, having barely swallowed the previous bite. The old doctor, Ébner mumbled, was to be replaced by his son, Dr. Kalman Szegedy Jr.

Ébner wiped his mouth with his hanky. He slid a penknife between his teeth to dislodge a sliver of meat that had stuck there.

A TORRENT OF rain in late summer was not unheard of on the Plains, and the showers in August had been heavy and sustained for three days. They had washed out the roads and swollen the Tisza, which had nearly burst its banks. The ditches had filled like bathing tubs, ready to overflow into the yards.

From the bedroom, Maria could hear Michael stomping at the floor. He was trying to shake the last bits of rainwater off his boots. There was a rag she kept near the door so he could wipe them dry, but Michael rarely bothered with it. She heard him grunt and swear as he tugged his boots off, and grunt again as he peeled out of his rain-soaked coat.

The rain had beat hard on the roof in the last hours. The drops fell like hard pips against the window. She held her breath in the darkness, keeping a fox ear on Michael to track his movements.

The sun set late in summer on the Plains, at nearly ten o'clock, and it was then, after Marcella had turned in for the night and before Michael had been chased home by the downpour, that Maria had hurried out to the stable to summon Franklin inside.

You can't stay out here in such weather. Come in where it's warm and dry.

He had followed her back into the house, first to her bedroom with her, and afterward out to the living room on his own, where he had unrolled Michael's diku, which was still damp and smelling of mold from the wet stable. He laid it out on the floor near the settee, sprawled upon it, sated, and fell asleep. Meat in Maria's trap.

She heard the squeak of Michael's rusty hand lantern. She saw flashes of light dart in the corridor. She lay curled on the bed, a pixie in the half-light. She did not flinch.

She had been alone in the dark for more than an hour, listening to the heavy drum of rain and waiting. She had heard nothing from Marcella's room, as the girl was as quiet at night as she was in the day.

Michael lumbered to the doorway. He paused, throwing a brief light on her, before jerking the lantern back with a tipsy grip. Maria watched the light's glow as he wandered back down the hallway, flashing first on one wall, then another, as if the lamp itself were woozy. She knew Michael had struggled to keep his lamp lit in the deluge, but now he cast it about freely. She could hear the handle squeak again as it swung in his hand. The swaggering light moved from the corridor to the living room and began its dance there. Maria steadied her breath.

She could hear Michael fumbling. She listened to his slow, deliberate steps. Even in stocking feet, his tread was heavy. They sounded like lead weights thumping at the floor. She could hear him joggle the rain from his hair, and the splatter of wet drops plunking onto the floor.

He pulled his lantern up in front of him. The flame flickered wildly as the lamp swayed, giving him brief snatches of the room: the clock, the cross on the wall, the table leg, the credenza. In a corner was Maria's phonograph machine and on top of it was her box of needles. The tin glinted in the light. Next to the phonograph machine was the settee, its high back and arms polished to a gleam by Marcella. Michael moved toward it. In the poor light, the room was all sharp edges and blocked paths, and Michael stepped among the furnishings as if there were snakes he was trying to avoid. One more step sent him crashing into a large, unexpected bulk on the floor.

Maria heard the noise and froze.

Michael's small flame lit frantic patches as he struggled to regain his footing. The little light zigzagged from wall to ceiling, from ceiling to table, from table to chair, until it finally came to rest at Michael's feet, where it illuminated the face of Franklin, who was awake now and staring dumbly into the brightness of the lamp.

Michael glared down at him.

What the hell are you doing here?!

Franklin scrambled up. He whipped the mat up from the floor and shoved it under his arm.

What are you doing inside the house?! At this hour?! Where is Maria?!

Franklin stumbled to find his way.

Get the hell out of here!

Maria sprang from her bed. She dashed in her bare feet to the hall. Her long hair hung loose at her back, tousled and untamed. She hurtled headlong through the corridor, in time to catch a last glimpse of Franklin as he slipped out into the rain.

She could smell Michael before she could see him, a mix of cigars and wine and fresh rain. He had sunk down onto the settee. She moved closer.

Most men Maria knew in Nagyrév kept a leather strap in the house, suspended from a peg near the front door. But Michael had never taken a strap to her, nor had she ever seen one in the house. Still, a flutter of fear brushed her, as if with wings. She felt a trace of thrill.

In the darkened room, his blue eyes looked gray, a cold metal of anger.

Why was he in this house at night?! Answer me, Maria!

Michael shot up from the bench. He, a man who rarely had capacity for fury, was consumed by it now. His muscles and nerves moved and twitched in it. His blood was heated by it, his thoughts trapped in it. The only part of him not possessed by rage was the tight, tired knot of feelings he still had for Maria.

He lurched toward her.

Maria inched backward. She scrabbled to the chair near the wall. She grabbed it by its curved rails and flung it into his path.

We aren't married! I can do as I please!

Michael pitched the chair back toward her. It cracked along the hard floor and came to rest on its side. The force rattled the phonograph machine and knocked the box of needles to the ground. They fanned across the floor, spangling it in slivers of silver.

You're not my husband! You can't tell me what to do!

The wet weather had made the house especially cool. A small draft reached across the room to touch Maria with its icy finger. She was shivering, from the chill and from the thrill, but an ichor of nerve still flooded her veins.

She stepped closer to Michael. His face was scarlet. Below him, there was a ghost of a space where the diku had been.

In the three years that she had been with Michael, she had vigorously erased every complication that had stood between them. Yet he had still not wed her.

He seemed suddenly smaller to her somehow. She leaned into him.
As long as I'm not your wife, I can do as I please.

Friday, August 20, 1920

The village hall was cooler by degrees than the air outdoors. Its stone walls were a decent barrier against the usual summer heat, which often hovered in the nineties. But the steady rainfall had reduced the sun's August fever, and the temperature outside had barely made it up to eighty degrees. The hall felt nearly chilly by comparison.

The hall was closed to the public. Maria stood in the very center of the room. She wore a silk hat adorned with feathers and small flowers. The hat was a favorite she had brought with her from Budapest that until now had been stored in a handsome hatbox under the wardrobe she shared with Michael. She had styled her raven hair herself. The silky tresses had been fashioned into coils and pinned underneath the hat, a method she had learned by trial and error from studying the way the Budapest society women did their hair.

Her dress was slim and long, with flowing, airy sleeves, but a bodice that was too tight. Maria had hardly gained an ounce over the years, but she could detect her body broadening in piffling ways: the snugger fit of her rings, the pinch at her waist. She resisted these inevitable changes by always giving the dressmaker the same measurements she had used since she was a girl of twenty.

Underneath, she had on her best pair of silk stockings. She hadn't worn them since Alex's funeral. They had sat for a long time in the back of her wardrobe, and because of that and the recent damp weather, they had taken on a faint fusty smell, which she had hidden with a dot of perfume.

But that scent was lost to her now, overpowered by something much stronger. She dared not take in more than quick gulps of air. She tried not to breathe at all. She could go long stretches holding a small bit of air in her lungs, and she dreaded every breath she did have to take. Every inhalation filled her petite nose with the horrible stench of horse manure.

She was accustomed to the smell out on the streets, where the open air dispelled it, but the odor inside the tight walls of the village hall was more than she could bear, and it was right next to her, discharging from Michael like steam from a train. He stood witheringly, miserably next to her. A castaway signaling with invisible clouds of stink.

He had arrived at the village hall just moments earlier. He had staggered down from his wagon and plunged his foot straight into a heaping pile of soft, smelly dung. The rain pelted at his back as he considered, bleary-eyed, what to do next. He looked at the fouled shoe, examining the excrement like a detective surveying evidence. He looked at his other shoe, as if it might offer further clues. He groaned and lifted his leg up, pressed his foot against the cart wheel as the rain dripped down his neck. He scraped his shoe back and forth across the wheel, trying to get the dung off. But it smeared across his shoe instead, and some of it flopped noisily to the ground, landing on his other shoe.

Michael had dripped the watery dung through the vestibule to the main room, where he now stood next to Maria. His shoes were still coated in excrement, and chunks of it clung to his trouser legs. His hair was uncombed. The tail of his shirt flapped openly under his vest. He had not shaved. His vision was blurry and his head pounded, but he was sure it was Ébner he saw standing in front of him.

Ébner held an open Bible in his hands. On his nose, he balanced his glasses, which he used for reading. He had marked the pages with the passages he required. He had not done this so often that the book fell open to the selections he needed. There had been so very few civil marriages since the law had changed to allow them. He scanned to the reading, holding his finger to mark the spot as he looked up at the couple. On Maria's face he saw the tight set of her jaw. He saw the lines that had appeared in recent years, causing her grimace to deepen. There was a slight quaver in her body. As ever, her crystalline eyes sparkled.

He looked long at Michael. A more defiant groom he had not known.

Ébner bent his head back to his Bible and proceeded.

November 1920

On the Tuesday following his appointment to the post, Dr. Kalman Szegedy Jr. arrived in Nagyrév early in the morning. The weather had not yet turned, and he had been able to make the five-mile journey from Cibakháza with no complications. He had taken over his father's main practice in Cibakháza, but he also had under his authority several regional villages besides Nagyrév, including Tiszaföldvár and Tiszakürt.

Dr. Szegedy stepped down from his carriage. Árpád Street was neither dry nor wet, but glistened from an earlier frost. The ground felt especially firm to him after the jostling ride. His bones were still humming with the journey. The carriage had jounced hard on the jutted wagon tracks, and the unmoving ground he now stood on was a welcome, soothing counterpoise.

Just like his father had done on Tuesdays in Nagyrév, Dr. Szegedy had parked his carriage in front of the village hall to check the appointment book the crier kept for him before setting up in his examination room. For the patients who couldn't get to him, he also made house calls.

The young doctor stepped inside. The vestibule was dark. It truly suffered on sunless days. Dr. Szegedy looked around and saw that nothing about the place was welcoming. Except for a map and a clock, the walls were unadorned. There was a bench along one wall. From the entrance, he could see a weak light emanating from the main chamber. He strode in, following a faint odor of paraffin into the room. The crier had recently refilled the streetlamp on Árpád, as well as the night watchmen's lanterns, and the air still smelled of the oil.

The crier was prepared for his visit. The appointment book was out and laid on the table, open to the date. But first Dr. Szegedy wanted to review the other logbooks. As the new doctor in charge, he thought a look at all records were in order, including the birth and death registers.

The volumes had the old Magyar crest impressed at the top of each page. The registers had once been well bound, but the stitching had started to loosen on some. They were all stained with decades of farmers' dirty fingerprints. The volumes still seemed much too ceremonial for the dreary village hall, even in their state of faded glory.

Dr. Szegedy drew the first log to him. He lifted back the cover and adjusted his spectacles, hunching forward over the book and resembling the old man his father now was. He ran his finger down the inky page, scanning for newborns' names, dates of birth, notes from the attending midwife. He was especially interested in notes jotted about any unusual circumstance of labor.

He saw instances of a line scrawled across the entry where a newborn's name should have been. A cursory note followed, explaining a stillbirth.

He flipped the page. The crackle of paper punctured the silence in the room. He had arrived just before the village hall was to open for the day, and the crier moved quietly around him getting the office ready.

The process was tedious for the doctor, though he scanned as quickly as he could. He was sure his father would never have been so exacting. Dr. Szegedy continued to read, but stopped his finger halfway down a page. He moved in closer. It was difficult to read the jittery scrawl. By now, the sun had fully risen, but the light in the room was still bleak. He looked around for a window that would offer more light.

He flipped back through the book to a previous entry. And further back, to another. He dog-eared several pages.

When he had finished examining the birth records, he moved to the stack of death logs in front of him. The death registers had thick, wide pages, much longer than they were tall. He pressed his finger to his spectacles and pushed them back up his nose. He opened the first volume. Outside, the peal of church bells announced the hour. The children had already set off to school carrying nose bags full of books, and he could hear their giggles and shouts as they played running games on their way to the schoolhouse.

He studied the death entries as hard as he had studied the birth log. Most of the births had been recorded in a hurried scrawl, memos dashed off without thought about how someone might read and make sense of them years later. The handwriting in the death logs was elegant and formal, a graceful script to mark the end of a life.

He ran his fingers across each entry, not yet sure what exactly he was looking for.

He trailed his finger slowly down the page. He stopped. He flipped back a few pages to a previous entry. And further back. In his medical bag were a notepad and pen. He took them out and began to jot notes of his own.

His neck and back were sore from bending over the logs. The crier circled around him, hinting at the appointment book.

In medical school, Dr. Szegedy had been taught how to look for evidence of disease. Observe the pallor of the skin, check the pulse, listen to the heartbeat, the breath. Each symptom and complaint was a clue to a bigger picture that formed a pattern.

Now, he was sure, he saw a pattern in the logbooks.

Dr. Szegedy straightened himself from the table he'd been leaning over. He removed his spectacles and massaged the bridge of his nose. He flipped closed the cover of the last book. A small whoosh of air let out from between the pages like a last breath.

"Who," he asked the crier, "is the midwife here?"

DR. SZEGEDY SPENT much of the day quizzing his new patients about Suzy Fazekas. He asked how long she had been the midwife in the village. Where had she come from and how well the people knew her. He asked about her family.

The young doctor was much like the man his father had once been, in so many ways. Early in the old man's career, his ambition had been unmatched. The elder Dr. Szegedy had put himself on boards and hospital committees, which kept him traveling often to Budapest and Szolnok for meetings. But by the time the war came, he had lost his edge. He became confused in his later years and began to drink. He had been inattentive to his patients. He had also allowed them to carry on with the centuries-old culture of midwives, which included a faith in herbalism and beliefs in witchcraft. But the younger Dr. Szegedy had been tapped to replace his father at this time because of the new regime. His appointment had come because Budapest was pushing regional doctors to bring outdated peasant communities like Nagyrév into the mainstream. He had known his job would be more than tending to the sick once a week. He knew he was being called upon to uproot the midwife tradition in the villages under his jurisdiction. But the morning's revelations had left him stunned. He had come prepared to cope with old customs, not to investigate potential crimes.

BY THE TIME he arrived in Nagyrév the following Tuesday, he was prepared to take action. When the crier met him with the appointment book, the doctor waved it away. Instead, he requested a meeting with Ébner. Dr. Szegedy settled in for a long wait in the dingy hall while the crier went off to fetch Ébner. This was pheasant season, and Ébner was likely to be somewhere in the area of his hunting lodge.

Dr. Szegedy took a seat on the wooden bench. The temperature had dipped recently, and he could feel an unshakable cold, a reminder to him that in another week, maybe in another few days, icy weather would set in and prevent him from coming to Nagyrév at all. The thought made him anxious. He had a lot of ground to cover.

On most days, the village hall saw little activity. From time to time, farmers or their wives stopped in to leave an announcement with the crier or to book an appointment with the doctor, and sometimes villagers came in small groups to make an appeal to Ébner to settle a difference between them. As often as not, there was a hooligan leaving in the morning after a night spent in the "jail" (the crier's storage closet), but it was otherwise an idle place. The crier spent a great deal of his time sweeping away silt that blew in through the cracks under the door. The telephone was usually silent.

From his seat on the bench, Dr. Szegedy could see into the office of the new tax collector, Count Molnar, who toiled quietly. The new administration in Budapest, in its push for change, had placed tax collectors in every village. Molnar was already reviled by the community. Dr. Szegedy couldn't help but pity him.

Ébner entered the hall, bringing with him a cold blast of raw November air that blew in with him.

He shook his staff at the feral dogs who had followed him there and slammed the heavy door shut before one of them could try to nudge its way in. Ébner often smelled of sheep goulash, or some other delicious meat, like goat or pig, which the hounds found irresistible.

He looked down at Dr. Szegedy, who had by now risen from the bench. He reached out his doughy hand to greet the doctor.

Ébner moved past the crier to his office. He jiggled the door open, then poked at it with his staff until it swung wider. He stepped in and removed his lynx coat, leaving Dr. Szegedy to close the door and seat himself. Ébner shuffled over to his desk, an expansive piece of furniture that fit the room not at all. It was as wide as it was long, and Ébner had to ease himself around it in the tight space. He plopped down into his chair. A typewriting machine was situated square in the middle of the desk, and Ébner sat behind it like a captain at a ship's wheel. Next to it was a candlestick telephone and some papers the crier and the postmaster had brought in.

Dr. Szegedy dropped his medical bag to the floor and took out his notes, which he had refined during the week. He had come back to the village hall for a second and third look at the birth and death logs, adding more evidence to support his theory. He adjusted his spectacles on his narrow nose and began to read aloud to Ébner, who kept a steady, immutable gaze fixed on the doctor.

When he had finished, he looked up at Ébner. Ébner kept a stash of brandy in his desk drawer, and the doctor could see it in the old man's glassy gaze.

The patter of hooves floated in from outside, as the traffic on Árpád began to pick up. Dr. Szegedy could hear the crier bustling about out there, sweeping the area in front of the hall.

Ébner stared hard at him. Dr. Szegedy watched in silence as the older man leaned back in his chair and quietly folded his hands across his wide lap. Ébner fiddled with his mustache, contemplating the situation. He was a reluctant bear poked awake by circumstance. Slowly, he leaned forward and reached for the telephone, grabbing the candlestick in his pawlike palm. He shouted into the receiver, instructing the operator to connect him to the gendarmerie in Tiszakürt.

AUNTIE SUZY LAY in her bed under a thick pile of blankets. The room was quite dark. She had closed the shutters to block out the day, and hardly any light came in from the rest of the house. The blankets pressed heavily on her, as if pushing her into sleep. Her head was resting on her favorite pillow.

She had come home and put herself to bed after her morning rounds, which had been capped by a few drinks at the Cser tavern. When she napped, she usually fell asleep quickly. This was in some measure because of the exertion from walking house to house with the heavy weight of her baskets, but also in part from the alcohol she consumed before coming home.

The house was still. Her grandchildren had been sent off to school in the morning, and Mari did lay healings during the day, massages for pulled muscles or sore backs, leeches for headaches. Mari also used some of her mother's herbs to make poultices for other complaints clients had, such as constipation or high blood pressure.

Auntie Suzy slept best when she was alone in the house. She also slept best during her naps. They restored her, and it was within their depths that she had her most divinatory dreams. But she had not been sleeping long when she awoke with a start.

The dog was barking furiously.

She thrust back the blankets and swung her thick feet to the floor. She was used to being awakened from a deep sleep, as babies came on their own schedules, but the old hound's urgency disturbed her. She shoved her stockinged feet into her wooden shoes.

She waddled to the window and pressed her pointy ear to the pane. She could hear nothing over the dog's frenzied cries. She hurried out of her room, mumbling to herself. Her dress had twisted around her while she slept, and she yanked it back into place as she scampered along the short hallway. Her wooden shoes clomped heavily, striking like blunt mallets at the floor. Her heart raced. The old dog could scent danger.

She darted into the kitchen. Long, silver strands of hair had fallen into her face. Her cheeks were still rosy from the wine and the sleep, and the embroidery from her pillowcase had etched a light imprint on one side. She looked around her.

The aromas of an earlier meal lingered in the air. Her apron, which she had removed before her nap, hung on a peg. The dog let out a long, shrill cry. Auntie Suzy dropped to the floor.

She crawled like a toddler toward the wall. The toes of her wooden shoes scraped and bumped along the floor, but her fat palms moved as fast as a crab. She crouched against the wall. She could hear now the crier's drumbeat.

Bastard!

Her putsi rested at her bosom. She reached for it, following the cord it hung on with her fingers until she found the pouch, which held her reassuring little talismans. Auntie Suzy held it tight and began to mutter the ancient incantations she had learned from her grandmother.

"SUZANNAH FAAAZEKAAS, COME OUT, PLEASE!!" sang the crier.

Auntie Suzy squared her hands on the floor and hefted herself up. She flattened her back against the wall and inched toward the window. The lace curtain hung down to the sill. The kitchen table, where she told fortunes, was directly under the window.

She crept one hand to the curtain and pushed it back a sliver. She leaned forward and peeked out with narrowed eyes. The dog was leaping at the fence gate, his back arching as he spiraled upward in a corkscrew. His jaws snapped at the air.

Auntie Suzy dropped the curtain back and took a quick survey of the room. Her empty baskets were on the table. She eyed her apron. She could see the small bulges in the pockets. The sideboard was tidy and the drawers were shut tight.

"SUZANNAH FAAAAZEKASS, COME OUT, PLEEEEASE!"

The pantry was in view. She put a hand to her galloping heart. She tried not to keep an extensive stockpile in the house. Her biggest supply she kept in small jars buried near her composting pile. And there was also a jar buried near the firepit, underneath the hound's favorite spot. But the vials in the pantry were empty, and each empty vial always had residue at its bottom.

Menj a fenébe!

May they be eaten by the devil!

She pulled back the curtain one more time. The sky was as overcast as it had been earlier when she was making her rounds. Her yard looked barren. The golden autumn leaves had already been raked and burned in her firepit. The creepers were denuded, making it easy to spot the unmistakable helmets the gendarmes wore, which were festooned with a grand plumage of rooster feathers. The feathers rose grandly over the top of her fence, as if a rooster himself were sitting on the gendarme's head, surveying the village from on high. Auntie Suzy quickly dropped the curtain back. She had never seen a gendarme in the village. She had only ever seen them in Tiszakürt when she visited her cousin.

Those meddling bastards!

She raced to the pantry. There was no time. She raced back over to the sideboard where she kept the flypaper. She tugged at the drawer, but she soon realized there was no way for her to dispose of her stash. She raced back again to the wall near the window. She was a mouse in a maze.

"A fene egye meg!"

"SUZANNAH FAAAAZEKASS, COME OUT, PLEEEEASE!"

She raced back to the table and sank onto the bench, panting.

"SUZANNAH FAAAAZEKASS, COME OUT, PLEEEEASE!"

She called out for help to her dead grandmother. She called in the spirits.

The midwife looked around the room for options. She wished Mari were there to help her. She heaved herself up from the bench and hurried down the hall to peer back into her bedroom. She could go back to bed, pretend she was asleep. Maybe the bastards would just go away if they thought she wasn't home. But her loyal old dog wouldn't bark like that if she wasn't at home, she knew that. And she was sure the gendarmes knew it, too. She scurried back to the bench and dropped herself onto it again. She considered an escape, but there was only one door to her house, one way in and out. She was surrounded.

She pitched her heavy body forward to haul herself once again from the bench, and when she did, her putsi dropped down into her face. She seized it and brought it to her lips.

Her skirt and petticoat bunched between her plump thighs as she scurried to her coat. She jammed her arms into the sleeves and wrenched the belt tight.

Outside, there was a haze of smoke from the open fire that had been smoldering in the pit since daybreak. She moved through it, fanning it from her like a magician. At the fence, she pushed back her frantic dog and, with a swift jerk, popped open the gate. The midwife could see the crier standing on the opposite side of the ditch. He was cloaked in a dark winter cape. His woolen, cone-shaped cap came down over his ears. His drum hung in front of him like a barrel.

The two gendarmes stood next to him. They wore double-breasted, olive-green overcoats. They had rifles with bayonets strapped to their shoulders. Both had large mustaches that dominated their faces. Their feathered helmets gave them each an extra foot of height.

As the midwife crossed over the ditch, the gendarmes grabbed her sharply by the arms and hefted her the rest of the way. She landed awkwardly on the other side, but the two men refused to loosen their hard grip. The crier stepped in behind them all.

Fraught at the sight of his mistress's capture, the dog began to whimper.

There was little activity on Orphan Street in winter. Farmers came and went in their carts, but the road stayed mostly quiet and empty. Still, no one, perhaps not even the crier, took notice of the neighbors who had pressed their faces to the gaps between the slats of their fences and eyed, from the safety of their yards, the midwife being taken by the officers. Among them was Petra.

The gendarmes took quick, harsh strides, their rifles slapping hard against their hips. Auntie Suzy struggled to keep pace. They wrenched her arms tighter every time she faltered. The crier stayed a few steps behind the trio, both hands on his drum to keep it from swaying.

With as much sugar in her voice as she could muster, the midwife assured the officers and anyone she thought might be in earshot that she had done nothing wrong. Surely, they were mistaken.

The gendarmes and their charge came to an abrupt stop when they reached Árpád Street. Carts ambled up and down the road haphazardly. The street was wide enough for wagons and animals of all shapes and sizes, and each, when it suited them, snuck up the wrong side, or suddenly changed course and turned around to go in the opposite direction. There was no method, no order, no nod toward the kind of traffic system larger towns and cities employed. Árpád was as much a mishmash of traffic as the jumbled arrangement of side roads that had taken root in Nagyrév. On the busiest days, the chaos created sudden tangles of carts and carriages, oxen and mules, that had to be carefully untied by the farmers caught up in the bungle before anyone could get moving again.

The gendarmes moved in even closer to the midwife. She could smell their stale tobacco breath. Their wool coats hinted at mold.

A tinkle of cart bells rang out up and down the street, but it was the jangle that streamed from the post and telegraph office that caught the midwife's attention. It was like a beacon calling to her, and her old heart fluttered with an idea.

The crier stepped forward to get in front of the trio and moved into the street with his drum. He held one hand up in the air and beat the drum with his other hand to signal the vehicles to halt. The traffic came to a confused standstill.

The crier motioned to the gendarmes. The midwife was bundled, as if by bandits, across the roadway, lifted over the ditch like a child, and deposited heavily onto the walkway.

By now, a tide of villagers had gathered to watch. They gaped at the sight of their wise woman, whose two baskets had been replaced by two gendarmes.

The officers formed a cage around her body. She could see little as she was whisked along the path, her eye catching only flashes of coats and boots and headscarves. She heard some women gasp. When she passed by the post and telegraph office, she shouted as mightily as she could.

It's all a terrible mistake!

I've not done anything wrong!

I'm sure I will be back home soon!

If her son was inside, she was sure he had heard her.

Auntie Suzy was ushered swiftly through the door of the village hall. Like a cell door, it was quickly banged shut and bolted behind her.

The vestibule was dark and gray. Cold rose off the flagstone floor. Auntie Suzy felt one final snap of pain as the gendarmes let go of her arms.

Three men stood in front of her. One of them she had only recently met. The second she knew well, and the third man she had never seen until now.

Count Molnar had been in Nagyrév less than a year. His peers on the village council had already come to know him as an overwrought technocrat who filled his writing tablet daily with notes on trifling offenses the council judges committed. Auntie Suzy had heard complaints about him, too. Nagyrév had never before had a tax collector. The villagers were incensed about the situation. When he had first arrived in the village, the midwife had made a special trip to the village hall to introduce herself to him, and he had already availed himself of her treatments.

The midwife had hardly seen Ébner in the last few weeks, because hunting season was well underway. He had hunting lodges on the land he owned outside the village, and he spent most of his autumn days there hunting fowl and, more rarely, boar. Sometimes he would give Auntie Suzy a pheasant he had killed and she would pluck the bird and roast it over the open pit in her yard. When she looked at him now, she was filled with a river of regret. She instantly remembered herself bragging at the Cser tavern. *"There is enough arsenic in this vial to kill one hundred men. No doctor could ever detect it."*

The midwife had never met the third man. He was approximately the age of her sons. He was of average height and had the beginnings of a paunch. He wore gold-rimmed spectacles. His face was marked by determination and intelligence, two qualities his father, old Dr. Szegedy, had never displayed much of, as far as she was concerned.

The crier's tiny room had been set up for the interrogation. A table and one bench had been moved inside. The cot where the troublemakers slept out their punishments, and where sometimes the crier slept, had been dragged over to the table and set up as a bench on the other side.

The cot came up to Auntie Suzy's calf. A thin wool blanket was laid on top. She lowered herself down slowly, feeling the squeeze of her tight coat, but she soon felt the flare of arthritis in her knees, and flopped onto the cot with a heavy thud. The ropes creaked with her weight as she landed. She righted herself, and clasped her hands in her lap.

The rest of the men filed in after her. Ébner and Molnar stood along the wall, as the law required at least two village council members to be present during a gendarme interrogation. Dr. Szegedy took a seat on the bench next to one of the officers. The second officer stood next to the midwife.

Her gray hair hung limp to her shoulders. Her coat was still cinched tight around her. She looked from one man to the next, but their faces were inscrutable, and she could find no safe place to land. She clasped her hands tighter. On the table was a stack of logbooks.

The crier's closet was small and airless. It had never been intended for so many people. The crier's broom, mop, and pail, and his assortment of vinegar-soaked rags, were piled in a corner.

Auntie Suzy looked across the table at Dr. Szegedy, who had begun to flip through the logs. She noted the small slips of paper poking out from the binding, where the pages had been marked. She realized now her mistake.

The father and son were alike in some ways, same hairline, similar height, but in few other respects. She watched the younger Dr. Szegedy as he fussed with his spectacles. He removed them, fastidiously cleaned the lenses, and then put them back on. He had separated the logbooks into two stacks, and one register was in front of him, opened to a marked page. The gendarme beside him had his notepad fountain pen ready.

The midwife's mind began to dash like a rat down various alleys. She fixed her eyes on the stacks of registers. They were piled atop one another like a pile of bricks. They had been opened and closed so many times over the years that their spines were now threadbare. They smelled like musty old leather, and the parchment of their pages had yellowed with age.

She eyed the gendarme with the notepad. He had begun to write copiously, the scratch of his pen a cat's claw dragging across the paper. She looked to Ébner, and he averted his gaze. She looked back to the logbooks. For years, she had maintained her own logs at home, privately recorded accounts of patient conditions, treatments, circumstances of birth and labor. She had shared them with no one.

She watched as the doctor leaned low over the book, his finger pressed to a spot on the page. She knew she had to shut him down. And quickly.

The lantern, which usually hung from the ceiling, had been removed from the hook and placed on the table for better reading. As Auntie Suzy took stock of the new Dr. Szegedy, she felt a rising determination. The young gadjo was going to get nothing from her.

Outside, the bells pealed, announcing the hour.

Auntie Suzy followed the doctor's finger as it moved down the tall, narrow page, and only then did she realize that Dr. Szegedy was reading from the birth register.

The midwife was baffled. She stared hard at the book, looking for answers.

The doctor had discovered a pattern in the birth logs. First, he had detected a high rate of stillbirths. Upon further investigation, he realized that an alarming number of village couples had only two children: a boy and a girl. The doctor had learned the troubling method of family planning in Nagyrév. He was sure that upon parents' seeing the sex of the newborn, lives of unwanted babies were terminated after birth. Not coincidentally, the system seemed to have begun at the time Auntie Suzy became the village's official midwife.

Dr. Szegedy pushed aside the birth log he had been reading from. He slid another book out from the stack and opened it to another marked page. This register, Auntie Suzy saw, had the broad, horizontal pages of the death register. Her breath caught. What had he found in there?

Dr. Szegedy read the entry: an infant death, a newborn who had lived a few minutes before expiring. This death, too, Dr. Szegedy considered part of the midwife's family planning method.

The midwife suddenly relaxed into the cot. The ropes sagged and squeaked with her weight as she adjusted herself. She realized now that the gadjo had nothing on her that she couldn't beat, and she became so relaxed that she stopped the mindless twirling of her thumbs. She and her sister Lidia both twirled their thumbs when they were nervous or upset, but now she rested her hands, palms up. She looked now like a sage, an untroubled guru. She could sense the answered call of her incantations.

A swift, hard kick at her calf came from the gendarme. She reeled forward, nearly hitting her head on the edge of the table.

ARE YOU A BABY KILLER?!

The gendarme kicked her again.

Auntie Suzy looked up at Ébner once more. He was leaning against the wall. He had nearly flattened himself into it, as if to make room for others, or to make himself unseen. The waxed tips of his white mustache were frayed where he had nervously rubbed them. He lowered his head and stared hard at a fixed spot on the floor.

Auntie Suzy felt contempt rise in her. Could the gadjo men really be this stupid? Did they not know that every midwife in every village in Europe had the power to bring life as well as prevent it? Midwives alone stopped mass starvation from happening, be it from too many children or milkless breasts. So she was a baby killer, the midwife thought, if that's what the gadjo wanted to call her. She preferred another term.

Yes. I am an angel maker.

At her pronouncement, the gendarme seated at the table began to scribble furiously, as Auntie Suzy spilled forth what was to her not a confession, but a manifesto on the role of a midwife. It was her obligation, she explained to the men, to help couples have practical families; not more than two mouths to feed, one dowry to pay, one dowry to receive, and only one heir to the property, usually a male. She maintained that she provided a critical service to the poor peasant families in the village, possibly something the upper classes could not appreciate.

When she had decided she was finished, she leaned back on the cot. Unheeding, she patted at her coat front, groping for her pipe.

By now it was dark outside. The merchants had closed their shops. The clanging at the blacksmith's forge would soon stop for the evening.

Dr. Szegedy stood up from the bench. He reached his fingers under his lenses and wiped his tired eyes.

The gendarmes closed in on her again.

GET UP!

The kick was much fiercer than the last one. It hit right at her shinbone, and the midwife yelped at the sudden spark of pain. She yelped again as both gendarmes yanked her up by the arms.

YOU'RE UNDER ARREST!

Dr. Szegedy leaned back down over the table and flipped the death register shut, unwittingly silencing the rest of Auntie Suzy's ghosts.

AT THE CSER cottage, long after the pub had closed, Anna lay awake, listening for the crier's drum, watching for the feathered helmets, wondering if she was next.

BY ANY MEANS, AND MAGIC

Deaths weighed upon the village like a nightmare.

—Count Molnar, Nagyrév tax collector

SZOLNOK

The Royal County of Szolnok's penitentiary was a one-story building with an entrance directly onto busy Gorove Street. It was several yards down from Kossuth Square, where the main market was held twice a week. Across the street from the prison was the White Dog, an iron workshop named for the picture of the white dog in its window; the National Casino, a men-only supper club for aristocratic city elites; and the Sugar Pharmacy. Next to the Sugar Pharmacy was a general store called the Angel House, an ironic moniker given its proximity to the prison. The jail had been built thirty years earlier (prior to that, it had been located in the nearby county hall) and could hold up to two dozen inmates at one time. There was, on any given day, a mixed population of petty thieves, hooligans, confidence men, and duelers— there were still Magyar men who settled scores with the swipe of a sword across the face of a foe. For days, the prison building had been coated with a soft winter frost. Icicles dripped from the eaves.

Auntie Suzy raised herself partly off the stone floor. The wool blanket she had pulled over herself fell away. Strands of straw were embedded into the blanket's fibers. They had been picked up from the pile of straw that had been laid for her the previous evening. Much of it had ended up on Auntie Suzy, too. She had pieces tangled in her hair, and marks on her cheek from the bits of straw that had fixed to her face where she had lain in it. She propped her back against the cold wall. Her eyes were swollen with fatigue. She had scarcely slept.

She finished the coffee the guard had brought her and placed it near the door for the guard to retrieve. It was some four generations from real coffee, and tasted like the blend of carrots and turnips that she remembered from the not-so-distant days of war rations. A filled chamber pot stood in the corner. Later in the day, a janitor would come to her cell and take it away. The air reeked of her urine and feces.

The cell was about six feet long and six feet wide. It was windowless, poorly heated, and with a corps of roaches that scurried about boldly day and night. The door was wide and heavy. There was a latched peephole on the other side, which allowed the guard to look in on her.

He was the only person Auntie Suzy had seen all morning. Some days, the guard was the only person she saw at all. When she first arrived, an examining judge had visited to take a statement, even though her full confession in Nagyrév was on record. She had met with her lawyer a few times. A doctor had come by to administer a reasoning test and to form a psychological profile. He had found her intelligent and psychologically sound.

The midwife spent much of her time in a heap on the floor. She would flop down on the straw and burrow under the blanket to keep the roaches away from her face. She would try hard to sleep. Once her trusted companion, sleep rarely visited her now. Instead, it sent its ghoulish friends. Whenever the midwife closed her eyes, distorted faces would manifest, in the semidarkness at night when one dim light burned, and during the day. They were all sorts of fantastical colors. Some had bodies, some had only parts of bodies. They were images from a wakeful, isolated mind. They came with consorts, laughing. She thought it was the mullo coming to torture her. They said horrible things to her.

Seclusion had been forced on her by circumstance, not design, as she was the only female in the penitentiary. In the weeks that she had been in her solitary confinement, Auntie Suzy had also been overcome with fits of claustrophobia. At times, she had a nearly irresistible urge to lunge at the walls, to slam her fleshy body against the stone until one or the other, the stones or her bones, gave way. Her heart would thump with a clap of fear. Her chest wall would tighten, constrict like a boa on its live catch, until she could barely move air in and out of her old, struggling lungs. The panic would eventually peter out, the rage of a hurricane dissolving to a mist, and Auntie Suzy would rub her angry tears and wipe her nose with a sleeve or the hem of her dirty black dress.

Attached to the west end of the prison was the courthouse. Its entrance was on a side road, a far less conspicuous front than the prison's prominent entryway on Gorove Street. Down a long corridor was the office of the prosecutor, where John Kronberg's office was located.

Prosecutor Kronberg was one among many from Transylvania now working at the court in Szolnok. A host of judges and prosecutors had, like him, escaped the Romanians the previous year when Hungary's new borders were demarcated. For its part, the Szolnok prosecutor's office had needed to grow. The tremendous influx of displaced persons into the county, people who had come from Transylvania as well as other parts of Hungary that had been severed, had greatly burdened the court. The higher population, coupled with the specific army of problems that came with so many refugees, had been a further strain on the judiciary system in Szolnok. Relief had come with the tide of displaced legal professionals.

There was also a newly appointed court president, a post that had been vacant since the execution of the previous president by the Lenin Boys. There were still bullet holes in the walls where he and others had been shot. Churches, houses, factories, schools, all were pockmarked with the scars of the Red Terror. In the months that Kronberg had been there, he had come to know Szolnok as a city that accommodated its new ghosts and new denizens equally.

Prosecutor Kronberg surveyed the docket. The caseload was heavy.

There were several thieves and people accused of public drunkenness, many of them refugees living in the railcars. There were also innumerable court filings on various issues related to the Red Terror. And, he saw, there was the abortionist from Nagyrév on trial. Her confession to the gendarmes had been well recorded by them. It was rare, indeed, to have such a detailed confession to carry into the courtroom, and Kronberg was certain that it made the case against her airtight.

NAGYRÉV

The mood since the midwife's arrest had been one of anxious anticipation. For many in the village, her capture had been exciting. The river regulation of fifty years prior—the same one that kept the fish out of the fishermen's nets—also kept the gendarmes out of the village. The forced waterway had formed a near noose around the village, severing Nagyrév from its Great Plains neighbors, so now only the very old had tales to tell of ever seeing a gendarme come to Nagyrév before, and no one in the village had ever known anyone who had served time in a real prison. They were used to the types of punishments the local council delivered, which amounted to no more than a few lashes on the whipping bench, or a night spent in the crier's storage closet. But these were petty offenses that deserved petty sentences. The midwife had been charged with crimes that were far beyond the bounds of village justice.

But the longer Auntie Suzy was away, the more she was replaced with gossip and suspicions. The large hole she had left began to fill with doubts and speculations. It was a wild vine that began to grow, with rumors and questions dangling from every small stem. The hiss of suspicion that had first passed around Alex Junior's friends on the night of his funeral now began to spread among more village men.

The gendarmes had apprehended an untouchable, a wise woman. Were her crimes so great that the gendarmes would risk her curse? Was it only stillbirths that had been found in the registers, or had there been something more discovered that the villagers weren't being told? Maybe, they wondered in their darker musings, Auntie Suzy had cast a spell on the women of Nagyrév. Some said it was the only answer to the rising number of deaths among seemingly healthy men. The rumors were so rife that one man who had recently fallen ill joked that he wanted his grave marker to read: HERE I REST, WHILE MY WIFE RESTS AT HOME.

Unnoticed by nearly everyone was Anna. She had been petrified from the first moment she learned the midwife had been arrested. She felt sure the gendarmes were about to stride through the tavern doors and apprehend her, too. Since the day the gendarmes had come to the village, her hands had hardly stopped shaking. She suffered blinding headaches that lasted for days. The little that she could manage to eat boiled restlessly within her to be emptied as loose stools.

She used her son and daughter as lookouts. Every time they went out, she questioned them when they came back about what and whom they had seen. She often thought she spotted a gendarme's feathered helmet at the gate. She would work up a panic, until she realized it was only a swaying tree limb, or a bird perched on the fence. As much as Anna despised and feared the midwife, she knew she wouldn't rest easy until Auntie Suzy was back home. Only then could she feel, even in some small measure, that she was out of danger.

EACH WEEK, AUNTIE Suzy's family made the long journey from Nagyrév to see her on visiting day. They brought clean clothes and baskets filled with pots of her favorite foods: bread from the baker, goulash, and lebbencs soup with a bounty of potato and paprika mixed in. Just the way she liked it. The stews and loaves were put on a table the guard had arranged inside the cell. The family stood hunched together in the cramped space and ate. They ignored the roaches that crawled at their feet and shook off the ones that crawled up onto the bread. Among the goodies her family always brought with them was her pipe, which she usually fished out of the basket and lit at once. The visits lifted Auntie Suzy's spirits immensely, and she slept better for a night or two following them.

During these visits, they talked about the goings-on in Nagyrév.

Early on, the midwife had feared the gendarmes would search her house, and worse, her yard, but the officers had not come back to the village since the night of her arrest. The weekly conversations centered largely on her upcoming trial. The family had pooled their money to secure one of Szolnok's top defense attorneys, Gabriel Kovacs.[*]

Hiring Kovacs was a wise choice. The midwife had been charged with nine counts of abortion, all based on premature births delivered as stillbirths. Despite her confessions, Kovacs had advised her to change her tack at trial. He told her to deny everything. Kovacs knew the prosecution had no real evidence. His best chance at an acquittal was for Auntie Suzy to recant.

On the morning of her trial, the midwife arose early and dressed herself in a petticoat and a black frock, both cleaned specially for the occasion. Her clothes had been heavily ironed and the dress had been starched so much it shimmered. With the slightest move, her dress crinkled and crackled like paper. Her boots had been freshly polished and picked clean of every last speck of mud. She wore a scarf on her head, like a proper peasant.

Her family had come up from Nagyrév the evening before and lodged at a hotel near the rail station. They had arrived at the prison when it opened, bringing with them her fresh clothes, her pipe, flour to pat on her face to lighten her complexion, and a flask of brandy, which they passed among themselves in her cell while they waited for the warden to come. Auntie Suzy took no more than a nip.

She was escorted into the courtroom by the prison guard. Her lawyer was already situated at the defense table. Except for her family, the gallery was nearly empty. A few reporters from the regional papers were seated together and some witnesses had taken seats near the front. Kovacs had called villagers to testify on the midwife's behalf. He chose farmers who had been successfully treated with her poultices and ointments. He had counseled them to tell the court how Auntie Suzy had helped heal their sick animals, and their sick wives

---

*No relation to the Kovacs family of Nagyrév.

and children. They were to talk about Spanish flu, and how Auntie Suzy had worked round the clock to save lives. He hoped to show that the midwife was indispensable to the people of Nagyrév, no matter what the charges against her were.

The two gendarmes were also there, along with Ébner, Count Molnar, and Dr. Szegedy. Auntie Suzy took her seat on the defendant's bench, her back to the gallery. The prison guard stood soberly next to her.

When her name was called, Auntie Suzy stood up. She waddled to the witness stand, lifting lightly the skirt of her dress as she made her way, as if she were outdoors and might have to dodge a puddle or cross over a ditch. She stepped up onto the stand uneasily, careful not to catch her boot on her hem. She tugged at her dress to adjust the waistband. She stood with her head bowed, her hands clasped at her waist. She looked like a fat tick.

Flanked by a junior judge on each side, the presiding judge read aloud the statements the midwife had made back in Nagyrév. The gendarme's copious notes were a pleasure for the judge, and he took a special joy in reading back to the midwife her own words.

He paused in just the right places to underscore the midwife's gall, her deceit, her perversity, her vulgarity. The gendarme's ink had poisoned the pages with the Romany midwife's bad character, and the judge had been suitably cued. The notes were hand-scrawled, and he sometimes tilted the paper to read comments that had trailed into the margins. He paused from time to time to take sips from a small glass on his table. When he finished reading a page, he placed it facedown on the table upon the others he had already read, creating a rather large and untidy pile beside him. The papers had been heavily handled and refused to lie flat.

The reading went on for several minutes, with the spectators attentive to every word. When finally the judge had concluded, he put down the last dog-eared page and looked up at the midwife. He stared hard at her.

What do you have to say about this?

Auntie Suzy's wide feet were planted on the platform like stakes.

Her fingers were still joined in front of her. Her thick thumbs twirled at her belly like a small spinning wheel. She fixed her narrow eyes on the judge. In the morning she had performed an incantation of protection. She felt it now like an armor around her.

Several weeks had passed since she had been captured by the gendarmes in Nagyrév. But Auntie Suzy could still feel the horrid grip of those gadjo hands on her skin. Those fingers digging into her flesh. Those blunt, searing kicks at her legs. She could still hear their despicable slurs and she could still see the glistening spittle that hung on the gendarmes' mustaches like hell's dew. Hers were not a victim's memories, but those of a witch who never forgave slights against her.

She summoned them now, those memories, and each spurn was a soldier for her cause, which she marched straight into the tale of her innocence.

She spoke quickly, hurrying to revise the record. Her voice was amplified by the size of the room. Except for the cavernous halls of the train stations in Szolnok and Budapest, which Auntie Suzy had only occasionally ever passed through, it was the largest room she had ever been in, and the grandness gave a weight to her words that surprised even her.

She told the court she had been afraid of the gendarmes. The bayonets and threats were so horrible that they had drawn lies from her tongue. The brutal officers had driven her to say things that were untrue. Her spin was fast and dizzying, and by the time she had completed her testimony she was nearly faint.

The midwife took an ungainly step down from the stand. She waddled back to the defendant's bench and dropped heavily onto it. Her putsi hung around her neck, hidden from view under her dress, and she could feel it now, pressing reassuringly at her chest as her breath rose and fell.

Dr. Szegedy was called to the stand. Auntie Suzy eyed him as he passed by her. She cast a silent curse at him.

A thin stream of cold drifted from the windows. The frosty air seeped in through the old seams and sashes and floated past the midwife, who sat as close to the edge of the bench as she could manage. She aimed to listen attentively to the doctor, ready to tear down every fact he presented.

In his office in Cibakháza, Dr. Szegedy had an overstuffed folder of papers and notes he had kept on the case, and he had memorized every scrap and scrawl. He had come prepared to answer with precision. To the judge's probing questions, he replied with dates, times, places. He was able to give such an intimate characterization of the inquest at the village hall that any capable artist could have easily reproduced the scene.

At each damning detail, Auntie Suzy lurched up from the bench.

That's not true! He's lying!

Sharp reprimands from the judge blew her back down like a strong wind, but she stayed seated at the edge, ready to jump again.

When Dr. Szegedy stepped down from the stand, more witnesses were called. Their testimonies were brief. Ébner said only what he had to. Even the fastidious Count Molnar kept his answers short. The count had not been in the village long enough to say much about Auntie Suzy. There were quick closing arguments from both sides, after which the lawyers went back to their tables.

The three judges drew together to confer. Their huddle was a small pyramid of justice at the front of the courtroom. The gallery filled with the hollow noises of coughs and scraping chairs. The reporters scratched at their pads and Auntie Suzy slouched on the bench, anxiously twirling her thumbs.

Few were surprised by the judges' decision. Auntie Suzy had given such a wide-ranging confession in Nagyrév that her guilt had been nearly impossible to dispute.

A flush of heat reddened her face when she realized what had happened. She snapped a fierce look over to her lawyer. Kovacs was already stacking his papers together, preparing to leave. Her eye caught the swift movement of the guard beside her, and just as she turned to him, he reached for his restraint, a long, braided leather rope with a cuff on one end that he kept looped on his belt.

As he unhooked the rope, Auntie Suzy scrambled down the bench away from him. She scooted herself along the wooden seat with her palms.

Burn in hell!

The guard seized her arm and jerked it up.

You're all bastards and you'll all burn in hell!

She flailed her arm back and forth. The guard finally cracked the cuff around her wrist with a snap so loud it could be heard throughout the courtroom. He yanked the rope like a leash, trying to drag the midwife back across the bench toward him. She screamed. She arched her back. She thrashed her head around in a convulsion of rage. The cuff tightened as she strained against it. She was not as strong as she once had been. She felt herself skid closer and closer to the guard. Her boots dragged at the floor. She hit the side of the bench with a thump and the guard grabbed her free hand. His clammy gadjo palm was on her skin, his tepid fingers wrapped around her own. Caught like a wild hog, she squealed again.

She balled herself into a seething mound on the bench. One arm was cuffed and sticking straight up in the air, and her other hand was pounding on the bench. It took two guards to lift her up. They dragged her back through the gallery as she howled and kicked and spit, and hauled her all the way back down to her odious cell.

She wouldn't stay there very long.

Her lawyer requested an appeal, which was granted. Days after her hearing, Auntie Suzy paid a hefty bail and was released. Soon, she was on the train back to Nagyrév. Her extended family welcomed her with a subdued gathering at home. The wait for a new trial would turn out to be a long one.

AUNTIE SUZY SPENT her first few days back in Nagyrév taking up her old routines. She went back to the pub and she dropped in at the sewing circle. But her freedom was hardly a cause for celebration. She had come home to Penia's dark cave of poverty, and her mood and her mind were as black as the deep chamber of fear she now inhabited.

She had spent a staggering sum in legal fees. The money that had been scraped together to post bail was the last of her savings, which included much of her children's nest eggs, and Lidia's, too. The midwife had emptied the money box. She had dug up every jar of cash that had been buried in her yard and had ripped the seam of every pillowcase or hemline that hid coins. She was penniless.

Yet, as terrifying as her finances were to her, it was the terms of her release that crippled her the most. The conviction had stripped her of her duties. Her lifetime appointment as Nagyrév's official midwife had been revoked. This troubled her beyond measure.

Her most immediate concern, and what kept her in a state of high anxiety, was the idea of losing her home. In November, another midwife would be elected to replace her, and with the position came the house. Until that time, the council would let her stay.

She was also deeply rattled by another decision the village council had made, this time in regard to Dr. Szegedy. It had been agreed that the doctor would fulfill the midwife's duties during the interim, although no one quite knew how he would manage the feat of delivering babies in Nagyrév, given both the winter weather and his host of other duties that would prevent him from being in the village most of the time.

The stress of her ordeal had so put Auntie Suzy on edge that she began to show a side of herself most had never seen. She would leave her house with as merry a face as she could muster, but the slightest disturbance—feral dogs too close at heel, the wind mussing her hair, the wine too bitter, the table too cluttered—would send her far off course. She would stop where she was and hurl a wad of spit. She would curse. She would stomp her feet. As a wide berth formed around her, she would ball her hands into round fists and give the air around her a beating. Yet these Strombolian eruptions were usually brief. Inside a moment, Auntie Suzy would marshal the scattered machinery of herself, fasten logic and her best imitation of peasant decorum back into place, and waddle onward.

None of her public outbursts could convey the cauldron of strife boiling inside the midwife. She was astir with worry. Every lay healer in the village was a potential candidate for the midwife position, and every one of them a threat to her prized homestead. The fears that had chased her much of her life were now wolves snuffing at her door. These losses seemed incalculable to her. She could see all the influence and favor she had worked so hard to gain, and that had given shape to her life, slipping down a well like rain. There were powerful forces at play against her, and Auntie Suzy knew that the only person who could save her was her daughter.

In the Romany tradition, wise-woman knowledge skipped a generation, passing from grandmother to granddaughter. It was true that Auntie Suzy had shared everything she knew about being an herbalist with her daughter, and she had involved Mari deeply in the other, more secret family business. She had relied on Mari nearly as she would have a twin. But Auntie Suzy had been saving midwifery for her granddaughter, who was still only eleven years old. For some time now, Auntie Suzy had been taking the little girl on trips into the forest to teach her rudimentary facts about the plants. The girl had helped her grandmother collect the herbs, just as Auntie Suzy had done as a child with her own grandmother. Auntie Suzy had always planned to begin training her granddaughter, who was Mari's daughter, in births when she became a teenager, in time for her to take over the chief role when Auntie Suzy retired. Now, that was not to be. She had to turn to Mari, who was both untrained in birthing and entirely unprepared.

DR. SZEGEDY HAD been savoring the midwife's conviction from the moment he walked out of the courtroom. The verdict had given him a stronger sense of mission than he had thought possible. All of his efforts, from his detective work in the village annals to his explicit testimony in front of the judge, made him more sure-footed now in his drive to uproot the old ways, and he had greater determination than ever to rid the peasants of their faith in magical cures and spells. It was time, he was certain, for them to put their trust in modern science.

As it happened, the groundwork was currently being laid for a new midwifery school and birthing hospital in Szolnok. The original institute had been in Nagyvárad, a city now under the Romanian flag. Dr. Szegedy held a vision that the new school would help banish the stranglehold the Romany had on midwifery in the Plains villages. The Szolnok Midwife Institute would train midwives properly. They would be instructed and supervised by men who were doctors of obstetrics. Until the institute was built, a temporary training facility was being set up at the county hospital.

In all of the other villages under his jurisdiction, there would not be an opening for a new midwife for years to come. As for Nagyrév, a midwife from the Szolnok Institute, even the temporary school that was being set up, could not be trained in time for the official appointment at the November election. A new midwife would have to be appointed from within the village ranks. Dr. Szegedy had insisted to the council that whoever replaced Auntie Suzy would apprentice under him first. He had not let it be known that medical school had given him no formal training in childbirth. Yet he was confident the scope of his experience as a medical doctor qualified him to do work that had for too long been left to uneducated lay healers.

Every day, Auntie Suzy waddled off on her rounds as she always had. Dr. Szegedy could hardly stop her from visiting neighbors, she reasoned, and if she carried elixirs and ointments in her baskets, he was not there to see it. There were many in the village who kept their distance from her now, crossing to the other side of the street when they saw her coming toward them with her swinging baskets. But scores of others, despite themselves, still counted on her medicine, including many council members. Ébner was among them.

The quick shot of enmity the midwife had felt toward Ébner when she was captured by the gendarmes had already dissolved. Even in her state of panic at the village hall that afternoon, she had noted his reluctance to be there. During his time in front of the judge he showed the same disinclination. Ébner's testimony had been unceremonious. He had given clipped answers. He had offered no insights. Though dutifully grim about the whole affair, Ébner had reliably done the minimum of what was required of him and not a stitch more.

Auntie Suzy curried his favor now, as well as that of others on the council. She plied them with free health care—massages and headache potions, foot creams, salves, aphrodisiacs, blood pressure tinctures—though she could ill afford it. She supplied them with free wheat from her sons' farms and free wine. She told fortunes for their wives and daughters. She was tireless in her campaign for Mari to succeed her. There were a handful of lay healers in the village who were better candidates than Mari, but that did not deter her.

One among them was a serious contender. To be rid of the threat, Auntie Suzy was considering a special plan for that particular woman.

In the meantime, her appeal to Ébner was paying off. Other council members were also coming around. Yet her Romany instinct asked more of her. Auntie Suzy spent evenings at her kitchen table with her array of magic tools, divining solutions to her problems. She examined her palms for answers. She read the coffee grounds. She heated her strip of lead. It was a small piece that she dropped in a crucible and held over the fire, seeing the remedy for whatever ill she faced in the shape it took. She searched her dreams. She looked for signs, messages, and instructions from the other world to guide her to her goal. With each divination, she felt more and more certain that Mari would succeed her.

DURING AUNTIE SUZY'S incarceration, Maria had not once made the journey to Szolnok to visit her friend at the prison. She had given little thought to Auntie Suzy's predicament, although she had often walked past the midwife's house. She would approach the house slowly, curious and probing, as if she had suddenly been given a puzzle to solve. She would lean against the rough-hewn fence and press her face to the slats. In the narrow gap between them, she would search the yard. Spiderwebs glistened in the frost. Dark ash had hardened to rock at the firepit, as no one in the family kept it lit except Auntie Suzy. At the kitchen window, the curtains were, as ever, drawn. Maria longed to be inside, seated at the midwife's table with the cards and coffee grounds and crucible laid out in front of her like offerings.

Winter always trapped Maria. When the roads turned into rivers of

mud, the village snapped shut on her like a snare. The sky was a smoth-
ering one, low and heavy, and most of the cottages were closed tight,
swaddling families within. Window shutters were clasped against the
foul weather. Tall bundles of kindling and firewood were stacked like
fortresses in the side yards.

The energy that moved through Maria was always halting, as if
looking for an escape. She fidgeted and twitched, as unsettled as a
small child, and the bleakness of the hibernal village only unsettled
her more. The absence of her friend had made the time nearly unbearable for Maria, so when Auntie Suzy finally returned, Maria greeted
her like the coming of spring.

Surveilling Auntie Suzy's house in those intervening weeks had
heartened her in some way. Her own home was little consolation to
her. She was as bored and edgy there as she had been anywhere. On
the worst days, her house felt like her own dark prison. She fought it
by thrusting open the shutters. She set the front door ajar, inviting
in fresh air like a guest to a party. She lit lamps all around the house.
She played phonograph records of her favorite Romany bands on her
phonograph machine. The thick clay walls and low ceiling wildly distorted the sound, as if the tunes were larger than the room could hold,
but Maria never cared. She hummed along with the music. She knew
all the melodies as if she had scored them herself.

Sometimes Franklin visited, coming straight in through the front
gate with the stride of a man who owned the grounds. At Michael's
insistence, Franklin and his sister had moved into Alex Junior's old
house, but Michael was often away now. He had been making frequent
trips to Budapest, and it was during these trips that Franklin came and
went freely from Michael's home.

Maria wasn't the only villager glad to have Auntie Suzy home. Old
Mr. Ambrusz was gratified to see her when she came back. He welcomed Auntie Suzy like an answered prayer. In a way, she was. Recently, his health had been tricky. He arose some mornings feeling like
there were bricks on his chest, and there were days when he could not
walk from his stable to his front door without feeling as if the breath
had been knocked out of him. The whole time Auntie Suzy had been

in Szolnok, Mr. Ambrusz had been without the tinctures he relied on, and he was sure he had suffered for it. It was the reason, he told himself, that his good health had slipped. He had not considered that at seventy-eight, his body was tired.

AUNTIE SUZY WADDLED up the road balancing her two baskets, a perverted Lady Justice once again commanding the village byways. One basket was filled with goods she had purloined, or that had been given to her outright; the other with herbal ointments and elixirs she had concocted at home. The cultivating season was upon the village, and she had nearly a full roster of clients to treat. The farmers, it turned out, were indifferent to her darker deeds if she could relieve their pain. Any new suspicions they had about her could not compete with their need for her help.

Her work had begun early. For the farmers who were in too much pain from hernias and torn muscles to make it to the fields, she came out shortly after sunup. She preferred to avoid the swelter of midday if she could. She also had a host of appointments scheduled for the evening, after the caravan returned to the village for the day.

The fragrance of locust blooms rushed at her as soon as she turned onto Árpád Street. Locust trees were dotted all around the village center, and each spring they perfumed the air. Auntie Suzy breathed in the aroma. She plucked some blossoms and placed them in her baskets. She liked to enjoy the scent as she walked. Her corncob pipe jutted from her lips, waiting to be lit.

She had not gotten far when she spotted the carriage. The horses stood facing the village hall, tall and dark, and as solemn as monks. They moved sparingly, flinching only when taunted by the bevy of flies that buzzed around their eyes.

The carriage wheels were covered with the soft dirt of the Plains. Hard chunks had lodged in the smaller crevices. The carriage doors were also powdered with it, and Auntie Suzy could see where the dirt had blown off around the rim when the door had been slammed shut.

She circled slowly around the carriage, a boxer edging the ring.

She chomped on her unlit pipe, considering what to do. She moved in closer. She gripped the top of the door and pushed herself forward until she was leaning far into the backseat. Auntie Suzy could see that the upholstery was not new but had been well cared for. There was minor damage from the sun, tiny splits in the seat the heat had caused. The floor was stamped with footprints. The whole interior smelled of warm leather and cigarettes. Stowed in the corner of the bench was Dr. Szegedy's black medical bag.

Auntie Suzy reached up and pulled her pipe from her lips. She closed her eyes. She swirled her tongue around her mouth. Her back teeth were missing, and she moved her tongue into those spaces, too, gathering her forces. She swirled and swirled until she had worked up a large pool of saliva. She could taste the stale tobacco as it sloshed in her mouth. She pitched farther into the carriage and, turning her body into a storm, thrust a gale of vicious spit onto the bench.

May you be damned!

She watched the slobber spread across the leather.

Auntie Suzy wiped the remaining dribble from her face with the back of her hand. She plugged her pipe back into her mouth and shoved herself away from the carriage. She pressed a hand to her dress to smooth it. She adjusted her baskets. She took a deep whiff of her blossoms and shuffled back onto the street.

Sunday, May 22, 1921

By early afternoon, the temperature had peaked at a pleasant seventy-five degrees, where it would remain until late in the day. The youth were busy preparing for the *csárdás*, which was held every Sunday afternoon at the tavern. Anna and her children had already stacked the tavern tables against the wall, one piled atop another, to make room for the dance. The Romany band would begin to play at four o'clock sharp. Over at the church, Pastor Toth was preaching to a nearly empty nave. Only a smattering of villagers came to hear the reverend preach each Sunday. Few had patience for his rambling and uninspired sermons, and most weeks he could not manage to fill more than a pew or two. Out near the banks of the river, there was a different kind of faith, where storks touched down in the open meadows, and where geese waddled behind village girls who led them out to pasture carrying poles with white ribbons waving at the top, which the gaggle had been trained to follow.

In the morning, Auntie Suzy had worked in her garden with her flowers. She had pulled weeds from the beds and had snipped several blooms and brought them indoors to put in ceramic pots and glass jars. She had them lined along her sills and had placed a large centerpiece in the middle of her table. The Calvinist households around her rarely had a petal pass over their thresholds. "A house with peacocks and pine trees in it cannot stand for long," she often heard quoted around the village. But she didn't care. Her house was abundant with flowers. On some days, it was as full as a flower market.

By the time Lidia arrived, Auntie Suzy had cleaned herself up from her morning garden work. She had taken a hard, scrubbing bath in her oak tub, which she did every weekend. Afterward, she had pulled her hair into a new bun and put on a freshly washed frock. Once Auntie Suzy had finished assembling herself, she examined herself in the small hand mirror she kept in her bedroom. She had powdered her moon-shaped face with a fresh pat of flour, and the air around her was still freckled with soft white specks. She could see them floating in the sunbeams reflecting from the mirror. She licked two fingers and smoothed back her hair. She pulled the mirror close. She looked for evidence of new wrinkles and new brown spots peeking through the coating of flour. She pulled the mirror back for a long view. She had grown as plump as a round, ripe plum, but her dress was crisp and clean. Her bun was spotless, not a hair out of place. The midwife put down the mirror. She was, overall, pleased with her appearance. It was her sixtieth birthday.

Sunday was the day for visiting, and Auntie Suzy was expecting a small crowd of cousins from Tiszakürt, including her cousin Kristina Csordás, to come to her house for the small celebration. They were saving the bigger party for her name day.

Kristina had been the midwife in Tiszakürt for about as long as

Auntie Suzy had been at the helm in Nagyrév. She had been an ally of Auntie Suzy since the trouble with the court had begun, although there was little Kristina could do to help her. Her cousin had been cautious about sending letters or telegrams to the prison, and usually tried to ensure her correspondence was handed directly to Auntie Suzy's son. Kristina would wait for him to arrive at the post office in Tiszakürt, and then she'd shove a scrawled note into his palm. Often, she just whispered a message for him to pass along to his mother. Auntie Suzy and Kristina both knew she had to act with care. Dr. Szegedy had rooted around in the Tiszakürt records, too, and although nothing had yet come of it, caution was in order.

Auntie Suzy visited with her family until evening. A table was set up in the yard and a feast was served of her favorite foods. Pitchers of wine and brandy were refilled countless times. By the time she went to bed, she was fully sated.

THE MIDWIFE HAD spent most of the day working outside. The soap had been boiled. The washing had been done at the well in her yard. She had hung the clothes to dry on the rafters in the loft. She had spread the new cloth she had made on a small patch of space in her yard. The linen had been bleached shortly after she had woven it, and now it had to dry.

She didn't hear her gate creak open. She didn't see the shadow of the young man who crouched there, nor the shadowy shape of the pistol he gripped in his hands.

Her dear old dog slumbered in the cool of the stable. A family of perching birds twittered in the bushes near the fence. They too had been busy most of the day, flitting back and forth between one bush and another.

Auntie Suzy's feet were swollen and sweaty inside her boots. Soil from the garden had worked its way onto them and blackened the soles. Sandy grit had formed little mountains of grime at her arch and between her toes. Her fingers and knees had also swollen in the heat. The sun had been burning as hot as a torch, roasting her.

She plucked at her dress to fan herself. She had an old cloth in her apron pocket that she used as a handkerchief, and she took it out to mop at her neck and forehead. She placed the damp kerchief back in her pocket and wiped her hands on her apron skirt. Auntie Suzy had always felt herself to be attuned to a primal order, so when the little birds fell silent, she looked to see what was the matter.

A lay healer had been missing for weeks. She had been Auntie Suzy's chief rival, the chief contender for her spot—Mari's spot—and Auntie Suzy had been determined that no one unseat her. Rumors were rampant that the woman had been poisoned and her body dragged into the river. When the woman's children begged Ébner to open an inquiry, he dismissed them. Worse, he laughed when they pointed a finger at Auntie Suzy.

At first, the midwife could see very little in the sharp light. Her property faced west toward the street, and the sun washed out her view. She only saw what was near her: the stack of logs on the woodpile, the low roof. And she could see the ground around her clearly enough. Some sprigs of grass had grown in the silty dirt. They curled around her boots. Beyond her feet there were more patches of grass and a few bright yellow dandelions. Whenever her grass got too high, she borrowed Mr. Ambrusz's cow to graze it, or she cut it with the old scythe in her stable.

The yard had grown eerily quiet.

She caught sight first of his boot-clad feet. Her eyes moved up from the ground like a ladder to see the whole of him come into view. She watched as he lurched forward. His face was wrenched into a scowl. It looked as tortured as his mother's face the last time Auntie Suzy had seen it. But unlike his mother, he had breath in him to shout.

"Menj a fenébe!"

The pistol fired. Auntie Suzy threw herself atop the drying linen, falling as hard as a tree to the ground. Another bullet blew from the gun, ripping across the yard toward the midwife.

The dog scrambled from the stable. He sprinted to the gate, barking. He ran circles in front of it, woofing wildly at the air. His frantic circles grew wider and wider as he fanned out his search, but soon his vigor began to wane. He came to an uneasy halt. He sniffed at the air, scenting the gunpowder. He had lost the scent of the man. He delivered another sharp bark of rebuke, then trotted over to his mistress.

Auntie Suzy lay on the ground, unmoving. She was like a heavy old statue toppled onto its side. The hound moved cautiously around her. He touched his nose to her, a detective tapping at the body. He held his long tail low. He loped over to her feet and sniffed, and to her head, smelling life. Gently, curiously, he wagged the tip of his tail. Auntie Suzy reached her hand up and patted the old dog.

I'm all right, old boy. Looks like he missed me.

Auntie Suzy's sons organized a manhunt. Along with a few of their friends, the men canvassed the village. By sunset, the would-be murderer was found.

Once again, the gendarmes were summoned to Nagyrév.

Wednesday, September 21, 1921

The Plains held on to the summer heat well into September, and as the days got shorter farmers were hurrying to get ready for the harvest. The women were out picking the grapes. The season had been a strong one. There had been hardly any flooding, and the temperatures had yielded plentiful crops. Most of the wheat and other crops had been sold to landowners, or brought to the markets in Kecskemét and Szolnok for sale.

On Orphan Street, the midwife had busied herself with her usual end-of-summer activities. All the canning had been completed, and her pantry shelves were now well stocked with goods. She had picked off every last weed she could find in her garden. Together with Mari and her granddaughter, she had boiled soap, made the candles, and churned enough cheese to last until next spring, thanks to the bounty of milk she got from old Mr. Ambrusz.

The midday sun shone through her lace curtains, dappling the kitchen with light. She sat at the table in the stream of sun filtering in. She lifted the findzsa and gulped back a last swallow of coffee. She settled the small cup back on the table and pulled herself up from her bench. The strings of her apron had loosened from her long morning sit, as she had forgone her rounds on this day. She reached around her waist to refasten them.

She opened the door and stepped out onto her porch. She held her hand to her eyes to shield them from the sun. She waddled down onto her path and patted and cooed at the old dog, who was still tuckered after an early morning in the woods with his mistress. She headed out of the gate, clucking cheerily at the chickens she saw splashing in a puddle left by a recent rain.

Slowly, she pressed at Mr. Ambrusz's gate. She held the gate by its edge, careful about its creaks as she slid it open. She had heard the women of the family when they had left for the fields in the morning. The midwife had been listening for them, but she could never be too sure. She called out to them. She called again, louder. No one answered. She pushed the gate all the way open and waddled up the pretty path to the house.

Auntie Suzy had known something about old Mr. Ambrusz for some time, and that was that his heart was failing. She had known it from his pulse, the sclera of his eyes, the pallor of his skin, the texture of the few threads of hair he still had left in his head. She had been treating him regularly for months, but each poultice and potion produced weaker results.

She opened the front door. The Ambrusz family had also been doing some final canning, and the air inside was scented with fruit. Auntie Suzy looked around the kitchen. The house had continued to impress her all these years. Nothing seemed to crack or wear. A veil of finery still graced everything. The glassware, the crockery, the little bowls that surely came from Budapest, or perhaps even Vienna, were all arranged in a tidy display on the cupboard shelf. Auntie Suzy nudged the bowls back and reached for the brandy. She poured herself a half glass and swigged it back in one swift chug. The glass settled back on the table with a rattle. She reached for a clean glass and poured more brandy into it. She plunged her hand into her apron pocket and ferreted for her vial. She unwrapped it from the paper and poured two careful teaspoonfuls of the solution into the drink. She stirred it with the small spoon and then again with her fat finger. She had come to do a good turn for an ailing friend.

Hours after she returned to her own house, frail old Mr. Ambrusz was dead, five years to the day since his grandson Stephen Joljart had departed the earth.

THE COUNCIL CONVENED in early November, and Dr. Szegedy was in attendance. The meeting usually went on for a while, since every manner of village affair was discussed and voted upon: whether to install an additional streetlamp, whether the cobbler could expand his shop, what to do regarding farmer complaints about the new taxes Count Molnar was levying, and who to hire to replace Auntie Suzy. On the last matter, the midwife's daughter was voted in.

As far as Auntie Suzy was concerned, her magic was working.

JUDGE'S LOSS

We, the women of Nagyrév, all knew what
Suzannah Fazekas had been doing.
We were as used to her deeds as we were used to seeing the flocks
of geese leave the village for the meadows each morning.

—Maria Szendi

NAGYRÉV

Dr. Szegedy's hands were bloody. His spectacles were fogged. The moisture in the room and his heavy breath had steamed them. The effect perverted his view of the blood so that when he looked directly through his lenses, which were precisely round and often smudged anyway, he saw a muted, vague hue, a red of plum stains or spilled wine.

The blood had dripped down and saturated his trousers. Some of the blood had pooled in the flat, smooth parts of the earthen floor, or ran in rivulets toward the wall along the small veins and cracks.

Anna's cottage had been bitterly cold when he arrived. The windows had been covered in rime. A soft band of snow had blown in under the front door, which no one but Anna ever bothered to sweep away. The floor had been made slick by the icy air, as if glazed in thin verglas. Frosty air blew in through the many broken seams of the house. With a fire lit, the room had quickly warmed.

He had been fetched earlier in the day while making his rounds in a village on the other side of the river. The wheel-track roads had been unnavigable in the deep freeze of January, but the river was solidly iced over. The doctor had been able to walk across the frozen Tisza and get to Anna's house on foot.

It was already dark outside. The light inside the room was dim and hazy. Anna's lamp had not been wiped clean since morning, and a layer of soot had collected on the glass, hampering the small flame from burning beyond a glimmer. Dr. Szegedy had placed his hand lantern on the floor near him. Its tiny flame cast a light around him like a nimbus.

His knees bore hard into the floor. They had grown numb. His back was taut. His shirt had been tucked neatly into his trousers when he arrived, but now hung loose. His boots, which had carried him so briskly across the river hours earlier, now felt laden with heavy stones. He was breathless.

Anna was motionless on the floor in front of him. A thin blanket had been placed over her hours earlier, parts of which were now wet with blood, too, as was her frock. She had her arms outstretched beside her in a sad posture of surrender. She was as idle as a fallen branch, yet she was still alive.

Nothing had prepared Dr. Szegedy for this. He looked down at the infant he had placed on rags on the floor. A patch of black hair was matted into curls at the baby's head. Its body was long and scraggy, with papery skin that puckered at the neck and knees. It was dead.

As far as Dr. Szegedy knew, the delivery had been proceeding fairly well, right up to the point where blood began to pour from Anna. Everything he had read about childbirth in preparation for this birth had not accounted for the proper way to stop a hemorrhage.

Except for the gusty winds slamming against the windows, the room was hushed. The winter was proving to be a severe one. The village had already experienced several snowstorms and blizzards. The air inside Anna's house was a swirling mix of raw cold at the windows and doors and dry heat everywhere else. Straw and twigs popped and snapped in the stove.

He could hear the light footsteps of Anna's son and daughter on the other side of the door, as the pair tried to move about silently in the home's one other room. He had not seen or heard Lewis. On the floor near Anna was Mari.

She had a rag in one hand, which she had pulled from the small bundle of rags she had brought with her from home. She used it to sop up the blood.

FRANKLIN GRABBED THE handle of the stable door. He gave it a hard yank and rattled it back and forth in the frame until he heard the loud crack of breaking ice. He had already been in the barn that morning, but another coat had formed since then.

He gave another hard tug and watched as the ice shattered, the shards clanking and tinkling around him as they hit the hard ground.

He could not recall such a cold spell. The earth seemed to have frozen right at her center. He pushed open the door the rest of the way. He could hear the livestock cooing at him. Animals had always seemed to favor Franklin.

Overall, Franklin and Marcella had settled well into Alex Junior's house, just as they had settled fairly well into Nagyrév. Marcella had a young bachelor pursuing her, a man she seemed to like, and Franklin had heard that talk in Nagyrév linked him to a girl named Piroska, whom everyone called "Pipsy." This was a relief to Franklin. Talk about him and Pipsy meant his neighbors had not noticed how often his landlady came over, or how long she stayed.

The stable bore all the marks of Alexander Senior, but none of his son. Five years had already passed since the elder Alex had died, but his diku was still in a corner behind the door. A pitted old plank of wood, which he had fashioned into a bench, was situated against the wall. Several low stools were beside it, as if waiting for guests to arrive.

On one end of the barn was the wagon shed, on the other, the tool area. When Franklin wasn't using the senior Alex's tools, he kept them neatly hanging from pegs or arranged on the shelf. Larger ones he stored in the old sideboard, and the biggest were propped along the walls.

The tiny window, barely bigger than Franklin's hand, had been covered with straw. Every bit of warmth mattered.

The two pigs, which Maria owned, were fenced by a low log pen. Franklin stepped inside the pen and onto the pile of straw. The straw had been strewn and flattened by the pigs, but it still had a fresh lightness to it. It felt soft under his boots, and Franklin waded through it like dewy grass.

He leaned down between the pigs. His heavy cloak pitched forward. It was an ornate, sheepskin *szür*, and the sheer heft of it nearly pulled him to the ground. The szür had belonged to Alex Senior and had been given as an heirloom to the younger Alex. It was highly adorned for a peasant's szür, and had cost the senior Alex a fair amount for the delicate embroidery work. The arms of the great coat had long ago been sewn closed to be used as pockets, so, as nearly all Magyars did, Franklin wore it like a cape.

He reached his hand up from under the mantle. He slapped the side of one pig, then the other. Fat. They were both fat. Very filled out. He pinched the skin of one and pulled it up. Nearly two fingers' worth of lard. Franklin was satisfied. The winter pig-sticking season was in full swing, and he was confident Maria's pigs would bring a top price.

MICHAEL'S FUR HAT hung on a peg near the woodstove. The heavy snowflakes that had caught on it had quickly vanished in the heat of the small fire. The hat was thick and round, not the domed cap of a peasant. A thin cigarette peeked from the band. Michael always kept a spare tucked there.

On the peg next to it hung Michael's vest. It had taken on his shape over the long years he had worn it, with the back hitched higher to accommodate his increasingly rounded shoulders. The front sloped forward.

His pockets bulged. In them were little notes he had scribbled on slips of paper, his container of matches, and his gold watch, the chain of which looped over the pocket flap. Maria could see it wink and shimmer in the light. His vest smelled of everything Michael had ever smelled of: brandy, tobacco, wood chips, horses, incense, cloves.

There were pockets on the inside, too, where Michael usually folded his tickets or other traveling papers. He had stuffed his penknife and an array of spices deep into the well of one—he always like to be ready in case he was unexpectedly invited to a meal—and Maria got a strong whiff of the spices when she pulled the vest open.

She had never been gamed by any man. But there were now rumors.

She patted her hands on the pockets. The slits had soiled over the years from Michael's constant use, and there was a soft line of grime across each one. She slid her fingers through the openings, rummaging blindly. Dry bits of dirt and stray tobacco that hid in the seams sunk into her nails when she poked there. She fingered the cold of a fountain pen. A lucky stone he had picked up. His spectacles case.

The letter had been folded in half and fit trim against the pocket side. Michael had handled it so often—unfolding, reading, folding it back up—that the paper had worn as soft as cotton. Maria dug at it with her fingernails and pulled it out.

She listened for Michael. The heavy blanket of snow made the sounds from the yard crisper and more distinct. The latch lifting on the shed, a greeting shouted to the neighbor over the fence. Maria could hear the stable door creak open, and faintly, the snorts and oinks of Michael's pigs.

The letter was frayed most at its fold, where the fine fibers of the paper had broken. She opened it gently, carefully smoothing out the fragile page.

It was dated from Budapest. The script was elegant. The letters looped and dipped softly across the page, each word neatly spaced, as if choreographed. The whole epistle, from date to closure, had the delicate mark of a woman, and the words jumped up and down in Maria's jittery hands, though she tried hard to hold the letter steady.

She could hear Michael by the woodpile now. The sweep of his hand across the logs to brush off the snow. Grunting as he picked them up. Her heart raced. She read more quickly.

The porch had some squeaky floorboards, and they announced Michael as he stamped across in his boots. She could hear the boots thudding as he tried to dislodge snow from the soles.

Maria fumbled with the letter. It felt like a feather in her hand, as if it could flutter from her grasp. She heard the rise of the door latch.

She folded the letter and slid it back into its home along the wall of Michael's pocket.

Michael brought in with him the smell of woodsmoke and snow. Maria watched him as he emptied the pile of logs into the wicker basket by the stove. His hands were red and raw. He rubbed them for warmth. He leaned down, placing his hands in front of the fire as it crackled and hissed.

How dare he?

THE EXTREME COLD had all but shut down the village. Hardly anyone ventured out, except for emergencies. Many had been frightened by a news bulletin the crier had read, which warned that nearby villages had been attacked by starving wolves, prompting the military to be dispatched to hunt down the animals. The young bachelors had formed their own hunting parties and prowled in the nearby forests.

The harsh weather had also kept Auntie Suzy indoors. With little to do, she occupied herself as best she could. She added to her stockpile of potions, mixing ever more elixirs. She organized and reorganized shelves to make them all fit.

When she wasn't fussing with her concoctions, she kept herself busy with numbers. The midwife had a good head for figures. She kept a writing tablet and a piece of charcoal in her sideboard, which she used for jotting her sums. In the warmer months, she liked to tally her numbers in the dirt outside, while sitting with her sister. Who owed what and how much?

Financially, the months since the midwife's release on bail had been impressive. She had imposed a stiff frugality on herself, which had helped ease her initial suffering. And she had also hounded old debtors. Auntie Suzy had always known the value of having a few key people in the village who owed her, but it was cash that mattered to her now. The midwife still had a rash of legal fees to pay, with more to come. All of her debtors had paid, except one: Michael had an unpaid tab for several sacks of wheat her sons had given him from their yield.

When spring finally came, it too was marked by wild weather. Temperatures would rise to sixty degrees one day and barely top out at twenty-five the next. Winds were dangerously turbulent. Trees were uprooted and delimbed. Villagers prone to superstition viewed the strange conditions as a bad omen.

THE MIDWIFE HAD been at the Cser pub since late morning. She had barely moved from her spot, and the idleness had cost her. The deepest, lowest part of her back had begun to throb, sending up small sparks of pain. A stiffness had settled into her legs and neck.

She had been sucking on her pipe for some time. She pulled it now from between her thin lips. She looked like a plump, angry bull as she blew the last bits of smoke from her nose. Ghostly clouds formed briefly around her before vanishing.

The midwife got her tobacco from a grower who worked on one of the estates. He typically sold it at market, but Auntie Suzy usually went to him directly and got large pouches in exchange for the potions she prepared for him.

She jabbed an extinguishing finger into the bowl of her pipe and patted it around the warm tobacco until it was tamped out. She leaned back on the bench. She plucked at her lap, a crisscross of folds, and when she found her apron pocket among the tucks and gathers, she dropped her pipe into it and patted the pocket firmly closed.

Auntie Suzy gulped down the last of the brandy that was in front of her. She waited for the burn in her chest to pass before pushing herself up from the old bench. She wheezed as she lifted herself from it.

The pub was nearly empty. A clutter of dirty soup bowls and wine jugs was on a table next to her, waiting to be cleared. At another table, there was a loose group of card players who came and went from a central game.

"I need you to pay your tab."

Auntie Suzy pivoted around.

The midwife had been watching Anna much of the morning, filling the pots and jugs, cleaning the bar in front of her with an old smelly rag. Anna sometimes studied a spot on the counter intently, as if it held answers for her.

The only daylight in the tavern came from the narrow window, under which Alex Junior used to sit. The air was heavy with stale smoke, but a thin trace of stew wafted through the dank room.

Anna walked toward Auntie Suzy as haltingly as a little bird. Her bony legs tottered in boots made for a larger person. Wood chips had fixed to the hobnails in the soles. Anna came within a yard of the midwife and stopped.

"Can you please pay?"

A large canvas sign hung over the bar: WE PAY OUR BILLS, SO PLEASE PAY YOURS! The sign had been tacked there after the war.

Auntie Suzy turned her head. She rolled her tongue around her mouth, searching for all the sourness she could empty. She pitched forward and spat a wad of saliva onto the floor. She leaned back over the table and scooped her baskets onto her arms. Their weight pleased her.

The midwife could feel the small flare of pain in her back stronger now that she was standing. Her knees, which she had been treating with a concoction of milk vetch, were still swelling. She felt, for the briefest moment, unsteady. She waddled to the door. The midwife didn't look back as she shouted to Anna.

"The good Lord will pay for it!"

SZOLNOK

Ever since the previous spring, Prosecutor Kronberg had been aware that a second villager from Nagyrév was awaiting trial at his prison. It was not rare to have someone from an outlying village in the Szolnok penitentiary, but it was quite uncommon to have more than one within the span of a few months.

The man's story had not changed since the moment he had been captured and interrogated by the gendarmes. He claimed to be seeking justice where none had come. He was certain the midwife had killed his mother. As a son, he claimed it was his duty to avenge her death.

To Kronberg, vigilantes were like any other breed of criminal. They wanted what they wanted and would stop at nothing to get it. His docket had always been peppered with "eye for an eye" crimes. He found those cases among the easiest to prosecute. The avenger's conviction of their own righteousness handed them a conviction under the law. The man's case was open and shut. As for his accusations against the midwife, that was another matter, and one the court could do little about. His mother was still missing. But without a formal request from Nagyrév to investigate—and without a body—the prosecutor's office had no grounds to proceed.

NAGYRÉV

During planting season, the streets in the village were far less congested than at other times of the year. Except for a few older farmers out making deliveries, their oxcarts creaking with barrels of milk or sacks of fodder, the traffic was usually fairly light. It was easy for Auntie Suzy to see across Árpád Street as she stood outside the pub. She spotted Maria right away. Her friend was feverishly waving her hands at her.

Auntie Suzy hurried across the road to meet her friend and the two crows walked together up Orphan Street. They were an awkward pair. Maria's anxious, flitting feet were a poor match for the midwife's waddling gait. Some feral cats joined them as they walked. The felines wove between the two women and circled around them in figure eights before darting ahead to a nearby copse to wait for the women to pass again. Auntie Suzy had always enjoyed the games the cats played with her. They liked to creep along her fence and observe her in her garden. She looked out over her baskets now and cooed in their direction.

A soft rain had lifted the scent of grass and fresh soil off the ground. The midwife breathed it like a tonic. The air had rarely been so still and gracious in recent months. She had come to appreciate every good bit of weather that came to her.

Perched like large hats atop some of the cottages with thatched roofs were the enormous nests the storks had built. They had been there for years, and each year when the storks flew south, the nests filled with fallen leaves and rainwater, which quickly iced over in winter.

When the storks returned, their first days back in the village were busy with restoration, mostly clearing debris and heavy mold that had grown while they were gone. The harsh winter had left many nests in near tatters. Large pieces of tightly woven walls of twigs, rags, and most of all reeds had blown out from all the deep freezes and cork-screw winds. The storks flew in pairs to gather new reeds down by the river, but just as many pilfered from the thatch of the roofs right under them. They clamped their pointy bills onto thick strands and tugged them free. Villagers could often hear the hollow whistle of a long blade being whisked from its place in the roof.

The hammering chatter of the storks piped down into the street, a rapid clack-clack-clack that the villagers had come to associate with the first signs of spring. But as the two crows neared the crossroad where Auntie Suzy's house was situated, it was the soft swish of a broom that caught the midwife's ear.

Petra's gate was open, offering an unhindered view of the yard. The shrubs were nicely trimmed. The firewood was stacked neatly under an eave. Most villagers kept two logs out and upturned to sit on as stools throughout the year. The Ambruszes' sitting logs, for Mrs. Ambrusz and Petra now, were placed neatly to one side. The edges of the path that led to the porch were not jagged like most, but crisp and straight. Even without old Mr. Ambrusz's touch, the yard was pristine.

Auntie Suzy eyed Petra, who was on the porch working her little bulrush broom. She watched Petra take quiet, certain steps, poking the broom into the corners and crannies to search out even the tiniest seed or grain of silt.

Auntie Suzy leaned in low to Maria. She flung her arm straight out and jabbed a finger in Petra's direction. Her basket jounced forward and nearly toppled her goods into the ditch. She pressed her jowly cheek closer to Maria's.

"That woman owes me!" she growled. "And she will pay!"

Once inside her kitchen, Auntie Suzy went directly to her sideboard.

The cupboard had come with the house when she had moved in more than twenty years earlier, and the top of it had long been cluttered with keepsakes she had received as gifts over the years. On a lower shelf she kept her strainer filled with tobacco. Her tobacco cutter was next to it. A goose bone, which she had gotten during a St. Martin's feast the previous November, was also on the shelf. She used it like a weather almanac. She had watched the bone grow darker, a forewarning of the harsh winter that had followed.

She pulled open the side drawer and fished out her cards. The deck had been left behind by her estranged husband. They were the same sort of playing cards her sons kept with them in case there was a chance for a game. She carried them, along with her matches, over to the table and dropped them in front of Maria.

She eased herself down onto the bench across from Maria. Her lap was jumbled with the skirt of her dress, her apron, and her warm petticoat, which were all bunched in a heap. She tamed the mass with her hands, petting the fabric like it was a dog.

She looked at Maria. Her friend twiddled with the bodice of her own dress. She moved up to the knot of her headscarf and twiddled with it, then down to the cuff of her sleeve. It was a circle of agitation the midwife had seen often.

She watched Maria draw a hand to her throat and stroke it. Maria did that anytime she was distressed and had something she wanted to say. In the brief time that she had been sitting at the midwife's kitchen table, she had rubbed it so vigorously, a red blotch had begun to form on her neck.

"It's his whorey nature!"

The midwife said nothing. She leaned back. She smoothed her apron pocket, then ferreted inside for her pipe.

"I can't bear a third divorce!"

Auntie Suzy pulled the pipe out and cupped its bowl in her thick hand. Expertly, she sifted the tobacco between her fingers, like a farmer inspecting his soil. The top was still moist. The small clod at the bottom was dry. She always saved that part for Ébner. He liked to use the chaw.

She tamped the tobacco down deeper into the bowl and lit it with her match. She took a long draw. Auntie Suzy reached for the deck. The cards were well-worn, tattered along the edges and as smooth as leather. They had taken on the scent of the drawer, old wood and incense; she liked to rub them on her dress as perfume. They also held the faint, sweet smell of her flypaper. She cut the deck in half and shuffled. She shuffled again, and fanned the cards out in front of her friend.

Maria looked up at her.

Sometimes Auntie Suzy kept her pipe to the side of her mouth so she could talk while she smoked. It was a method she had mastered when she was young. The pipe stayed at the edge of her vision, bobbing as she spoke. She talked for a while, explaining what she saw and jabbing her finger at the cards as she made certain points.

Maria didn't question her. Maria never questioned Auntie Suzy's prophecies or plans. But she needed reassurance, and the midwife was quick to deliver.

"If it wasn't noticed with your boy," the midwife said, "it won't be noticed now, either."

BY THE TIME Maria left the midwife's house, an afternoon chill had set in. She tightened her headscarf. She hugged herself for warmth. She walked swiftly yet guardedly past Auntie Suzy's old dog and out the gate.

The Ambruszes' gate was still open. Maria looked in as she passed, appraising the yard as if with Auntie Suzy's covetous eye. Petra was on the porch. She had pulled a shawl over her head and was in her coat, as if she had been waiting out there a long time. Maria watched as Petra hurried to her across the yard, stopping just before the ditch.

"What did Auntie Suzy say to you earlier?"

Maria looked back at Auntie Suzy's house, then again at Petra. She leaned forward, signaling Petra to do the same. The two met over the ditch, close enough for a whisper, while Maria fed her Auntie Suzy's warning that she would exact her dues.

Petra gasped. She stepped back.

"That woman has taken everything from me!" she shouted. "And it is still not enough for her!"

WITHIN DAYS OF the divining, Auntie Suzy and Maria had worked out a schedule as well as a payment plan. Maria had agreed to pay nine thousand crowns in cash. It was an inconceivable amount of money to most villagers. Part of the money, as far as the midwife was concerned, was to cover Michael's debt to her sons for the wheat he had bought but never paid for. She had not forgiven him for cheating on the deal. Time after time she had come to him for payment, and time after time he had said he would have the money for her the following month, and then the following month, and then the following one, but it never materialized. Whenever he saw her, he would tip his hat to her and say things like "Your purse will be here soon," or "Your patience is kindly appreciated," and then he'd duck off to the reading circle, or to Budapest, or to a party at the hunting lodges. It had never been Auntie Suzy's intention to play the part of a fool.

But Auntie Suzy was most satisfied with another part of the deal, which was, finally, the acquisition of Alex Junior's house. Maria had been promising it to the midwife for more than two years, but had always found a reason to hang on to it for one more year, or one more season. The house had been a long time coming to her.

AT THE READING circle, Michael liked to sit in the "couch room," a small chamber off the main hall where the card players and chess enthusiasts also liked to gather. The room was crowded with settees situated around low tables. Portraits of Magyar lionhearts hung on the wall. A paraffin lamp hung from a wire secured to a rafter in the ceiling.

Michael had a weekly newspaper in front of him, still bound in its rattan frame. He leaned forward over the newspaper, pulling back a page and pressing it flat against the frame with his fist. He picked up his wineglass and steadied the stem between his blocky fingers. At home, Michael drank jug wine harvested from his own vineyard, but that was largely to wash down his meals. At the reading circle he preferred the sweet grape of the Tokay wines. He sipped it slowly and luxuriously.

Nearly every morning that Michael came to the reading circle, he was joined by his friend Joseph Sulye, whom most everyone knew as "Judge." Michael and Judge had grown up together, they had farmed and hunted together, and both had served as judges on the village council (Judge was still a council member). It was Judge whom Alex Junior had stolen the three chickens from. Michael considered him his closest confidant.

Their friendship was a thousand brushstrokes; small facts slipped in between the sips of wine and the slow turn of news pages—*I visited Maria Szendi in Budapest; Maria's train comes in this afternoon; the farmhand slept inside the house last night*—until the larger truths seemed somehow always to have been there.

Michael's marriage to Maria the previous year had hardly come up between them.

Neither man was given to introspection or dwelling in regret. Michael had accepted his circumstance, but he took a rogue's pleasure in defying its constraints.

He slipped his hand into his vest pocket and pulled out his letter. By now, tiny holes had worn through the folds and the edges were so tattered the paper nearly tore apart each time he handled it. He lifted the letter to his nose and sniffed it. He opened it and smoothed his hand across the page, unaware that Maria's fingers had recently traced a similar path.

Michael had known when he met Maria that she was some kind of a trap for him. He was an animal walking around with his foot in a snare. Disdain had loosened much of it, but there was still a ghost of a hold. In his heart's shadows, he was still drawn to her.

The woman in Budapest was a widow. Michael had been seeing her for weeks. *I love you,* she had written. *Let's get married.*

Michael waved his letter in front of his friend's face, smiling and teasing. It was his current favorite souvenir from Budapest, and he had been carrying it with him like a prize he had won.

As he had often done over the years, Judge batted the letter away.

"You play with women like a cat with a mouse."

WHENEVER THERE WAS mail for Auntie Suzy, either a telegram or a letter, her son would sort it from the pile and bring it to her after he'd finished his route for the day, and he would stay long enough to read it to her. One day, just as spring was coming, he brought two notices to her, both of which were sent from the Royal Court of Szolnok. The first was that her attacker had been convicted. The young man had fought to have the charge against him dropped, but the court had ruled against him. Auntie Suzy received the news with a great deal of satisfaction and would enjoy spreading it around the village before the crier could announce it in his bulletins.

The second letter regarded her own conviction, a notice that her trial date for her appeal had been set for the following January in Budapest, at which time the higher court would hear her case. The midwife had months of invocations and incantations ahead of her, and she began right away.

IN THE WEEKS that followed Anna's stillbirth, Dr. Szegedy had questioned himself hardly at all about the delivery. He had spoken briefly with his father about the bleeding, and both men had determined that the sad event had been unavoidable, though neither could really speculate about the cause. The senior Dr. Szegedy had less experience delivering babies than his son. He had never delivered one at all.

Before he had become a hard drinker, the elder Dr. Szegedy had been an avid advocate for what he considered proper health care in the region. He had been on the board that championed the construction of the Szolnok County Hospital. He had urged the matter at a public meeting, arguing that the poor and the elderly in the area had no access to care when they got ill, beyond what he could provide once a week from his black doctor's bag. It was to this hospital that the younger Dr. Szegedy, in his relatively short tenure as regional physician, had occasionally moved some of his patients. Sending sudden, acute cases there was out of the question because the long journey made it too impractical. But those with withering illnesses, such as consumption, he always sent.

The new Dr. Szegedy had no desire to be on the board of the new Midwife Institute, though it was true no one had asked him. He had become emboldened by Auntie Suzy's trial, and he knew the best place for him wasn't on a board, but in his villages, keeping a watchful eye on the goings-on of the midwives there.

THE PLAIN LITTLE corn bunting stood on its perch. A light breeze blew through its small feathers. It twittered a jangling chirrup and lifted briefly into flight, its whisker-thin legs hanging down like two loose threads, and landed gently on the dry grass. The little bird hopped a few paces, causing the chickens to scatter, and was soon in flight again to a nearby bush.

Michael had been listening to the birds all morning. He had been able to hear them cawing and chirping and warbling through the thin panes of the bedroom window since daybreak.

He had often watched the birds erect their nests on his property. They had built them in the hedges, the walnut trees, and the plum trees, and at least one year a family of warblers had made their nest in the stable. He would sometimes catch sight of a golden oriole, a clump of horsehair in her beak, preparing her roost, or a warbler collecting little tufts of hay. Michael hadn't been outside in days. He could only close his eyes now and imagine them dabbling at the well.

He often listened for Maria. Her darting footsteps were like mice scurrying in the hall. He had an ear to the orders she gave Marcella. They were conveyed in the singsong he had once found alluring. He saw little of his wife as he moved along what had become his trail through the house: from the bedroom to the privy and from the bedroom to the porch. In the afternoons, he sat outside to be with friends who dropped by to visit. From there, he also watched Franklin, who had been helping with the animals.

As soon as Marcella opened Michael's door, the smell of goulash rushed into the room. The aroma engulfed him. He arranged himself in the bed, sitting up to rest his back against the headboard. He clumsily freed his bedclothes, which had twisted on him while he had been lying down. He watched while Marcella set up the tray of food on his bedside table.

He had seen a lot of Marcella in recent days. It was Marcella who brought him his meals and Marcella who washed his clothes and bedding. It was Marcella who got up with him in the night, and Marcella who emptied his chamber pot.

Michael surveyed the meal. The bowl was filled nearly to the rim, despite his weak appetite. As ever, a full glass of brandy was beside it. Neither appealed to him, but the brandy, he believed, was helping to settle his stomach. He lifted the glass to his lips and took a gulp. He had noticed for some time that the taste was off, somehow different than the brandy he had cultivated.

Perhaps it was an effect of the malady, but he was curious and he asked Marcella if the brandy was from his batch.

The midwife prepares your meals. Maria pours the drinks.

Slowly, Michael placed the glass back on the tray. He stared into it. He looked over to the bowl. The scent of paprika and garlic still wafted from the hot stew.

He dropped his head to his chest.

He was quiet, as the pieces assembled in his mind.

Everything made sense now.

"Those two bitches have been putting something in my food!"

JUDGE HAD NOTICED certain things at the Kardos house when he visited. From the time Michael had first taken to bed, Judge had not once seen Maria enter the bedroom where her husband was. Most days, he didn't find Maria home at all, and when she was there, she was in the most unlikely places. Tending a shrub in the far yard. Inside the stable fussing with tools, or even odder, tidying an already tidy space. It was a peculiar attention to tedious chores that he had never seen in her before.

Judge had always viewed Maria as a curious thing. When she was a very small girl, he had watched her skip like a darling sprite through the village. She was a pop and dazzle of a child, who, from the moment she could toddle off her front step, had enthralled Nagyrév with her little-girl charm and cleverness. But he had seen as she grew a bit older the disquiet that took hold in her, and he witnessed the means by which she began to obtain the items and people she wanted most. By fiddling with truth and setting traps.

He had shared his misgivings with Michael only to a point. There was a low ceiling on his influence over his friend. He could never have convinced a man as smitten as Michael had been. But Maria deeply troubled him now. What kind of wife would leave her husband's bedside?

Once Auntie Suzy learned what Michael had screamed out to Marcella, she frantically set about trying to fix the situation. She had to act quickly. She knew she had to make her move before another friend of Michael's came to the Kardos house.

The first thing she did was hurry to her pantry. Behind her supply of vials she kept a paper packet, which was filled with small white pills. They were as round as buttons and no bigger than a pinch, and she had kept them all these years for an emergency such as this. She had used them on Stephen Joljart to help him sleep. She had obtained them from an apothecary she had visited on one of her rare trips to the city. She felt glad now for her prescient mind. Auntie Suzy reached behind her vials and snatched the packet. She spilled out a few pills into her palm. She picked up one and pressed it between her finger and thumb, but it didn't give. The stoic little sleeping pill didn't crush or crumble at all. Auntie Suzy was relieved by its apparent potency. She pocketed that one and one other, and stowed the rest back in the paper packet. Two would do for now.

It had not taken much to convince Marcella to give the pills to Michael. In the two years that Marcella had been in Nagyrév, the young woman had come to think of Michael as a father. She often confided in him. She talked to him of Transylvania, where he had never been, and she asked his opinion about the bachelor she was seeing. When she was alone, she would ruminate on what he had told her, reflecting on each bit of wisdom as if it were a mental jewel to consider.

Marcella would do anything to relieve Michael's suffering, so when the midwife told her the little white pills would calm him down, Marcella was eager to help. She was even willing to lie to ensure he took them. She was sure that Michael's rantings—"those bitches," he had screamed—were brought on by his illness. Pure delirium. She had been horrified when Michael had refused to eat another bite or take another a drink, even from his own flask. Marcella trusted Auntie Suzy. She had grown up under a midwife's care and believed in their methods. So when she opened her palm to reveal the two pills and Michael asked where they had come from, she told him it was she herself who had purchased them from an apothecary.

JUDGE HELD A handkerchief to his face. He took short, shallow breaths, trying to avoid breathing in the stench. The windows in many Nagyrév homes couldn't be opened, which worked well for the villagers. They considered a breeze in the home a cross to bear, as they were certain they brought on colds and fevers. The people of Nagyrév felt safer in a well-sealed room, but Judge would have given anything now to break open Michael's window and let in some fresh, breathable air.

Judge pulled his handkerchief away from his face and balled it into his hand. He touched it to Michael's face. He dabbed the sweat from his friend's brow.

Judge eased himself onto the edge of Michael's bed. He reached for his friend's hand and patted it. The room was dark. Judge looked around for a lamp to light. Somewhere outside, he could hear Maria humming. Her reedy voice quavered as she struggled to reach a high note. He wondered again, *What kind of wife . . . ?* When he left

Michael's house, he went straight to the village hall to schedule an appointment for Michael with Dr. Szegedy.

It would be too late.

Friday, April 7, 1922

The heavens were gray and melancholy. The sun had been missing for at least two days. The temperature had topped at a raw fifty degrees and was now rapidly dropping. A persistent mist touched everything with its moist hand. The air was wet to breathe.

Judge cupped his wine in his hands. It was a small drinking jug that fit squarely in his palm. He locked his thumb through the small handle. His fingers were still stained with soil from the morning's work. He could smell the dirt when he lifted the little glass jug to his lips.

The yard was crammed with mourners, some of whom he had never met. He had secured a spot to stand that was farthest from the band. Maria had hired Henry Miskolczi and his trio, who played at the tavern every Sunday. The music was piercing.

He eased behind the other men until he was near the gate. He peeked out. A family of dogs had settled in under a tree across the street. They were the same mongrels Judge had seen trailing behind Michael's procession earlier in the day. The dogs had wandered over to the house when they saw the coffin being loaded into the wagon. Alerted by the fuss, they had set off into rounds of barking and hadn't quit until the cortège started off. The pack trotted silently with the bereaved until the wagon had made its way past the square before they turned and trotted back. He could see them resting easily now. He glanced up Árpád. The village hall was closed. The post and telegraph office was closed. Not a single business on Árpád had opened. Even the pub. As far back as Judge could remember, it was the first time everyone had closed their doors to attend a funeral.

A long row of wagons stretched from Michael's house as far as the village hall and beyond, and single mules were hitched to trees and to the hitching posts that randomly lined the street. He had examined the wagons on the way back from the cemetery, and it was clear from the plates mounted onto the back of carts that mourners had come from across the entire region.

He had gone twice to the cemetery. The first time, he had set out before dawn with friends to help dig the grave. By the time they finished, Judge had barely had time to change his clothes before the funeral procession was ready to begin. Maria had arranged for the burial to take place early in the day to allow more time for the burial feast.

There was hardly a place for him to stand in the yard. When he had first arrived back at the house, he made his way toward the stable, expecting to gather with Michael's other close friends, but the entrance had been blocked by the band. Judge had never before heard of a band being invited to play at a funeral, and he was quick to find that few other customs would be observed, either.

He gripped his glass tighter. He had learned already how to navigate in the tight, unbreathable space. He raised the glass slowly, drawing it up through the thin channel he had created in front of himself. When Judge had safely landed the glass on his lips, he knocked back another swift gulp.

He could determine where Maria was by the slight parting in the crowd. It was a soft ripple in the fabric of people.

He watched as she wove a slow but determined path toward the band. There was an area directly in front of the trio that was so loud no one had dared step into it, and she aimed for this space. The music was thrumming. Maria could feel it like her own heart beating. Her arms were pressed to her sides, the flat of her palms against her silk dress. She patted the rhythm lightly onto her thighs. She had given Henry Miskolczi a list of her favorite songs and he seemed to be playing every one. As she waded forward, she eased her hands up over her head and waved with the melody. Her arms looked like thin periscopes peeping over the thicket of mourners. Many mistook her gesture as a signal that she was about to make an announcement or declaration of some kind. They turned to watch.

Maria sidled through the final wall of guests. She waved her arms wider now, painting a small arc in the air above her. She clapped her hands together. Slowly at first, then faster. Soon, Franklin joined her.

The pair swayed and twirled, their cheeks flushed by the brandy and wine they had drunk. They were two lovers dancing in a glen, surrounded by a forest of shocked onlookers.

AT SUNSET, THE temperature dropped even further. The sky darkened to deep blues and silvers, and the few guests who still lingered in the yard walked about in silhouette. The tables set out for the food had been cleared. Auntie Suzy and her relatives had done most of the work, aided by Marcella. The food had been prepared the previous day at the Cser tavern by Anna, with help from her next-door neighbor, Mrs. Kiss.

If Anna could have called anyone in Nagyrév a friend, it was Rosa Kiss. She was older than Anna by at least twenty years, and gave Anna both advice about her personal life and practical support in the tavern. Mrs. Kiss provided the lion's share of the food for the pub. She cooked stews in her own kitchen and brought them over in large, steaming pots. In turn, Anna paid her a share of the earnings. In the morning, Mrs. Kiss had helped Anna carry the extra tables over from the pub to the Kardoses' yard for the funeral feast.

Carrying them back was proving hard for Anna. She was fatigued. She had awoken that morning more tired than she normally was, and the lethargy had worsened as the day wore on. Energy merely passed through her on its way to somewhere else. She was a sieve for it, nothing more.

She knew the signs well enough to know just where her energy was going.

She seized the underside of the table and hoisted her end. Her scrawny arms shook from the weight of it. Mrs. Kiss was strong and able, and Anna moved with the bulk as if it were she being lifted like a balloon across the road and settled noisily back in the dark and empty pub, where the table was dropped onto the floor with a clatter. Anna released her grip. She examined the mark the wood had made on her hand.

Maybe this baby would live, she thought. Maybe it would not. Her bland acceptance of her circumstance was a heartbreak to no one but herself.

BY THE TIME the midwife got home and put herself to bed that evening, her temper was so worked up she couldn't sleep. She thrashed about. She yanked the blankets over her, then thrust them off again. She plumped her pillow with her fist, first one side, then the other, unable to get comfortable and all the while muttering and cursing to herself.

She had come to Maria when the band was packing up and as the guests were leaving. Women were clearing away tables, pouring stews from smaller bowls back into the bigger pot.

She pulled Maria aside and, in a whisper, reminded her friend of the agreement they had struck. In her pocket she had secreted papers, drawn up to complete the transfer of deed on Alex Junior's house.

Maria waved the papers away. She shook her head and clucked a no, and all Auntie Suzy could see was the demolition of a friendship, with only a treacherous gadjo left standing in its place.

She vowed never to speak to Maria again. She would remain true to her word for years.

THE CRIER LEANED down over the bulk of his drum. He placed his hand lantern on the ground beside him and pulled himself upright again. He slid his drumsticks from their sleeve, which he kept under the strap. He unrolled his scroll.

He read slowly each announcement: who was marrying, who had livestock for sale, and each bit of news from the county and the capital. He closed with a curious piece that had snaked its way to him over the telegraph machine: townspeople near the Plains had reported that a mysterious rain of spiders had poured down on them from the heavens. The sky had been speckled with spiders, black, hairy raindrops flinging and splattering onto rooftops, porches, inside carriages, dropping onto hats and headscarves and tangling in children's hair.

Some saw the extraordinary event as a harbinger of the end times, but every wise woman knew that spiders were an auspicious sign. Auntie Suzy knew plenty of good fortune was on the way.

KRISTINA CSABAI LED her horse back to the stall. Taking small steps and edging slowly to the barn, she stared down at her bare feet, which were marred with tiny scrapes and had strands of straw embedded in the cakes of mud still lodged between her toes. Her right foot had ballooned, its hue a deep purple, and she could feel a pain in her hip now that she hadn't felt the night before. If she could have looked in a mirror, she would have seen that her forehead was marked with droplets of dried blood, and her swollen cheekbone still held the faint imprint of a chain link. Her vision was blurred, and she could see out through little more than narrow slits, as a bruised bulge arced over her eyes like a cliff.

Kristina secured the horse back in his stall and rested her head for a moment on his side, absently stroking his hair with her fingertips, aware of the slight ridges of his ribs. She sometimes hummed because she thought it calmed him, but this morning she lingered with him quietly. His steady breathing, the fact of his solemn body, the fact of his ribs, his coarse hair, were like a shelter.

She thought she would be driving to Auntie Suzy's house and had earlier struggled to hitch up the wagon, but it had been too heavy. She fitted the harness easily enough, taking the task at a pace her sore body would allow, but she was surprised by a quick snap of pain that struck her when she lifted the hefty shafts of the cart to secure the straps to the harness. She let out a sharp cry and let the wagon fall from her grasp. Kristina knew then that she would have to walk the distance to Auntie Suzy's house.

Each time her tender foot touched ground, she winced. She at first tried to take long strides, leaning heavily on her one leg and pivoting her other leg as far ahead as she could, hoping to gain more ground and speed up the journey. But the quick motion and the rush of air pushing against her battered foot made it throb more. Small, shuffling steps were more tolerable.

It was still early in the morning, but the sun was already heavy with heat. She tugged at her frayed scarf, which itched where it was tied in a matted knot under her chin. She tugged also at the top of it, pulling the scarf forward and using it to pat at the sweat on her forehead. She kept touching her hand to her swollen brow. Her apron smelled of hay and sweat, and her black dress was filthy and sticking to her clammy skin. There were sharp creases in the skirt, wrinkles from where she had lain in the pile of hay the night before.

The evening came back to her in sharp currents, like jarring electrical impulses. At some point in the night, she had awoken shivering, uncertain where she was. She tried to pull herself close, to fold in for warmth, and was surprised by a shock of pain that burst forth, signaling in from so many places. It was knifelike, and she froze her body as a weapon against more. Then, very cautiously, she unfurled, gently and gradually, so as not to trigger more pain, and eventually eased her way out of its grip.

She became aware of the smell of dampness and animals, and knew she was in the stable. She carefully pried herself from the hay on which she'd passed out, and crawled on her hands and knees to the horse stall, feeling her way in the dark and twice getting tangled in her dress. The ground was cold and numbed the palms of her hands. Her foot throbbed. On the floor at the back of the stall was the horse blanket. She unfolded it and swaddled it around herself, huddling against the wooden slats of the stable. The occasional rustling of the animals in their slumber was a comfort, and Kristina's body began to quiet into it. She settled enough to try to piece together what had happened that afternoon . . .

KRISTINA HAD SWEPT up the old cow bedding and piled it outside the stall. The ground was muddy, and she was anxious to lay the new hay and get her feet out of the muck. As she scattered the straw about, she talked softly to the calf, who sidled up to her to be scratched behind the ears.

The blow came fast. Her husband's boot struck her brow, pitching her against the stall wall. He shoved his boot into the side of her head, slamming against her ear. She grasped the cow tie railing for support, but another blow struck, this time in her stomach. Kristina lost her grip on the railing and fell to the ground. The calf began to let out shrill cries. Her husband staggered backward a bit and then steadied himself. He leaned down, grabbed a fistful of Kristina's hair, and yanked her up so that she was face-to-face with him.

With his free hand, he seized one of the unused cow chains that hung from the railing. He stood up straighter and widened his stance. The chain was about five yards long and he gathered it like a rope, swinging it in circles above Kristina's head, faster and faster, until it was whirring and snapping at the air. The metal chain came down heavy on her face, her arms, her back. He let go of her hair and Kristina fell onto the ground with force.

He stood back. He released his grasp, the mass of cold metal clunking as it landed in a heap at his side. His hand was red where he had clutched the chain, and he rubbed at its soreness. Kristina lay on the floor between the stall wall and the calf, whose shrieking had turned into whimpers. Julius got down on his knees. He sat back, leafing his fingers through the straw bedding and contemplating his wife.

He stood up and lifted one foot to his knee to examine the bottom of his boot. Kristina looked up at him, watching his face darken more. He slammed his booted foot down on her once again, this time targeting her foot, and heard a snap. She screamed.

IT TOOK MUCH of the morning to walk to Auntie Suzy's house. Kristina had heard it was best to go around to the back. Kristina entered and tapped on the door.

When Auntie Suzy opened the door, she thought it was an old woman teetering on her stoop, or maybe a Romany beggar, but then she noticed that the brown hair that hung down from the scarf didn't yet show gray, and the skin was too white to suggest Romany blood. Both of the woman's eyes were swollen nearly shut, and her clothes were soiled and torn. She reeked. Her foot looked broken.

I'm Kristina. My neighbor told me I should come to you.

A HASTY CHRISTENING

Romany anger is like the wind. It comes and goes.

—OLD ROMANY SAYING

BUDAPEST

Auntie Suzy stepped onto the courthouse portico and into the brutal wind. Cold and biting, it swirled around her. It slapped and shoved her like a bully, and she reached for the nearest pillar to steady herself. A dusting of snow that had been on the ground when she arrived in the morning had largely disappeared, but slick patches of ice still covered the stone steps.

Despite the harsh weather battering her, she couldn't help but grin. The victory was hers. By some great hand of gadjo logic, Auntie Suzy had been acquitted of all charges against her.

Anyone following the case was most certainly going to be stunned by the reversal. Her confession to the gendarmes had been like sealing wax on a letter. Absolute. Incontrovertible. She had described her criminal acts with a flourish. And at the Szolnok trial, when she claimed her confession was false, no one had believed her. How was it, then, that the higher court acquitted her? Was it possible it had found her story credible? Was it possible the higher court believed her over the gendarmes? Or had her ace lawyer gotten her off on a technicality?

Auntie Suzy didn't care one whit about any of it. She only cared that she was free. She was filled, supremely, with an unshakable trust once again in her own good sense.

The noise from the boulevard below was terrific. There was, to her ears, a deafening rattle from passing motorcars and carriages, and the midwife covered her ears as best she could to muffle the noise. Her lawyer, Mr. Kovacs, was somewhere down on the street amid the hubbub, holding his hand to his bowler hat and climbing into a carriage.

Thursday, January 18, 1923

Anna's straw sleeping mat was laid out against the wall. It was an old mat that she had used for years. The sides now puckered where they had been stitched and restitched to keep the straw bound together, yet several strands had managed to escape the seams and now encircled her like a fence.

Her sleep had been profound. It had been misty and distant, and she had awoken from time to time, fluttering her eyes against the daylight before falling again into a deep well of slumber.

An evening and most of a day had passed. The room had been scoured, all the blood soaked up with rags and tea towels. The burlap sack she had been on for the birth was drenched in blood, too. It had been discarded—buried, or burned—Anna didn't know which.

Lewis had come in during the night, defying orders to stay away. His odor and his clanging knocks into the bench and other hard surfaces in the room had barely woken Anna, and she had soon slid back into her well.

The children slipped out of the house by morning. Her daughter had gone to school. Anna rarely sent her daughter to school in winter, as the little girl's shoes had holes in them and the walk to the schoolhouse was far too cold. But Mari, who had stayed most of the night and arrived back before dawn, had sent her off in a borrowed pair. Her son, at thirteen too old for school, had gone to help Mrs. Kiss in the tavern. Mrs. Kiss had been with Anna off and on through the night and had opened the tavern in the morning.

Pleasant sounds streamed in from the outdoors. Through Anna's thin windows came the patter of horses and oxen, the clank of milk barrels as they rolled in the carts, the jangle of cart bells. Yet each musical note that rang outside was punctuated within by Mari's heavy-footed thuds. Her boots made a dull thump every time they struck the floor. She moved as if with each step she was stamping out a small fire. It was the same ponderous, pitiless walk as Auntie Suzy's.

Mari bore a striking resemblance to her mother, and to her aunt Lidia as well. From behind or from afar, Anna could not tell one from the other. Someone she thought was Auntie Suzy at the square would turn around and reveal herself to be Lidia. Or Mari, emerging from the post and telegraph office, was really Auntie Suzy. They shared the same shape, the same lips, the same voice, the same twiddling thumbs, and the same dawdling walk. When Anna had occasion to leave her house or the tavern, she felt a trifold threat of encountering Auntie Suzy.

It was a poorly kept secret in Nagyrév that Auntie Suzy assisted her daughter with births, regardless of Dr. Szegedy's orders forbidding her. Mari had finished her apprenticeship with Dr. Szegedy and had been given his go-ahead to perform deliveries on her own, but in nearly every case, Auntie Suzy still showed up. And on many occasions, some would say most, Auntie Suzy delivered the babies, with Mari assisting her. Anna had been relieved beyond measure when Mari had shown up the previous day without her mother.

Anna had only been awake for a few minutes before she felt another strong tug toward the lap of sleep. She was being pulled away from the sounds and sights around her, as if snipped from them with a scissor, fiber by fiber. She struggled to keep her eyes open long enough to catch another glimpse. She held her focus on Mari. Nagyrév's newest midwife had on an old but well-kept dress, the color of which had hardly faded over the years. Mari was growing thicker around her middle, and the dress bunched at the hips where her apron was tied. Her headscarf was pulled down tight at her forehead. It formed a little triangle at the back that bobbed when she walked. Anna watched it now. With Mari's back to her, Anna could see the back of Mari's arms, and from them the dangling, wiggling red feet of her newborn son. With his little toes curled, he kicked at the air around him. He yowled.

Anna had already chosen the baby's godmother. Anna's isolating life left her little chance to grow friendships with other women. Mrs. Kiss had become her confidante largely because of proximity, and because she knew what took place in the house. Mrs. Kiss had seen what Lewis did to Anna. She often helped prepare the compresses for the bruises he left.

But Mrs. Koteles was closer in age to Anna and, more important, she was Catholic. She lived quite far out Árpád Street, toward the edge of the village. Weeks ago, Anna had sent her son out to her on foot, with the invitation to be the new baby's godmother. Mrs. Koteles had accepted. Anna thought now that she would need to send him out there again in the next few days. A christening needed to be planned. Anna had said little to anyone about the stillbirth she had endured the previous year, the child Dr. Szegedy had delivered. That's how it went with her babies who didn't survive.

AUNTIE SUZY CAUGHT the first train home that she could. She had stayed at her cousin's place during her brief trial in the capital. Some of the Csordás family lived in Budapest, and she lodged with one of them on the rare occasion she came to the capital.

By late afternoon she had arrived at the Újbög depot. Along with her suitcase, she had one wicker basket with her, which she had filled with a meal to eat on her journey. There were also tasty treats for her family in Nagyrév, which her cousin had prepared.

The midwife stepped off the train into the twilight of the day. The wind still had teeth, as gales on the Plains were stronger than any in the Magyar land. But Auntie Suzy was sure-footed on her own home ground and without fear of the city rush. She lowered her head, moving into the wind like a bull.

The wind yanked at her shawl. It blew through her basket, making off like a thief with the aromas that had been tantalizing her for hours. She took a deep breath to fill herself with home, but the wind snatched that from her, too. Auntie Suzy clutched the basket closer to her. She grabbed a fistful of shawl and pulled it tighter. Somewhere beneath, she could feel the small weight of her putsi, warm against her skin.

Her tussle with the wind had confused her, so when there was a push at her side, she felt it as a blow. She looked to see her granddaughter flush against her, flung there by her own excitement. The girl wrapped her thin arms around the midwife's wide trunk. Young Lidia pressed her head hard against her grandmother's chest and spoke into it all that had happened in the few days that Auntie Suzy had been away. The tinctures the dog had been given for his ailments, the small branches that had blown down in the yard, the villagers' squabbles with Count Molnar about the rising taxes. The winds in her young mind blew about as recklessly as the Plains gales and she mixed big news with small.

"Miss Anna had her baby last night. It's a boy. She'll call him Stephen."

BY THE TIME Dr. Szegedy boarded the train in Budapest, the withering shock he had felt upon hearing the verdict had jelled into deep distress. It had taken the higher court nearly eighteen months to hear the case. Dr. Szegedy had spent that time rooting through the registers in the other villages. A conviction at the higher court would be the go-ahead he was waiting for. It was all he needed to request full investigations into the affairs of every village midwife under his authority, including Kristina Csordás in Tiszakürt. But with Auntie Suzy's conviction overturned, his investigation was as good as dead.

Auntie Suzy's appeal had been granted largely because the midwife had recanted the original confession she had made to the gendarmes. Dr. Szegedy had been confident the higher court would uphold the Szolnok decision. An acquittal had been unthinkable to him.

It was midweek, midwinter, and the train was nearly empty. The window was spattered with dirt and old snow. The Plains unfurled before him, bland and vapid in January. They were abandoned, except for a host of crows that pecked at the cold ground.

His seat was hard and unforgiving. Dr. Szegedy slumped in it, summoning his best posture of defeat. On the good patches of track, the railcar swayed in a boxy rhythm side to side. On the turns and bad patches, it jolted and shuddered. Dr. Szegedy surrendered himself to the train's temper. He loosened himself to it, feeling the locomotive's chug rattle up through his body.

When he closed his eyes, he took himself back into the courtroom. As the miles passed, he reimagined every word he could remember hearing, every action he could remember seeing. With his physician's eye, he searched for the fissure, the point of weakness he hadn't seen before, which had caused such a catastrophic break in the bones of his case.

BY THE AFTERNOON, the din from the tavern had grown louder. Anna could hear the scrape of chairs and benches as they were dragged out from the tables. She could hear the throaty, wine-soaked guffaws of her patrons.

The light from outside was steely and severe. It cast her room in harsh silver tones. There were pockets of the room Anna couldn't see. She tried to give shape to what was in those darkened spots, fixing her gaze until she had worked up a dim memory: the ceramic pot with a broken lip she had brought with her from her mother's house when she moved in; the chipped, splintered step stool that her daughter still used as a chair. In her light-headed state, the room was foreign and unpredictable to her. She poked at it with the soft paw of her foggy memory.

Her recall of the birth was also out of her grasp. It was black and formless, a field at midnight. She groped her way toward it.

What had Mari said to her?

Delicately, with the care she usually showed only her children, Anna propped herself up on her mat. She leaned back gently against the icy wall, resting her head there. She could feel the cold fan out across her scalp. She drew her blanket closer around her, tucking it tight to her bony body to retain any warm air that was trapped there.

Do you want . . .

She could close her eyes and know where Mari was in the room. The hobnails on Mari's boots tapped at the floor when she walked, as if hammering out a dull message. The boots smelled of sweat and wet leather, and the soles held a faint trace of horse dung. Whenever Mari walked near her, Anna caught a sickening whiff.

Do you want this one . . .

She could hear faintly the sound of children's voices. A soft melody. The children often sang on their way home from school, and she could hear strains of their ditty drifting up the road. When it was warm out, Anna's daughter liked to sing out by the ditch, where she braided the grass and played with her corn-husk doll.

Do you want this one to go . . .

Sometimes her daughter's friend would walk over with her pet lamb, a piece of twine tied around its neck as a leash, and the two girls and the lamb would sit on the grassy patch. The girls would sing to the lamb and coil its soft hair around their small fingers.

Do you want this one to go away? I can make it go away, just like Mama did with baby Justina.

It was all there. The dark field of her memory was now lit with horror.

For nearly seven years, Anna had carried the secret shame of Justina. She had heaped it onto her already shame-packed soul. For a long time after Justina's death, she was so racked with guilt and fear that she could barely function. She was dazed and disoriented, and her pain was always someplace beyond her reach. She felt even less connected to herself than she had felt before any of it had happened, and her worry, not only for Justina's soul but also for her own, consumed her.

She had worried endlessly when the gendarmes came to Nagyrév, but they had never questioned her, and at least in that regard, her fear had eased. During all of that time, Anna believed that what had happened to Justina was a secret known only to the two sinners. It had never occurred to her that the midwife had revealed anything to her daughter about that night.

Little Stephen had been born sharply at midnight. The church bells were tolling the hour the moment he came slithering into Mari's hands. Blood had poured from Anna's body and pooled around her like some grim foreboding. Blood seeped onto her hands from the sackcloth, which was soaked in it. She bled nearly as much as she had the last time, and she could barely hold on to consciousness. Anna had already begun slipping into her deep well when Mari posed her question. It came to her as if on a slow-moving river, a dreamlike query floating gently past her, then drifting away with the current.

Her breasts were full and sore. They leaked onto her filthy dress.

How had she answered?

KRISTINA CSABAI NEARLY buckled as she ran in her old boots down her path. She could feel her son's hand pressing hard against her back. At sixteen, he was already as tall and as strong as his father. He pushed at her, urging her to hurry. With his other hand, he gripped the hand of his ten-year-old sister, who was struggling to keep up.

Her husband stood in the doorway screaming at his fleeing family. *I will kill all of you!*

Kristina didn't look back at him. She just kept running. They all kept running.

"I will kill you and then I will kill myself!"

Mr. Csabai slammed the door shut. It met the frame with a sound like the crack of a rifle. He opened the door and slammed it shut again.

Kristina and the children scrambled through the fence gate. Her son yanked his little sister over the ditch and pulled her into the roadway. Kristina charged ahead in her unwieldy boots. Fresh welts covered her face.

She saw her neighbor, John Tary, at his gate, motioning them silently to come to him. The three bumbled toward him, her son still holding his sister's hand. They all hurried up Mr. Tary's path and into his house. They would be safe there. At least for the night.

NINE MONTHS HAD passed since Michael's funeral. In that time, Maria's life had not changed much. She still lived in the same house that she had shared with him, although she owned it now. She had inherited the house and all of the other properties in his name.

She was a landlord now, and that felt to her like the granting of authority she had always been expecting, but had never gotten. Not when she arrived back in Nagyrév to take up with Michael, nor when she became his wife. As for Alex Junior's house, she was even more satisfied that she was still in possession of it. She had never intended to sell it to the midwife, not really, and it gave her an extra bit of satisfaction to ride by it and know that what had belonged to the Kovacs family now belonged to her. The only action she had taken on her dead son's house was to move its occupants out and bring them to live with her.

For the first time in her life, she needed no one.

In particular, she no longer needed Auntie Suzy. When she buried Michael, she was sure she had buried the last of her troubles. Once again, she had erased what no longer fit, and was swiftly coloring in the contours of a new life. She didn't need the midwife to divine answers anymore. She could not foresee a single problem.

Friday, January 19, 1923

The streetlamp was a hazy point of light far up the road. The low row of buildings that stood near it, dreary even in daylight, were gray slabs under the lamp, mottled with the dull shadows of naked tree limbs.

The small light around Anna was weak. There had been no time to clean the soot off the hand lantern, and the little flame struggled to glow. It burned atop the long wick, a tiny bud of fire throwing a hazy glimmer at her feet. A faint smell of paraffin hung in the air. The violent winds of the previous days had died completely, and an arresting stillness had taken their place.

Anna could feel the warmth of Mrs. Kiss beside her. Mrs. Kiss was not much taller than Anna, but she was heavier, and she pressed comfortingly against Anna's side. Mrs. Kiss had locked her own arm in hers, funneling a strength to Anna that kept her upright.

Mrs. Kiss gripped the lantern and Anna cradled the baby in her arms. He was swaddled, with a little piece of twine tied around his toe to ward off the devil. Anna had hastily fastened it there as an emergency measure. A blanket was draped over him.

She was wrapped in Lewis's coat. It was much sturdier and warmer than her own, but the stale odors of sweat and brandy were trapped in the fibers of the wool. It was Lewis, lying in wait.

A couple of trusted patrons had been put in charge of the pub for the evening. Lewis had already exhausted his usefulness by fetching Mrs. Kiss. Even if he had been sober enough to make it all the way to Mrs. Koteles's house, there still would not have been time for Mrs. Koteles to do all that needed to be done in such a short time. She simply lived too far away. For this single duty, Mrs. Kiss had agreed to stand in as the baby's godmother. It was a matter of saving his soul.

Mrs. Kiss had hurried to track down Pastor Toth. He was usually spotted leaving for his ranch early in the morning, stomping in double-soled boots with his shotgun slung over his shoulder. Like Ébner, he was an avid hunter, who often spent the entire day hunting in the forest and usually did not return until dark. It was well past dinnertime when Mrs. Kiss had finally got to him.

Anna and Mrs. Kiss walked as quickly as they could toward the chapel, passing along the way the night watchman and a band of young bachelors, sixteen- and seventeen-year-old teenage boys, out for the evening. The young men were headed down to the riverbank with a jug of brandy and cigarettes. They sang as they went, their voices floating dreamily back to the square.

Anna pressed her baby to her chest. She listened for a breath.

Inside, the church was dank. The massive stones of its walls emitted a cruel, wet breath into the musty air. The church had never known warmth, not from a woodstove or a summer sun, and the cold within was settled and stubborn.

The narthex was unlit, and it was only by the glow of the lantern that Anna could see at all. A crooked row of mouse droppings lined the edges of the floor. A tiny hill of dust that had also escaped the reach of a broom was heaped in a corner.

The altar was lit with candles. They illuminated Pastor Toth, who stood waiting for her there. She could see a figure in the first pew, too. Sometimes Pastor Toth's wife accompanied him. Anna had invited no one to this late-night christening, the baptism that would save her infant son from an eternity in purgatory. Justina had not been baptized, and Anna refused the same awful fate for this soul. With Mrs. Kiss at her side, Anna moved as quickly as she could up the aisle of the nave.

Except for perhaps weddings and holy days, the church was usually empty. It had been built more than 150 years earlier, before the village was even named. It had had a thatched roof and, except for its prominence on the square, could have been mistaken for another cottage. Eighty years later, it was reconstructed and the steeple was added, making it look like a proper Calvinist chapel. To Anna, it seemed as old as the ages. It felt like a tomb, and smelled to her of the musty pages of the hymnals that were stacked in the pews.

The altar candles were thin, but together they offered enough light. As Anna neared, she could see Pastor Toth, who stood waiting for her there (just as there had not been enough time to fetch Mrs. Koteles, there hadn't been time to arrange for the priest, either). She could see his girth, poorly hidden by his robe. There was a small table draped with a cloth, as if set for an intimate dinner, behind which the pastor usually delivered his sermons. Elaborate webs had been woven by spiders under the table and in the window behind it, spotlighted now by the candle flames.

Anna looked again at the front pew, where the uninvited guest sat. Her head was wrapped in a knitted shawl, which draped across both shoulders. Her coat was the color of charcoal. A crease was marked across the back, where she had pressed heavily against the back of the pew.

There was an orphanage in Cibakháza where the nuns worked, and Anna wondered if perhaps by some mysterious manner one had been sent to her now. Anna had never known a nun to come to Nagyrév. The priest came twice a month in good weather, but even he was a rare sight to most of the village, especially the children, who trailed behind him and mocked his cassock when they saw him walking the dusty road into the village. They had certainly never seen a nun, and

Anna was sure the rest of the Calvinist villagers had never laid eyes on one, either.

She looked harder now. The miracle of a sister appearing as if by magic at this hasty, secret ritual was all Anna needed to leap to a hope of a far greater miracle at hand. She had prayed, for more than twenty-four hours she had prayed that her son would survive what had been placed on his lips and tongue by the midwife's daughter. And she had begged God to let her raise this boy that He had given her, and to whom He had given milk in her breast to feed him, which He had not done with Justina. She had not given consent to dismiss this life. Of this she was certain——or nearly certain.

But it was not a nun. Anna saw that now. She surveyed the uninvited and it was some small gesture that informed her, the familiar twiddle of thumbs perhaps, that crushed her brief hope of a blessing. Anna walked the last few steps to the altar, feeling the curse of the midwife's eyes upon her.

Anna clutched her dying baby closer. She could feel the devil's grip on him already.

AUNTIE SUZY STAYED at the church to help Pastor Toth clean up, then walked to the Cser pub, where she and Mari had agreed to meet. Ever since Mari had been appointed to fill her mother's post, she too began to frequent the tavern. Now there were two women in the village who dared to swing through the doors of a pub.

Mother and daughter drank for more than an hour, and in part were celebrating Auntie Suzy's success in Budapest. It seemed to the midwife now that her victory had always been a foregone conclusion, and she felt an immense lightness in her being. By midnight, the pub was getting ready to close, so Auntie Suzy poked around behind the bar and grabbed a bottle of brandy to take with her. It was the rare occasion when she had no baskets, so she slid the bottle into the breast of her coat and headed out with Mari.

As the two women came up Orphan Street, they could see light coming from old Henry Toth's place. Henry was a barrel maker who lived near the midwife. He and Auntie Suzy had been neighbors for nearly twenty-five years. Henry's gate was ajar. Auntie Suzy peered through the opening. Firelight glowed from his workshop.

Inside the yard, a low din of voices could be heard, the hum of a midnight hive gathered for a nightcap. Auntie Suzy and Mari moved toward it in the dark. Auntie Suzy liked old Henry and she was not yet ready to go home. The wine had put her in a festive mood, and she was sure he had one more glass to share with her.

She was laughing as she approached the workshop, unaware or unmoved that the gathering inside had fallen silent when they saw her. Word had already spread that she was back from Budapest. Rumors had begun to circulate about what had happened at the court. Much of the conversation in Henry's workshop that evening had been speculation about her witchcraft. Some had convinced themselves that the only way she had beaten the conviction was through the work of her magic.

She stood in the doorway, the heat at her front, the cold at her back. The workshop was large, perhaps twice the size of a stable, and well lit by the fire that burned in the pit. The iron cage Henry used to heat up staves abutted the wall behind him. A tidy row of staves was laid out nearby. His tools hung from the walls, as did the pin barrels. Most of the larger barrels were packed along the back of the workshop, but two or three had been turned over to use as tables. Some of Henry's guests were now seated at them. The floor was carpeted with fresh oak shavings.

Auntie Suzy and her daughter stepped in close to the fire. The midwife welcomed the flush of warmth on her face. The wine had already reddened her cheeks, but the heat from the blaze turned them into bright cherries.

"Where have you been at this late hour?" asked Henry.

Auntie Suzy snuffed out her lantern and placed it at her feet. Her hands were pink with cold. She rubbed her palms together, then held them to the fire.

"We've been at a place drinking good wine," said the midwife.

There was an open jug of brandy on Henry's makeshift table that had been making the rounds. A few dirty glasses surrounded it, left there by friends who had already gone home. Auntie Suzy eyed the jug.

"And where might that be?" asked Henry.

With a rag, Henry began to wipe the inside of one of the glasses.

"At the Cser tavern."

Henry filled the glass with brandy and handed it to the midwife.

Auntie Suzy gulped back a swallow. She let out a laugh. The quick shot of brandy made her even more loose-limbed, giddier. She locked eyes with Mari. The pair were dressed nearly the same. Both women had heavy, dark shawls pulled snugly over their heads; both wore dark, drab, woolen, belted coats and heavy boots. The actor and her understudy.

The secret Auntie Suzy had been holding began to stir. It wriggled on her tongue and she knew she had to open her mouth and let it out.

"Baby Stevie has given his last will and testament."

"To whom?" Henry asked, after a beat.

The midwife put her glass down on the upright barrel. She rubbed her hands together and put them to her cheeks to feel the heat coming off her face.

She leaned in close to Henry.

"It was just for my ears."

IN THE DARK, the crier reached for his matches. He cupped the flame, shielding it from the winds that blew through his raggedy front door. He reached his hand down into the glass bowl of his lantern and lit the wick.

The dinginess of his old cottage didn't bother him. He had hung the frayed tapestry when he moved in, and never thought about it again. He never noticed it fading more year after year, or growing more tattered, or the thick layer of dust that now covered it. The wood-burning stove worked, which mattered to him a great deal. His bed, situated in the little room off the kitchen, was a sturdy cot with a thick straw mattress, high enough off the ground to be comfortable to him. He had lived in the run-down cottage for more than a dozen years and had yet to change a thing about it.

He slept in his boots. On the coldest nights, he slept in his hat, too.

The crier reached for his cloak, which he kept on a peg near the door, and slipped it on. He bent down and picked up his drum, lifted the straps over his shoulders, and fastened the drum to his waist. He grabbed the lantern and stepped out the door into the night.

The mongrels trotted over to him when he turned onto Árpád Street. He whacked his drum with his drumstick to shoo them away. The crier continued to the village hall, where he read through the crier's book. He scribbled down the new announcements onto his scroll. Back out on the street, he headed in the direction from which he had come to go to the well on the square. His lantern dangled as he walked, casting strange, ghostly lights on the road. The handle was rusty and squeaked as it swayed.

He passed by the caped night watchman. From time to time, the crier had seen the watchman sneaking nips of brandy from a flask he kept concealed under his cape. He knew the watchman also kept a loaf of bread secreted there. He had seen him tear off large hunks and eat them.

When the crier arrived at the square, he could already see windows of nearby houses lit with lamps. The sun wouldn't rise for at least another two hours, but the working day was about to begin.

He unfurled his scroll. There were several announcements, but he scanned to the last one and read it first: *Take heed! After two years, the attacker of Mrs. Suzannah Olah Fazekas has served his time in the Royal County of Szolnok prison and will be returning home to Nagyrév.*

Just as the sun was rising, baby Stevie died.

Late September 1923

Kristina Csabai opened the door of her bedroom. She had not slept there in weeks. Her son had taken her place in the room. His single bed had been moved in and placed opposite his father's bed. Both father and son had been ill with dysentery for weeks.

Kristina moved past her sleeping son toward her husband, who was also asleep. On Dr. Szegedy's last visit, he had given each patient a high dose of codeine for their discomfort.

The putrid, sour odor of their watery bowels mixed with the acid scent of vinegar, which Kristina had plied generously on the walls and floors.

She looked at her husband in the bed. Fever and pain made his sleep fitful, but it was still a more restful slumber for him than she had seen in years. For her, it was a glimpse of her prewar husband. Her prewar love, who had been kind and calm.

He had marched off to the Italian front. He had climbed up the sheer, ice-covered rock faces of the Alps. He had crawled on shaking hands and knees along the narrow ledges. His brothers-in-arms were in front of him and behind him, single file. He had crept into crevices and caves to fire at the enemy and waited for an avalanche to come, as the shelling often triggered one. He killed the enemy and the blasts killed the mountain, such was the deal that had been struck in this vertical war in which he had been called to fight. On such a battlefield, his rage had been born.

Kristina shook her husband to rouse him. She propped him up with pillows behind his back. She gave him the small glass of water she had prepared in the kitchen. Auntie Suzy had suggested this was an ideal time to administer her solution. Disease always provided a good cover for the midwife. Masked by an existing malady, poison would never be suspected.

By anyone, including Dr. Szegedy.

Friday, October 5, 1923

Kristina's black kerchief was sopping, and the knot fastened under her chin had hardened in the rain. Strands of her hair were matted to her forehead. Steady streams of water dripped from the rim of her black shawl and water seeped into her boots. She blinked back raindrops.

She stood in front of the privy. She gripped the pot with both hands. The scent of the rainwater helped tamp down the stench rising from the bloody excrement and vomit sloshing in the bottom of the pot. She flung the pot upside down. The watery mix slapped onto the sodden ground. Traces of mucus, stained pink with blood, were the last to swirl down into the hole in the earth.

The privy door swung shut behind her as she turned to go back inside the house. The soles of her boots sank into the soft ground, wet mud clinging to the worn leather as she hastened back across the yard. The night air, usually filled with the sounds of baying mongrels and cockerels crowing, of reed wolves and foxes, of fighting feral cats, had been silenced by the hard rain. The torrent had also snuffed out the meteor shower above. The Earth was barreling through the path of cosmic dust kicked up by an unknown comet—a warning for villagers, had they been able to see it—of deep trouble on the way.

In the morning, Kristina Csabai's husband was dead.

EIGHT CRYING ORPHANS

When I was a curious little girl, I asked about it and my parents
told me when my great-grandfather died, nobody investigated.
There was no investigation, because everyone knew
"my mother wouldn't do something like that."

—LIDIA KUKOVECZ, GREAT-NIECE OF AUNTIE SUZY

Ever since old Mr. Ambrusz died, Auntie Suzy and Lidia had shucked corn at Lidia's place on summer afternoons. For a while, they continued to join Mrs. Ambrusz at her house, but the old woman had become increasingly reclusive in the wake of her husband's death, and by the time she passed away late the previous year, in '23, the sisters had already moved their ritual in nearly all respects over to Lidia's house.

Lidia's cottage was similar to Auntie Suzy's, and inside she had small, well-ordered collections. Porcelain findzsas, silver teaspoons, decorative plates. They were treasured items she had inherited from her mother-in-law or purchased from the antiques peddler, or that had been procured for her as souvenirs from Budapest. Her house was kept scrupulously neat. Lidia swiped a rag across her tabletops and cupboards at the first hint of dust or dirt. If ever an item was out of place, Lidia hurried to put it back. But the home held a persistent yet vague scent of fresh loam, carried in anew each evening by her husband. Valentine was well into his sixties, but he still worked the fields each day with his sons.

Though Lidia had not thought of it in years, there was a glass bottle hidden underneath the cornerstone of the tidy whitewashed cottage. Valentine had placed it there when the house was built. Inside the bottle was a scrap of paper noting the date the home had been constructed, for whom it had been built, prices of items, such as sugar or tobacco, and a short record of key events that had taken place around 1880, when Lidia and Valentine Sebestyen—a gadjo—were newlyweds. The time capsule was a family fingerprint sealed beneath the earth.

Lidia's porch was as spruce as the rest of her house. She swept it several times a day, assiduously brushing away the fine dirt that had been pecked into a powder by the fowl and blew onto the porch as dust. A long, low bench was near the front door, under the dried *kukurut* and paprika, which hung down in ribbons.

A large basket of corn sat beside the bench. Next to it was a twig basket that had begun to fill with shucked ears. Another basket was filling with the papery husks, to be saved for use in the privy. Among the wicker containers was a heavy jug of red wine.

Auntie Suzy was seated on the bench. A small jumble of corncobs lay in a pile on her lap. The air was tinged with her pipe smoke. She hefted the jug under one arm like a small barrel and tilted it downward. She watched a wide stream of wine belch into the glass that she held steady on the bench. When she was finished, she pushed the jug toward her sister. She pulled her pipe from her lips like a cork, lifted her glass up, and guzzled.

Sometimes the midwife cast a studious eye on her sister's yard. The garden was nearly as pretty as her own. There was a well in the middle. There was a bounty of flowers. Lidia's two sons, when they were younger, used to pluck the flowers and stick them in their hatbands on their way out to meet dates. Auntie Suzy's sons had done the same thing with the flowers in her garden. Vast creepers clothed the fence, a curtain to shade the yard. There was a gap at the gate line, and with the gate open, the sisters had a view to Rose Pirate's house.

Rose had been the talk of the village for months. Auntie Suzy had been relieved to have the focus off herself. The midwife's acquittal in Budapest had set off another round of rumors and speculation. Villagers took note that her magic had been put to the mettle. They convinced themselves that her sorcery, and her sorcery alone, had upended the Szolnok decision. For a while now, they had been coping with their own suspicions about the midwife by keeping their distance whenever they could, although the farmers still sought out her poultices for their aches and pains. But the truth was, for every villager who crossed to the other side of the road when they saw her coming, there was yet one more woman furtively rapping at her kitchen window. It was a corps of women that continued to grow.

Auntie Suzy's falling-out with Maria Szendi had also not gone unnoticed by the village. The two women hissed and cursed when they saw one another, creating public spectacles that sometimes drew a small crowd around them. Auntie Suzy's alliance with Maria had been a blind spot that now shamed her. She was anxious to have the tarnished friendship behind her, which was another reason musing about Rose had been a welcome distraction for her.

Mr. Pirate's suicide the previous summer—he hanged himself from the rafters at home—had caused the villagers to study Rose more closely than they ever had before. Few had given her much thought until then. Rose had been born in Budapest, and because of that the villagers had always treated her with a certain caution. There were plenty of people in Nagyrév who had been born elsewhere, but they had come from places well known to the locals: Tiszakürt, Cibakháza, Tiszaföldvár. Their families knew one another, or at least had ways of finding out about each other. But no one knew Rose's family. No one knew whether she could be trusted. She spoke differently. She carried herself differently. But Mr. Pirate had been one of their own, and they had come to accept her through him.

Initially, the community had rallied around Rose in the days after Mr. Pirate's death. They helped her bury him, brought food over to the house, and helped her with the cleaning. But the period of bereavement turned into an opportunity to take a closer look at Rose, and in the weeks and months that followed, many had become convinced that Rose had driven Mr. Pirate to take his life. They hunted for proof, finding it in the couple's only son, Desi, who joined the army directly after his father's grisly death. Why, they reasoned, would a son leave his mother in mourning, unless he thought her guilty?

They found further evidence in the gossip that circulated about Rose's numerous affairs. Every whisper about Rose provided a trifling yet gratifying thrill to the vultures of the village, a pleasure in pain that kept them circling back for more. While the probing villagers cleaned the bones of the rumors, Rose gave them a shock they never expected. To their absolute astonishment, Rose suddenly wed Charles Holyba, a widower from Cibakháza, in a rushed ceremony held nearly a year to the day after her husband was found dead. She had known Charles only two weeks.

Charles was not a familiar face in the village, but nearly everyone knew the most unfortunate fact about him, which was that he had been left to raise eight children. The story of his whelping wife was widely known. The youngest child had been less than a year old when Charles's wife died. That was four years earlier. The child was nearly five now. The oldest was sixteen. All of the children lived with their father on his property in Cibakháza, which measured a respectable three and a half acres.

Anyone who knew Charles could spot him from a distance, and this was because of the other unfortunate fact about him. He had been born with a clubfoot, one that turned so far inward that the soft, pink sole had never met the ground. He moved unevenly, lurching like an injured yet eager animal. The skin on the side of his bad foot was as tough as a hide, but the complicated structure of small bones it protected had grown fragile over the years and caused him unbearable pain. For that, and for the array of stomach ailments that dogged him, Charles regularly sought treatments from his longtime friend Dr. Szegedy. The doctor had known Charles his whole life.

Charles was badly crippled, plagued with pain, and burdened with a gang of children. How he had been able to convince Rose to marry him was a question many were asking.

One other union in Nagyrév had been noteworthy, at least to the midwife. After eight years of widowhood and of caring for her late husband's grandparents, Petra Joljart had decided to remarry. Petra had inherited old Mr. Ambrusz's house, the very house she had lived in the last several years. Her daughter had been left a sizable amount of land, twenty acres, by Mr. Ambrusz when he had passed back in '21. Petra's new husband, Mr. Varga, moved in with Petra and her daughter after the wedding. He was a farmer from Nagyrév and well-known among the villagers.

Shortly after the wedding, Mr. Varga purchased a bicycle. He rode with the bicycle all through the village and often left it outside the gate so that it was visible to all who walked past the house. He was only the second man in the village to own one, and Auntie Suzy was not impressed with the way he put it on display. Auntie Suzy had never thought much of Mr. Varga.

ROSE'S NEAT LITTLE house gleamed from a recent whitewash. The creepers that clung to her fence were still neatly trimmed. Inside, the atmosphere was undisturbed. She had taken hardly a thing with her to Cibakháza, except what she could carry in a bundle in her own two hands. Rose had gone from her home in Nagyrév nearly as quickly as her late husband had gone from this earth. It had the appearance that she hadn't left at all.

From the front of Charles's house, Rose could see through the window to the very long wooden table, which at dinner was cluttered with chipped bowls of potatoes or lentils. The plates were worn, also chipped, with one or two displaying a crack down the middle. None of it was like she imagined it would be—a look at the disappointing table was a look at the rest of the house—and there were moments here and there when she wondered if she had made a mistake.

She had already endured nearly a month at Charles's house, which meant dozens of evening meals crowded at the table with the eight children, the youngest of whom had eyes as puffy as pillows from the crying she had done since Rose arrived.

The yard smelled of moldy hay and fodder. Behind the house there were outbuildings with narrow paths stamped from one to the other, a network of functional, if inglorious, veins. A muddle of fruit trees dotted the bald yard. Small clusters of cherries had fallen from their branches and lay rotting on the ground. Charles's property was not a sweeping estate, as he had made it out to be. His grounds were made up of uneven patches of land that had been joined together from smaller plots, and it seemed to Rose that behind every overgrown hedge and through every dirty window there was a dirty-faced child peering at her. And always, there was Charles. He limped behind her. He circled around her like a lame dog, hopeful and besotted. She loathed every lurching step he took. Yet, in that crippled footfall, she was sure lay some small fortune.

The fact of his children had not troubled her at first. Charles had assured her he would find other places for them to live. But just as he had talked up his property—describing a manor, not a mill—he had also exaggerated that notion.

As for the real manors, Rose knew them well. She was a ten-year-old girl when her parents sent her up from Budapest to work as a servant on one of the estates. When she was eighteen, she left the manor house and married Gabriel Pirate.

The manors were enclosed with stone walls that hid broad green lawns. Rose remembered trees whose limbs stretched out wide like raptor wings, providing shade for the children who played underneath their cover. She remembered the heavy iron gates at the front that allowed ample space for the lord of the manor's motorcar to pass through, or teams of white horses pulling grand carriages.

The manor she served was so large that it was easy for a young girl to get lost in her first few days of employment. She would aim to go to the kitchen but find herself in the study or the parlor. She would venture to a child's room but land instead at the door of the master's bedroom. She had been both terrified and intrigued.

Rose's memories of the manor were unhampered by nostalgia. When she looked back on those days, she knew she had learned the switches and signals of her new life as fast as the track on which it seemed to be running. When she set her feet onto the manor steps in her child's frock and shoes, straightaway she had grasped that the master and mistress were her employers, not her guardian parents, and their children her straw bosses. She became a peregrine perched high on a branch, surveying the foreign landscape. Her childhood had been sold, but she blinked away the cloud of fear and saw the take: A house of brokered deals. Steady warmth instead of the cold. Food. Clothing. Lessons in manners and diction. Over time, with her falcon's eye, she had become practiced at spotting opportunities.

SZOLNOK

Kronberg arrived at the courthouse steps. Dust blew around at his feet. He stood in front of a makeshift entrance pathway and a massive pile of ashlar, which jutted out into the street. He surveyed the mess.

In early spring, the city had approved a large budget to renovate the courthouse and prison. Funds would come from the League of Nations, which had approved war reconstruction loans. The plan was twofold: to flip the positions of the courthouse and the prison— giving the courthouse an entrance directly onto busy, prominent Gorove Street—and to double the capacity of the prison so it could hold up to seventy inmates. This part seemed absurd to Kronberg. Why a fairly small city such as Szolnok needed such a large-capacity prison was beyond him. God help him, he thought, if there were ever that many criminals locked up at the same time.

But the funds had been frozen. A bureaucratic delay. The court had severely overreached financially. It barely had enough money to prosecute the current caseload. Meanwhile, the pile of stones had sat untouched for weeks.

THE HARNESSES WERE hung on the side wall of the stable. Rose pulled hers from the peg. She loosened the tangle of buckles and straps until she heard them clank on the floor. As she lifted the bridle toward her, she felt the sudden heaviness of the harness in her arms. It felt like an anchor bearing down. The leather and ropes were cold to the touch and struck a chill through her.

Stop being cruel to the children! Charles had begged her.

There was a deep pile of straw blanketing the floor. Bits had embedded into the bottom of her wooden shoes, which were wet with dew. She could feel fragments of straw poking through her stockings at her skin.

You bruise them!

She moved lightly to her horse, greeting him with a soft hello. The lantern brought only a dim light into the stable, but she knew her horse so well it was as though she were viewing him under a bright midday sun. She knew every long, arced lash on his eyelids and every risen vein on his muzzle. She put her hand to his side and stroked his hair with her fingertips.

She gently brushed her horse with her palm. She spoke to him sweetly. He lowered his head. She placed the bit in his mouth and tightened the noseband. She fastened the throatlatch.

. . . *without the children, it would have been easy with a man like Charles* . . .

Rose had waited until Charles had left for the fields. She had with her the same bundle she had brought with her to Cibakháza.

. . . *a match lit to his bed . . . a fall from a ladder* . . .

She collared her horse and tightened the girth. She slipped the breeching into place. She leaned down and slid the crupper under her horse's tail and buckled it.

To hell with him.

She trod across the bedding to her cart, her long dress picking up pieces of straw at the hem. She leaned down and hefted the cart by the shafts and dragged it into place behind the horse, sliding the shafts through the tug loops. With any luck, she would be back in Nagyrév by breakfast.

She'd had enough of Charles.

THE SUMMER PASSED gently in Nagyrév. The cobbler's hammer tapped like a woodpecker as he mended shoes for the children in time for the new school year. The watermelon farmers were having one of their best seasons. The fruit markets in Szolnok and Kecskemét were loaded with their fare. The bad roads always ruined about half of the produce on the way to market, but that didn't matter this season. There was such a delicious bounty that there were still plenty of good watermelons to sell.

A parade of minstrels and peddlers had already passed through the village, including Mr. Goldmann, the wandering merchant. He arrived each summer in his partially covered wagon, in which he kept his large, hard case full of wares and small bags filled with smaller items, like sewing needles, spools, and spices, that one couldn't get at the Thursday market. Mr. Goldmann would stop at the end of a street and pull his hefty case to the ground. He would drape his smaller pouches over one arm and tramp door to door with them, dragging his case with his free hand. "What do you have for us today, Mr. Goldmann?" the women would ask. He would flip open his case on a turned-over log in the garden, or in the stable if it was raining, and make his best pitch.

Before leaving the village, Mr. Goldmann would stop at the blacksmith's forge for his wheels to be checked or repaired. The cascade of sparks flying from the smithy's hot iron would stop when the peddler entered. The blacksmith would move away from the manor gate he was crafting or the horseshoe he was mending to chat with Mr. Goldmann. A peddler always brought with him news from other towns—who had died, who would be wed, who had shot the biggest pheasant—and, like a gazette, the news that fell into the blacksmith's ear flew out of his mouth like birds across Nagyrév. In summer, the smithy rivaled the crier's best efforts to inform the villagers.

It was not through the whispers of the smithy, but by the bellows of the crier that word got to the villagers that a change was afoot in the village council. The bell ringer post was vacant, and until it could be filled, Dr. Szegedy would be in charge of signing all the death certificates.

A new appointee would be named to the post at the November meeting.

Auntie Suzy had a perfect someone in mind for the job.

ROSE BROUGHT THICK glass jars out of her pantry and placed them on the table. The tablecloth had been pulled away and she had moved the pitcher to the side to make room for them. The jars were old and etched with small, delicate scratches, and their veneers had dulled over the years. Above the table was a small window, through which sunlight came and pooled inside the cloudy jars.

On the bench was a large basket of freshly washed and peeled fruit. Plums. Apricots. Cherries. Rose had picked some of the fruit from her own small garden and the rest she had plucked from the fruit trees that grew wild in the village. Rose had been peeling the fruit most of the morning. Her fingers were stained with it and bore tiny cuts where she had nicked herself with the knife.

Rose had not worried herself over Charles since she came back to Nagyrév. She was not one to spend time ruminating on the past, and she reached only far enough into her future as was needed. It never served her spirit to dwell on bygones, nor the distant road ahead.

The first day home had been given to restoring some order. Unpacking the bundle she had taken with her. Taking stock of her kitchen. Opening the shutters. Sweeping.

Some of her neighbors had stopped by. They were more curious than helpful. Lidia had come. The two women had always been on equal footing, in spite of Lidia's age, as she was older than Rose by twenty-six years. Both believed they shared a practical sensibility about the village that only an outsider could have. They had compatible dispositions, although Lidia was more anxious. Like her sister, Lidia was fidgety, with thumbs that twiddled and a leg that shook heedlessly. Rose, on the other hand, considered herself to be cool-headed and stolid.

In appearance, Rose was ordinary in nearly every way. She was not fat, but muscular. She had long, limp hair. She had a long nose set on a long face, and her mouth had the even, balanced line of a level. She rarely bent it into a smile, and when she did, she was quick to withdraw it. She stared without apology, looking straight through a person as if they were a window.

She heard a soft ping. Then another. It was the familiar sound of a jangling cart bell. A noisy wagoner was ambling up her road. Rose listened to the clanging bell grow ever more insistent.

There were some visitors who announced themselves well ahead of their arrival by ringing their cart bell as soon as they turned onto the street, or sometimes even before they rounded the corner. Some wouldn't stop ringing it until long after they'd pulled up in front of the house. By the time the noisy wagoner had pulled up in front of Rose's house, the clanging had reached a hysterical pitch. The horse and cart lurched to a halt. The bell rang out for a moment longer.

Rose often left her gate open. Sometimes she left her front door ajar, too. These two narrow openings offered a snaking view to the road.

The cart was toppling with objects. There was a small stack of wooden trunks tied loosely with rope. Goods had been bundled in blankets and piled onto the floor and onto the wooden seat. A few farming tools, clumps of dirt caked on their tines, lay at the seam of the cart wall. Seated like a mouse among the crooked mountain of effects was Charles.

Rose watched as he removed himself from the cart. He fumbled until he was able to swing his good leg over the side, careful to preserve the precarious tower he had made. He straddled the wall of the cart. The sides bulged with the burden of his belongings. He pulled his other leg over the cart wall and hopped down gingerly, landing on his good foot. A brief surge of pain shot through it. The years of overuse, one foot doing the work of two, had weakened his ankle. The bones of his good foot were as worn and fragile as those of a man of ninety. He steadied himself, then pulled his back up as straight as he could and began to walk toward the house.

Rose could see the effort in his face as he pulled himself heavily onto her porch. He grimaced against the pain. He stepped inside. He was covered in a fine mist of soft gray silt that had blown at him relentlessly on the wheel-track road from Cibakháza. There was a ridge of darker dirt at his hat line and smudges on his face. His heavy trousers were wrinkled and his back was damp. Rose could smell the sweat coming off him. And the smell of the horse, of leather and hay and the horse's own dusty perspiration, was still strong on Charles. He had worn it in like an extra garment. The scents were an affront to the fruit-filled, sugary aroma of the kitchen.

Except for the sad belongings in the old cart out front, Charles had sold every single thing he owned. His house. His vineyard. His farm. All of his humble assets had been turned into cash.

He had put his children in foster care. Some of the older ones were being cared for at the orphanage in Cibakháza.

I can't live without you.

Rose had a neighbor up the street who kept goats, and every day he walked them to the Tisza and grazed them down where the ferry docked. She could hear them now, bleating at the unsteady cart Charles had parked in their path as they passed her house.

Charles held his hand out to her. What she had thought couldn't happen, had happened. He was unhitched from his children, with cash in his pockets. Rose invited him in to see the rest of the house.

SOMETIMES LIDIA ACCOMPANIED her sister on her forays into the woods, where the wild ducks liked to lay their eggs. Lidia kept her eyes to the ground, looking for batches of leaves or sticks or dried grass the mother ducks used to conceal their clutches. Lidia and Auntie Suzy would hike their dresses up high enough to see any snakes slithering beneath them. When Lidia spotted camouflage, she would brush back the cover with the toe of her boot. She would lean down, select what she thought was the best egg, and gently deposit it into her apron pocket. At home, she would give it to her hens. They would hatch it with their own clutch. When the stolen duck grew big enough to fly, Lidia would clip its wings. When it grew big enough to eat, she would wring its neck.

Whenever it was just the two sisters on these walks, it was a chance for them to speak freely.

Recently, the subject had circled back to Rose. Auntie Suzy knew Rose was back in Nagyrév. She knew, too, that Charles had followed her there.

Why is she still bothering with him? the midwife wanted to know.

DR. SZEGEDY LEFT most mornings with the farmers' caravan. After the farmers veered off to the fields, his horses knew the rest of the journey to the villages he had to visit. The horses needed little prompting from him. He had heard stories of men, too drunk or sick or tired to drive, climbing into their carts and falling asleep while their draft mules trotted them home. Dr. Szegedy could sit back and have plenty of time to think during these long morning sojourns. His mind often ended up at the gates of his burdens.

Dr. Szegedy had been troubling over Charles all summer. He had always taken Charles to be a man delivered uneasily to his circumstance. His friend had a long list of woes to recite, starting with the misfortune of his clubfoot and moving along to any number of large or small sorrows that Charles was sure had rolled down the mountain of jeremiads to his front door. Dr. Szegedy had heard Charles complain of a luckless fate, and of the dark forces of the Curse of Turan, the great curse that had been put on the Hungarian Kingdom nearly one thousand years earlier. Charles was sure the Curse had singled him out for punishment.

But Dr. Szegedy knew that it was tenderness that made Charles so susceptible to the winds of his life. He moaned about his miseries. Yet he just as fervently hailed his blessings. His offspring were his great source of pride. He had looked beyond the insults the people of his village traded about his unusually large family and had taken comfort in his children. He had always been a loving, unfailingly attentive parent, which made the sudden and complete abandonment of his children all the more puzzling to Dr. Szegedy. Charles seemed spellbound. Charles's children agreed. They cried that their father was bewitched by Rose.

Several of Charles's older daughters had come to Dr. Szegedy at his practice and told him that their father was not in his right mind, and that they had retained a lawyer. They had filed a petition to have their father committed to an asylum, as it was the only way they had a chance of recovering any of what he had sold out from under them. He had sold the home they were living in, and the land they were living from, and had given all the profit to his new wife, a woman he barely knew. Having their father declared mentally unsound was the Holyba children's only chance, Dr. Szegedy knew, of reclaiming anything from Rose's hands. They could survive without their father, but not without his means.

LIDIA'S PORCH WAS a sanctuary for Rose in the days after Charles moved in. Her new husband no longer had any farming to do. He had no children to take care of. He had no friends in the village, only some acquaintances. He spent his time trailing behind her from room to room, from stall to stall, from shop to shop, and it was a challenge for her to find a place to be where he was not. Rose knew there was one place she could go where he wouldn't follow, and that was a neighbor woman's house.

Sometimes Rose would bring her embroidery over to Lidia's and the two women would sit together stitching while they discussed Rose's situation. On the back side of the porch was an overhang where firewood was stacked, and they would each sit on a log and embroider under the eave. Both Rose and Lidia had a wooden chest stuffed with the *varrotas* they had stitched over the years: intricate, brightly colored patterns woven onto pale ochre cloths that age had antiqued.

"Just finish him," said Lidia one afternoon.

Rose was handy with a needle. Sometimes she used the cross-stitch, sometimes the twist-stitch. She had been taught to sew by her mother and grandmother in Budapest, and had mastered the skill at the manor house.

"Go to our Suzy. She will give you something."

Rose poked the needle at the back of the cloth. She peered close. She pulled it through the other side until the thread was taut.

Sunday, October 5, 1924

Rose could feel the sun reddening her cheeks. It was just past ten o'clock, but the day was already warm, unusually warm for autumn. The village hall was cool enough, but her business there had been brief and now she stood outside in the heat again. She looked down at her wooden shoes. They were coated with silt that had swirled up from the unpaved road.

Rose looked up toward the square. She could see a band of black dresses fanned around the well like an umbrella. She could hear a light din of chatter. As ever, there were more folks gathered outside the church than inside, even on the Lord's day.

Wooden buckets were dotted along the dusty ground. Many crows now had wells in their yards and only came to the square for the whispers. But some still toted water home. Rose often saw Anna there. Anna had begun to bring her daughter, who was now ten and strong enough to carry two pails back to the Cser cottage on her own. Anna's daughter had also begun working as a "goose girl." Petra's daughter, too. The girls, along with a host of other children in the village, raised and fattened the geese for the estate owners, who in turn sold the birds to Schneider's, a goosery near Kecskemét. The girls could often be seen holding their long sticks high up in the air, tattered strips of white cloth waving at the top like a flag, and their gaggles of geese waddling obediently behind them to the oxbow to feed.

Rose had followed the midwife's instructions to the letter. The first dose she had given Charles was enough to make him ill, but not dangerously so. He was to be sick enough to warrant a visit by Dr. Szegedy, but not sick enough to rouse suspicion, went the midwife's command.

It was not a new edict, but the midwife was adhering to it more strictly since Michael's death. People in the village were still whispering about the fact that Maria had never called the doctor for him.

Now Rose made a second appointment, also as the midwife had ordered. As soon as she had entered the hall on this morning, the crier had right away reached for the logbook. Word had gotten around that Mr. Holyba was still sick.

Charles had complained all week of his pains. He sat on a bench, placed for him outside the gate by his new wife, and petitioned passersby to sit with him. He told them he was sure he was dying. His stomach had finally gotten the best of him, he told some. Rose suspected he would say this. She did not know about the much darker story he would also tell.

During the first visit, the doctor had noted that Charles "looked exhausted." He had given Charles some codeine to help with a cough, and for his nausea, had prescribed mira water, a mineral spring water that was often used to treat digestive disorders. He applied a hot compress to Charles's chest before he left, another effort to ease the persistent cough and help his friend breathe easier. But Charles's condition had changed little in the week since Dr. Szegedy had examined him.

ROSE ENTERED THE square, passing through a faint scent of hogs. The herdsman had been there earlier with the pigs and their odor still floated in the air. The blacksmith's forge was quiet, out of respect for the church service. Rose approached Lidia. They were two corvine swindlers set on their spoils.

"Has there been any change?" asked Lidia.

The deal that had been brokered was the midwife's standard arrangement: half paid up front, and the second half due some six months later. As the broker, Lidia was earning a sizable cut.

"Not enough."

Rose could hear children playing out beyond the churchyard. On flat stretches, especially near the river, in the untamed meadows, boys set up bowling games; sticks propped at one end were knocked down by balls spun toward them from the other. The boys' roars could be heard up by the church and beyond.

"I will cook him something," said Lidia.

SUNDAYS IN NAGYRÉV before the final harvest were perhaps the most pleasant. The younger farmers who camped in their fields for weeks on end in the summer were back at home. They spent their Sundays courting their favorite girls. Sunday was also the day for young married women to visit with their parents. In nice weather, whole families would go for strolls together, either down along the river or up and down Árpád. On this warm autumn day, the village buzzed with life.

At noon, Lidia left her house and made her way across the road to Rose's place. She held her cast-iron kettle out in front of her. The thin handle dug into her fingers. The pot was heavy, but the lid was secure. She strode with force, cutting into the path of cats that had gathered in front of her, drawn to the aroma. She took care not to let anything slop out, lest the animals lick up the spill, and with it the elixir she had poured in. Who among her neighbors was watching, Lidia didn't know, but she was sure that bringing duck soup to a neighbor's home at lunchtime was an ordinary enough deed on a busy Sunday to go unnoticed.

Lidia stepped onto Rose's porch. She pried one hand from the kettle handle and rapped on the window. Rose's face appeared, and a moment later Rose stood in the doorway, a warden at the threshold.

"Give this to your husband."

ON SUNDAY AFTERNOONS, Henry Miskolczi usually left his cottage around three o'clock carrying his viola. His blouse was white and his jacket red, but mostly red, and he wore a black hat with a dramatic round rim like a saucer. Miskolczi and his trio performed at the pub weekly for the csárdás the young people held. It began at four o'clock, but Miskolczi liked to get there early enough to warm up his fingers and his voice.

He was about to leave for the pub when he was summoned to Rose Pirate's home—he had not yet gotten used to thinking of her as Holyba—which is where he now found himself. Rose herself had come to fetch him. She told him Charles was begging to hear music.

Charles's room was chockablock with belongings. His worldly goods were piled along the walls, leaving only a narrow passageway between the bed and the door. The odor in the room was sickening. A window looked onto the yard, where Miskolczi could see Rose tending her garden.

He pressed his chin to the instrument. The wood was as familiar to his cheek as his wife's kiss. He held his fingers to the strings. The tips were hard and white and had been callused since he was a boy, when he first learned to play.

Charles kept requesting mournful songs, and Miskolczi kept playing them. Charles tried to sing. His voice was weak and faltering, but Miskolczi found a certain beauty in it, and he played as subtly as he could so Charles could hear himself.

CIBAKHÁZA

Tuesday, October 7, 1924

Dr. Szegedy placed his lantern on his desk. He drew his hands close to the warm flame. His office had grown very cold in the night. Drafts blew in under the door and could only be repelled by a well-lit stove. Dr. Szegedy never bothered heating the practice on mornings he was bound for the villages, nor so early in the season. He pulled his cloak tighter.

He folded down the hard handle of his medical bag and opened the clasp. The case was sturdy, but the leather was dry and starting to crack. A few years of dirt, from windblown roads and dusty footpaths, had lodged in the dimples of the tough leather, painting the black bag in dark, chalky grays. When he opened it, strong smells of his tinctures were released.

The bag weighed several pounds, as much as a traveling salesman's case. When Dr. Szegedy picked it up or set it down, he could hear the clink of glass and metal and wood inside, scraping together in the tight space. Opened, it presented a small apothecary—glass bottles filled with opiates, iodine, rubbing alcohol, alkaline ointments, chlorogenic powders. He kept his spatulas bundled together, as he did his glass receptacles, which he used to collect urine and other fluids. At the top of the bag, he kept his cotton and gauze bandages and his largest utensils, which were also the ones he used most often: his wooden stethoscope and his steel ear cornet. His scissors and tweezers were kept in packets on the side, along with his emergency forceps. There was a fountain pen and a writing pad. When he fished down to the bottom he could reach his pocketknife and the bottle of brandy.

A tall sideboard stocked with medicine was located along the wall opposite his desk. The process of refilling his daily supply was quicker than when he had first taken over from his father. He no longer labored over each drop or spoonful as he had done in those earlier days. The routine had become second nature to him, and he could fairly determine what had to be replenished before examining the bottles each morning. As soon as he opened the cabinet, the smells of ether and rubbing alcohol rushed at him.

He stopped for a moment to listen to a curious beat of hooves outside. It was still too early for the caravan, of course. Dr. Szegedy expected to be in it within the hour. He could not see to the street. The window was still shuttered and latched. Perhaps it was only a passing wagon.

Dr. Szegedy could see his stock only in shadows. A few small spiders were camped in corners. They did their business mostly along the back edges of the shelves, where they could go unnoticed. He moved the lantern closer to the shelves and began pulling out the remedies.

The patter of hooves halted.

There was a small beat of silence, followed by the clink of a harness. Rustles and snorts followed.

Dr. Szegedy held up a thick brown bottle he had taken from the sideboard. He removed the top and sniffed at the potion, a habit inherited from his old man. With a steady hand, he poured the tincture into his smaller vial without spilling a drop. Skillful and efficient, he liked to think.

The door handle rattled. He looked up. He watched as the door creaked open, revealing a figure standing in the entrance. Her shawl was swaddled tightly around her neck and draped over her head, so that only a tiny round hole was left for her face. She peered through it as if it were a portal. Except for her telltale gait, the muscly legs that moved like wooden planks, Dr. Szegedy might not have recognized her. Rose had an old nose bag folded in her arms, and he watched as she unraveled it and reached inside.

From time to time, Dr. Szegedy's regional patients drove the distance to Cibakháza to see him, rather than wait for his weekly appointment schedule. He would look out the window to see a wagon pulling up and a farmer being helped out by a friend. Sometimes, he saw a husband leaning gravely on his wife. This was usually at dusk, after he'd already finished his working day. But Dr. Szegedy was due in Nagyrév at sunup. What pressing business did Rose have that could not wait two hours?

Rose cast around in the nose bag. She ferreted around inside until she pulled out a paper and held it out for Dr. Szegedy to take.

"I need your signature."

Dr. Szegedy snatched the paper from her. He pushed up his spectacles and brought the document to the lamp. He knew the form well. In the doctorless villages, like Nagyrév, they were either kept at the village hall with the vital records, or with the bell ringer. He kept Cibakháza's supply in a folder in his office.

He took stock of Rose. The downcast eyes. The nose bag held tight to her chest, like a shield. He understood now why she was there. Charles Holyba was dead.

By order of the village council, Dr. Szegedy was required to sign all the death certificates in Nagyrév. It would be that way until the village appointed a new bell ringer to resume the roll.

But why had Rose traveled in the night to get the death certificate to him on the very day he was due in Nagyrév?

He unclasped his black bag. He placed the death certificate inside and clipped the bag shut. He had no idea why Rose had come to him, but he was not about to sign anything without first examining the body.

HAD IT NOT been for the caravan about to leave, Rose would have raced back to Nagyrév to get there before the doctor. The urgency she felt was like nothing she had ever experienced. But the caravan *was* leaving, and if she didn't travel with it, she knew she would create unwanted attention. As it was, she would have to drive back, possibly wagon to wagon, with Dr. Szegedy. She deeply regretted her decision to come to Cibakháza. She knew now she should have just stayed at home and waited for him back in Nagyrév. All she had accomplished by coming was to ring an alarm. But she had done as Auntie Suzy had instructed her to do.

Auntie Suzy had assured her that Dr. Szegedy would not come to Nagyrév that day. The midwife had bet that the doctor wouldn't come if the rains expected later in the afternoon, the first of the season, had any chance of stranding him there. She had been wrong. Now Rose would have to go with him in the caravan, wondering and worrying what would happen when they arrived.

Auntie Suzy had always told her clients that "not even one in a hundred doctors" could notice the work of her solution, but she knew that was true only to a point. A host of clues observed together could inform a coroner who had a watchful eye. The midwife had never intended a body to be viewed up close by anyone but herself. She had always been the one to dictate to the bell ringer what the cause of death was, no matter who had died and how. Without a bell ringer in Nagyrév, the stakes were considerably higher.

But Auntie Suzy, perhaps still riding high from her acquittal, had taken Rose on as a client, knowing the threat Dr. Szegedy posed. That Charles had passed away on a Monday evening, and not any other day of the week, she considered to be very poor timing, indeed. The midwife knew that had he expired any other day, it would have been practically impossible for Dr. Szegedy to get to Nagyrév before the body had to be buried. He would have been forced to sign the death certificate without seeing Charles. She blamed her sister and Rose for hurrying the job.

By the time Rose and Dr. Szegedy got to Nagyrév, the sky was already a deep and forbidding gray. The sun seemed to have not even bothered to come up. Dr. Szegedy could see lanterns burning in some of the homes. He slowed his carriage to a halt in front of Rose's cottage and climbed out. He reached back in for his black bag. Rose had pulled in behind him.

Inside, the doctor removed his coat and hat. He entered the bedroom, where Charles was laid out on the bed. Dr. Szegedy's hands were slick with moisture from the damp morning air. The drafty window let in a chill. The room still smelled sour, of diarrhea and vomit. He dropped his black bag onto the earthen floor. He moved over to where his friend lay. The body had not yet been cleaned or prepared for burial. There had been recent vomiting. Dr. Szegedy could still see trace evidence of it on the front of Charles's shirt. Dr. Szegedy pulled Charles toward him. He lifted the soiled linen shirt and looked underneath at the skin. He examined the back and the chest. He eased Charles onto his back again. He tugged the shirt back into place.

The body showed the marks of a heart attack. But why?

The rain began. It had come much sooner than expected.

A SMALL PUDDLE had formed at the entrance of the village hall, where boots had been stomped and rainwater brushed off. A few villagers were hovering near the crier. Dr. Szegedy had missed his morning appointments, and his patients were milling about, trying to find out what was going on. Dr. Szegedy moved through them with terse apologies, and when the crier handed him the appointment book to check his schedule, he waved it away.

He leaned over the counter to move in close to the crier. Rainwater dripped from his overcoat and plunked onto the table. The crier leaned in to meet him, ready to receive the whisper in his ear.

Get Ébner. Get the gendarmes, too.

THE RAIN QUICKLY washed out the roads. A day would pass before the gendarmes arrived. Dr. Szegedy would spend the night in Nagyrév at a council member's house.

In the meantime, the rumor spread faster than the raindrops fell that Charles Holyba had been murdered.

Wednesday, October 8, 1924

The hard rain had finally let up by morning. The ditches had swollen to rivers, the rivers to a sea. Soaked, shivering dogs had sheltered where they could during the downpour, under bushes and eaves, and had come out when it let up to pursue food. Árpád Street was still a slippery mire. The deluge had pelted holes into some of the thatched roofs and men were out on ladders making repairs. There were tales told of cats and other climbers that had fallen through the sodden thatch, landing dazed on the earthen floors inside. Reminded of this, and seeing the messy puddles already forming in their homes, the men worked quickly.

By the time the gendarmes arrived, Nagyrév was already a knife edge of tension. Nearly everyone had spent their time caged by the rain discussing not only Charles, but other men, too.

The two officers, John Bartók and John Fricska, looked like they could be brothers. They were about the same height. Both were trim, grandly mustachioed, with dark brown hair, and around thirty years old. They had bayonets strapped at their waists. The gendarmes set up in the crier's storeroom, just as had been done four years earlier for the midwife's interrogation. Dr. Szegedy followed the gendarmes in. Count Molnar was there to formally witness any testimony. So was Ébner.

Several villagers had been summoned to give testimony. They milled anxiously, like gamblers at a track. They paced in the tight space in the vestibule, smoking and tapping the ashes into their hands. A loose band of onlookers had wandered in among the witnesses, trying to catch word of what was going on. The crier had ushered them out of the building, but they grouped together outside, anyway. Some stared barefaced into the window.

It was Rose's neighbors the gendarmes wanted to hear from, the ones who had seen Charles during the short time he was living in Nagyrév. The ones who had sat with him on the bench.

The coffin maker had sat with Charles on the bench the day before he died. Charles had told him that he had just eaten some soup that he thought was bad, and he worried that maybe his wife was trying to poison him. Charles told the coffin maker that he wanted to end his suffering right away. He threatened to eat a box of matches, believing the matches had toxic ingredients that would kill him.

Henry Miskolczi told the gendarmes how Rose had fetched him to come play his viola for Charles. He told them how weak Charles had appeared, and about the sick man's desire to hear sad Hungarian songs.

"He told me he would die soon," Miskolczi told the gendarmes.

Lidia was also called in. Some villagers had reported seeing Lidia and Rose together often in the days before Charles's death, and the gendarmes spent much of the day questioning her.

When it was Rose's turn, she sat stonily inside the crier's storeroom. Her black shawl was draped over her head. Her hands were folded in her lap, as if in prayer. The cot she was seated on shook every time an officer kicked it. A small tremor spiraled through her each time. She could feel their steamy breath on her face when they leaned down into her. She could see the long, bristly hairs of their mustaches. They smelled of stale tobacco. She squeezed her eyes shut when they shouted. They were so loud, she was sure their voices could be heard all the way to the square, and beyond, down to the potter's graveyard, down to the meadows, to the riverbanks.

DID YOU KILL YOUR HUSBAND?!

Rose stared into her lap. She had put on a petticoat in the morning, as the foul weather had brought cooler temperatures, and her hands sank into the bulk of her dress. She could feel a heat of fear rising in her. The musty storeroom seemed inescapable.

ARE YOU A KILLER?!

Rose remained silent, immune to the shouts and kicks, flying beyond the cramped space of the crier's closet to that high, high branch, out of reach.

BITCH! DID YOU MURDER YOUR HUSBAND?

After rounds and rounds of fruitless questioning, the gendarmes strode over to Rose's house, where they searched for fly stone, potash, anything that could be used to poison someone. But they found nothing more than what they had seen in their own mothers' and wives' cupboards—salt, vinegar, paprika.

ÉBNER JABBED HIS office door with his walking stick to open it. He shuffled to his desk and threw himself down into his wide chair. He had grown heavier with age. He was in his sixties now, and his knees and back had begun to trick him, wrenching if he turned in a way that disagreed with them. He reclined back far enough in the chair to open his desk drawer and retrieve his brandy. He was sweating heavily after being in the crier's closet most of the afternoon. He hadn't taken a comb to his hair since morning. He looked as disheveled as an old pig.

He could hear the gendarmes outside mounting their horses. The inquest had ended as abruptly as it had begun. All they had found was a doctor and a few neighbors filled with suspicion. Ébner twisted the top off his flask. He would pay a call on his way home to the coffin maker's workshop. Charles's body was being kept there for lack of any better place to keep it, and he could now tell him to proceed. Ébner took a swig. He felt the slow warmth of the brandy as it moved down his throat.

THE LAST THING the crier did before he left the village hall for the evening was to clasp and bolt the shutters. More wind and rain were on the way.

Inside, the clock ticked a steady beat as the hours passed. Some mice nibbled on a table leg and the bottom of the front door, where the rain had made the wood soft and easier to chew, but the hall was otherwise still.

Sometime in the night there was a slight disturbance at the front door. A shuffle of boots outside. Muffled knocks and bangs. There was a narrow slit at the bottom of the door where it was no longer plumb, where in summer silt blew in, and in winter snow, and through this slit, this little open lip, an unsigned note was slipped. It skated partway across the floor before coming to a twirling, tidy halt.

It is not only Mrs. Holyba the gendarme officers should look at, but also Mrs. Takacs, Mrs. Beke, Mrs. Farkas, Mrs. Foldvari, Mrs. Kardos, Mrs. Kiss, Mrs. Csabai . . .

THE NIGHT WATCHMAN held out as long as he could in the rain. His cape was soaked. His lantern had been snuffed by the downpour. He tramped to a friend's stable to warm and dry himself by the fire in the pit.

Before he gave up for the night, he had patrolled the zigzag of side roads closest to Árpád. He had passed 1 Orphan Street, where a light burned in every window.

The midwife had been awake all night.

Thursday, October 9, 1924

Dr. Szegedy had left Nagyrév the evening before with an uneasy feeling, and he awoke in the morning with the same unease. He wasn't sure the gendarmes had done their job. Rose's interrogation had been half-hearted. He couldn't put the blame entirely on the gendarmes, because he himself had asked few questions. At the midwife's abortion inquest, he had stacks of vital records to support his claims, but this time he had much less to go on. The witness testimony, though it had taken the bulk of the day, was only hearsay. He needed more than a suspicion, rumor, and eight abandoned—now orphaned—offspring to prove Charles had been murdered. He needed forensics.

Charles's funeral took place in the early afternoon, directly after his body arrived in Cibakháza. His long procession snaked down sodden roads and his eight children trailed woefully and tearfully behind the wagon that carried their father's body to his grave site. The younger of the brood cried uncontrollably. Rose, the sole heir, led the cortège.

After the funeral, Dr. Szegedy went back to his office and drafted a letter to the high sheriff of the Royal Court of Szolnok, Henry Alexander. He requested that Charles Holyba's body be exhumed and autopsied, as he, the coroner, suspected foul play. He hurried to the post and telegraph office with the letter before the end of the working day. Following protocol, he sent duplicate letters to both the gendarmerie in Tiszakürt and Ébner's office.

He would wait three anxious weeks before getting a response.

AUNTIE SUZY HAD dozed off sometime after the sun came up, but she was too drained to sleep well. She woke often, each time with a start, which sent her heart rate soaring. A tight pain presented in her sternum and she thumped at it with her palm, as if trying to dislodge something.

The peak of her terror was subsiding, if for no other reason than that it had exhausted her. She had spent the previous day crouched by her kitchen window, checking to see if the gendarmes were coming for her. She had spent the evening pacing every room of her house. In the afternoon, her son had come around with word that Bartók and Fricska had gone back to Tiszakürt, but she was still panicked by the notion they would return for her. It wasn't until the sun rose on a new day that she could see the village had calmed, and then she was able to calm herself. For good measure, she mixed up a batch of herbal spirits known to soothe. She poured the mixture into a cup and guzzled it down.

Once her private storm had eased, Auntie Suzy realized there was one thing her long night had made clear to her. Something would have to be done about Dr. Szegedy.

IN AUTUMN, THE vineyards were a tranquil landscape on the Plains, with leaves rustling in the wind and rabbits hopping along the ground. The stillness was broken when the time came for the grapes to be gathered. The villagers always brought in their grapes together, and after the harvest of each small vineyard, a table was laid out on the grass for a picnic. The children recited poems, toasts were made, brandy was served, and everyone went home at twilight, to return the following morning to do the same thing at the next vineyard. It was a tradition the villagers looked forward to each year, and one that involved a lot of eating and only a little working. It was the last outdoor season of feasting before the cold weather came.

In the midst of the grape harvest, the murder inquest was still on the minds of many in Nagyrév, and in the last week of October, the official word from Szolnok reached the village hall. For his part, Ébner had tried to remain indifferent to the whole affair. The stir had gotten the peasants ruffled for no good reason, proof being in the fistful of anonymous notes addressed to him that had been slipped under the door in the last weeks. He had deposited each one as he received it into a folder inside his desk drawer. He dared not leave them in the trash for the crier to find.

He knew that if an autopsy for Holyba was approved, the restlessness would only grow. The peasants would wildly imagine that every death, no matter how old or how sick the deceased, was suspect. The commotion surrounding Charles had been an agitation in the village, and Ébner was eager for it to be over. Ébner was often amused by the hysteria the peasants could work themselves into over trifling affairs. Over the years, he had received countless anonymous notes alleging offenses like stolen milk pails or stolen firewood, and every now and again an allegation of vandalism, but the frenzy that would be whipped up over a full-fledged murder investigation was quite something else, and he wanted none of it—which is why the letter from the high sheriff's office in Szolnok, the response to Dr. Szegedy's request, was a relief to him. There would be no autopsy.

The answer might have come from the high sheriff, but it was a directive from the Royal Court of Szolnok. The court allowed that it could not authorize an investigation, based on the current lack of funds to support one. The League of Nations loans the court had been waiting on had yet to come through. The grand renovations were still on hold, and the offices of the Royal Court of Szolnok, including the prosecutor's office, which oversaw murder probes, had to hold on to every cent.

Early November 1924

Daniel stood behind his barber chair. A cigarette dangled from his fingers. A thin vein of smoke trailed up from the tip, at once frail and forbidding. He brought the cigarette to his lips. He watched the tip grow brighter in the dim light as he inhaled.

Twilight had dressed the narrow shop in blacks and grays. A mirror hung in front of the chair, and Daniel could see the room reflected back to him. His horsehair shave brush sat in a small porcelain bowl. His shaving oils and soaps were on a tarnished silver tray next to his scissors and clippers. His razor was tucked inside its leather case. His mustache waxes and hair tonics were aligned on a shelf behind him.

He had a view to the window, as well. It looked out to the road. It was streaked with handprints he had not yet washed clean, and smudges from a recent rain had stained it with dirt. The light outside was quickly growing faint. He eyed her, she whom he had always feared, growing smaller as she waddled away down Árpád Street, fading into the blur of sunset. He could still smell the sweet tobacco of her pipe in the room.

Her sorcery terrified him.

He looked once more at his reflection. He watched himself bring his cigarette to his lips once again. He blew the smoke out, covering himself in a cloud. When the vapor cleared, he examined his face. He looked ashen. The color of dread. His was the face of the new bell ringer.

FORGING AHEAD

It was a "business of poisoning". . .
—JACK MACCORMAC, *NEW YORK TIMES*

Auntie Suzy had put on layers of petticoats in the morning to ward against the cold she knew she would be facing. Together, they were as warm as eiderdown and were far too hot for her as she bustled about the house preparing for her trip. She had risen in the night to bake a special bread. She could still smell the aroma wafting in the air in her kitchen as she waddled to the sideboard to the drawer where she kept her sheaf of white paper. She slid a piece out from the stack. She wrapped the paper twice around the bread before placing it in her wicker basket. She pressed the loaf gently to the side to make room for the other goods she was bringing—jams she had canned the previous spring, hard candy she and her daughter had made, a poppy seed strudel. In her pantry, she snatched several vials of her solution from the shelf. She had distilled a fresh batch. She wrapped each vial in the white paper and tucked each one carefully into the basket, pushing them down toward the bottom to secure them. The midwife waddled over to her coat and slid her arms through the heavy mantle. She cinched the belt tight. Auntie Suzy fixed her basket on her arm—she needed only one basket for this trip—and headed out the door. When she met the blistering, blustery air outside, she was grateful for the extra layers she had donned.

The midwife held her head low against the cold and wind. She fixed her eyes on her old black boots, carefully navigating the icy patches that remained after a recent ice storm. She looked up only when she reached Árpád Street. The Cser tavern was still shuttered and latched at this hour. The area outside looked especially barren. The mongrels who were usually there had gone off to slumber in a warmer spot.

She turned toward Maria's house. With no one there to see her, the midwife paused to take it all in. In the more than two years since Michael had died, the midwife had not spoken a word to Maria, not even when the strange news spread that Franklin and Marcella were about to become "Szendis." Maria had announced she was formally adopting the adult siblings.

The midwife inched up to Maria's fence. The rotted parts had been recently replaced and she could still smell the fresh-cut wood. She flattened her face to the slats and put her eye to the gap. She took in a roaming view of Maria's property. The roof had been beautifully tiled. The stable had been nearly rebuilt with fresh timber. A new door had been fastened to it. Most irksome of all to the midwife, the one-horse cart had been traded for an ornate two-horse carriage, which in the snowiest, iciest weather could be turned into a sleigh. The carriage was more magnificent than the midwife could bear. She pushed back from the fence and spat hard onto it, issuing a curse into the frosty air. She doddered back onto the street and crossed Árpád. The spittle would stay frozen to the fence until the next thaw came.

When she got to the post and telegraph office, her son was already outside with the mail cart. She waited while he grabbed the mail sack and flung it into the low-lying cart. While the postmaster delivered in Nagyrév, her son carried the mail to the surrounding hamlets and villages. The midwife got in next. She grunted as she raised one foot and leveled it onto the cart floor. She gripped the sides and heaved herself inside, landing with a thud on the frost-covered bench. She wheezed as she righted herself. She pulled her basket close. She adjusted her coat, tugging it this way and that until finally she cinched the belt, a sign that she was at last comfortable. She planted her feet firmly on the flooring. Her boots sank into the hay that had been spread there. It was an extra band of warmth for the cold journey.

Her son swung himself inside. He reached down for the blanket he kept tucked in a corner and spread it across his mother's lap and his own. Tiny ice crystals had formed atop the wool overnight. They sparkled in the early light of the day.

Auntie Suzy reached for her basket once more, patting at the contents. She had more arsenic with her than ever before. She had never carried so much out of the house until now.

Her son shook the reins. The horse edged onto the roadway and began a slow trot up Árpád. When they exited the village, they headed to Tiszakürt, where Auntie Suzy's cousin lived. It was time to enhance the business, and Kristina Csordás was the type of partner she had always been able to trust: family.

PART II:

THE INVESTIGATION 1929

MR. ÉBNER'S SECRET

The Café Louvre was located just yards from the post and telegraph office and the new Radio Austria, which is why it was the "journalists' café." The reporters would scribble their stories at the café, then dash across the street and send them by telegram or over the wires to their editors in time to make deadline. It was as good as a newsroom to the foreign correspondents, who had even trained the headwaiter, Gustav, to be their copyboy. Gustav kept the café's ample supply of newspapers in a cabinet along the wall. He kept a ream of paper behind the pastry counter, as well as ink and pencils. News bulletins were sent directly to him, completely bypassing the pressroom that was set up for the reporters at the telegraph office.

Jack MacCormac and his wife, Molly, had arrived in Vienna at the new year from Jack's post in London. The *New York Times* had appointed him the new bureau chief in Vienna. His territory was vast and included Czechoslovakia, Romania, Bulgaria, the Kingdom of Serbs, Croats, and Slovenes, and Hungary. MacCormac knew the countries well when it came to news pertaining to politics or matters of the postwar era. But he had only a vague sense of what went on outside the capitals. "Slice of life" pieces made their way into the paper from time to time—perhaps a charming jump-roping competition in an unheard-of hamlet, or a bizarre weather incident of some kind— stories sent in to the bureau by local stringers. There was so much happening in Budapest under the authoritarian regime in place since the chaos after the end of the Great War—and the country climbing back from ruins—that anything going on in the provinces would be low-level enough to stay in the provinces, he felt certain. Rare was the story that would take him out of the capital cities.

NAGYRÉV

Count Molnar pulled hard on the desk drawer, tugging and jiggling it until finally it loosened. The wood screeched against the frame as it jerked open. He leaned forward, crouching over the drawer like a wilted flower. The musty smell of old paper rushed at him. A spangle of dust motes dotted the air around the open drawer. The files were crammed in so tightly that many folders had ripped, with papers bulging from the sides. Several documents had escaped their folders and lay crumpled between the drawer joints. He reached in to yank them free.

He had been meticulous about tidying Ébner's mess. The wooden desk tray had been stacked with old mailings, empty envelopes, scrawled notes, catalogs, bulletins, Budapest train schedules—a pile of irrelevance. The small treasure chest that occupied a corner of the room was supposed to be filled with items precious to the village but had been used instead to keep Ébner's personal trove of very old hunting trophies. The count had been working tirelessly at sorting and sifting, and had saved the biggest battle, the file drawers, for last.

Ébner had died suddenly in late October (his wife had followed him to the grave not long after), and at the November village council meeting, council members had voted for Count Molnar to take the helm. Most had already come to regret their vote. Where Ébner had treated the villagers like his playthings, it was already clear the count viewed them as a ragtag army that needed his correction. Within hours of the election, the count had begun pacing the streets with a notepad, jotting down any infraction he saw, whether it be a poorly hitched mule or a lamb on the loose. Every trifling offense was worthy of his eye, and no one was free from his scrutiny. When he wasn't making notes about the peasants' faulty ways, he was, in his fastidious, technocrat's script, inundating the county seat with letters detailing violations he felt the village judges were committing.

His appointment had become official Wednesday, the ninth of January, and the first task he had given himself was to bring order to the office at the village hall.

He leafed through files much of the morning. When the light grew dim, he relit the lamp for a brighter glow. By lunch, he had culled a sizable amount. He frowned now at his wastebasket, which was nearly filled to the top. He reached for another file. When he opened it, a flurry of handwritten notes fluttered out like moths, landing in a circle around him. He picked them up and brought them to the light for a better view. After reading them, he realized they held the reason for every fallen man.

The count turned to his typewriting machine. He inserted a fresh sheet of paper. This was one letter to the county seat that he prayed would not be ignored.

YOURS ANONYMOUSLY (AGAIN)

It was a quick stroll to the village hall from his house, and the count usually took it at a clip on his way back to work after his lunch break.

Even on fine days, he wasn't inclined to relax his pace and take in the easy atmosphere that otherwise fell upon the village on warm afternoons. People often left their gates open in spring so neighbors could come and go. If he had wanted to, he could have slowed, taken a peek inside. He could have seen the older woman braiding the young girl's hair, or the old man out on the porch step, resting his head in his wife's lap. But it wasn't the count's desire to slow anything. He moved like a machine, not a man. He saw himself as a cog in the wheel of a much bigger apparatus.

Inside, the village hall was quiet. There were certain creaks and groans, the breathing of an old building, that tended to unnerve the count when he was alone in there. The crier had gone out to read his news bulletins and wouldn't be back for an hour.

The rooms inside were always clean, broom-swept twice daily and mopped weekly, and the slip of paper on the floor in the main chamber stood out like a white boat in a gray sea. It caught the count's attention immediately.

He reached down for it. The note was folded in half and half again. The paper crinkled when he unfolded it, making crisp pops in the quiet of the room.

The script was legible. He couldn't tell if it was a woman's hand or a man's. Educated? Possibly, maybe to the third grade or so. He searched for a signature, but didn't find one. A little pot of ire and excitement began to stir inside him.

The count seated himself behind his desk. He placed the note in front of him. He flattened it gently with his palm to smooth it out, then lifted it at its top corner and held it to the light, like a detective mindful of fingerprints. He read it once more, this time more studiously.

Why now? he wondered.

This was the first note on such a serious matter that had come in on his watch. Ébner had received a veritable mountain of them.

He pulled out Ébner's old folder. The count held the new note in his hand as he riffled through the older ones. He looked for a handwriting match, or a match in syntax, and the more he went about his sleuthing, the more infuriated he became—he had alerted the high sheriff of the notes when he had first found them, yet no one, as yet, had bothered to investigate. And now there was another.

The count removed a fresh sheet of paper from a tidy stack he kept in his front drawer. Carefully, he fed it over the platen of his typewriting machine and began to type:

Attention: High Sheriff, Henry Alexander
As my previous correspondences to you regarding years-old claims of
suspicious deaths has gone unanswered, perhaps you will be interested in
this latest anonymous letter delivered only today. . . .

MAY DAY FESTIVAL

Auntie Suzy tapped her boot to the beat. Her fat hips swiveled a bit. Down at her side, she snapped her fingers together, swinging her hand in a little arc of delight.

The music and warm sun had already started to work on her like a balm, despite the bone-rattling ride out to the Jurenák estate. The bit of dancing she was doing, the swiveling and the finger snapping, had helped to ease her tight old muscles.

She had always liked a good tune. She liked to purchase penny song sheets from the peddlers, and she always brought them home for her grandchildren to learn. Many of them were songs she had sung when she was a child. She had always kept an ear out for violins, and she would rush to where they were when she heard them striking up together. The other kids would gather. She would try to sing louder than the rest when she was younger, better than the rest when she was older. As for her father's violin, his sound was singular to him, and she was tuned to it like a bird to its mate. No matter where he was in the settlement, her ear could follow the strains of his violin strings to locate him.

As a child, she had come to the May Day festivals piled into the back of a rickety cart with the other dark Romany children like so many logs of wood, her uncle or father at the reins, singing all the way there and all the way back, their violins in worn cases at their feet.

Squire Jurenák was a pig seller with a big gold watch chain that hung from his vest pocket like an ornament. His estate was one of the largest of those that girded Nagyrév, and he had a fleet of the most beautiful carriages the midwife had ever seen, all drawn by regal white horses. Jurenák rented the carriages for balls and other extravaganzas in Szolnok, and offered drivers in top hats and tails as part of the arrangement. The squire hosted a spring festival every year. Against the backdrop of his grand mansion, his lawn filled with Romany musicians and magicians, candy sellers and storytellers, and the midwife looked forward to the event every year.

This year, she had looked forward to it quite a bit, and saw it as a much-needed shaking off of the loneliness that had landed in her life. It had been a while since the midwife had lost her dear old dog, but she still felt the pain of his absence like a hollow cut into her. She couldn't walk past the firepit without seeing him lying in front of it, and she couldn't eye a rabbit sprinting across her yard without seeing him jumping up to give chase. Sometimes, she still heard his slow, measured breathing, which had been about the most soothing sound she could have ever hoped for. And she often revisited the first minute of his long death, the collapse, the convulsion. She had dropped down to the ground where he was and dragged him partway onto her lap, as far as she could get him.

Mari had moved out around the same time to live with a farmer whose cottage was a short walk away from Auntie Suzy. Auntie Suzy's grandchildren still came and went from her house—which, according to the council, was technically Mari's—as if they still lived there. They were often there for breakfast and just as often slept in their old beds. Mari was there nearly as often as she had been when she lived there. But she didn't live there, and Auntie Suzy felt that absence, too.

Auntie Suzy looked around now for old friends to catch up with. Festivals were a favorite meeting place for Romany folk. Some families made the whole circuit of spring fairs, coming in caravans from as far away as Transylvania and Czechoslovakia. To the midwife, they were clients as well as friends, and she never liked to miss a meeting with them if she could help it.

"THE GENDARMES ARE HERE!"

Anton Bartal opened the wide door of the gendarmerie and hurried through it. A brief gust of air blew at his back before the door banged shut again. Inside, he stood for a moment to catch his breath. The door was not so heavy. A very young child could open it if they used both hands. But so weak was Anton that the small effort winded him.

The gendarmerie was in a low building with a pitched roof, topped with a cupola like a gentleman's hat. It was situated just off the dusty square, directly across from Dr. Szegedy's examining room, which, like his practice in Nagyrév, was open one day a week. Anton passed by the gendarme office every day, yet he had entered it so rarely he could recall nearly every visit. Nothing about it had changed since the last time he had been there. There was still an old, fusty smell drawing off the furniture. It was the same dark-brown wood, the same scuffs and nicks, the same spray of dust across the backs of benches that he remembered.

The room was sparsely furnished but still managed to look cluttered. The officers were seated behind large wooden desks, which faced out like a fortress. Anton started toward them on shaky legs. He moved as quickly as he could, his heart beating with the thrill of a near miss. Nothing this dramatic had ever happened to the old man before, and he was anxious to lay it all out.

Officers Bartók and Fricska had for years been the two gendarmes assigned to Tiszakürt, dispatched from the headquarters in Tiszaföld-vár. They were supposed to patrol on foot, horseback if necessary, but more often than not they could be found at their desks doing paperwork, or thumbing through hunting catalogs or the stack of weekly newspapers, each with a cigarette balanced between his fingers. Their conversation stayed at a trickle most days, a slow drip of comments and quips that filled in the hollows of boredom. When they weren't reading, they often sat with their hands folded under their arms and their legs propped on the desk. It was a posture of suspicion adopted for the job, and they barely moved from it when Anton came in.

The gendarmes knew Anton, the old schoolteacher who had played the organ and sung at Sunday services before retiring from both positions a few years back. They had never had any trouble with him, though both could see the drink in Anton's ruddy cheeks and in the small network of purple veins on his fleshy nose.

Anton scurried over to them in quick jagged steps, like a nervous mouse, and stopped abruptly when he reached their desks.

His breath was heavy. His round belly ballooned in and out with the long, frantic intakes of air. His heart was a pattering storm of beats. He could never remember feeling so exhausted, so weak, so empty, as drained as the bottles he left by his bedside at night. There was very little strength left in Anton on this morning, but he had been saving every gram of it for this.

Esther Szabó tried to murder me!

Hearing himself say it, he was immediately disappointed in how the words had come out. They seemed somehow flat. The gendarmerie was compact and had a way of dwarfing sounds that, to Anton, would have soared in a bigger space, like a church.

What had happened to him was still a jumble in his mind, but he retraced it for Bartók and Fricska, starting with his walk home, just twenty-four hours earlier.

Late in the afternoon, he had come along past Esther Szabó's house when she called to him from her front porch. Anton had been drinking much of the day. He had started at his favorite tavern, moved on to a chum's house, and then to another chum's house, then back to the tavern before he set out for home. His days since retiring had proven to be longer and more lonesome than he had imagined they would be. The stretch from sunrise to sunset was a long yawn of nothing, so he filled the void by filling himself with wine, his favorite liquid friend.

Esther's singsong had startled him. He never saw much of Esther. He had taught her when she was very small, six or seven years old, but she was twenty-eight years old now and married, with two very young children. He peeked in at her gate, teetering precariously over the ditch. She gestured for him to come in.

"She asked me if I wanted to have a glass of wine with her, but I told her I had to go home."

Esther held up a glass to him and told him she had already poured it for him. Anton thought it would be rude to decline.

After leaving Esther's house, he passed the evening quietly, dinner with his wife and then to bed early. But he awoke with terrible pain. His stomach was roiling. His body was in a heat, and he hurried from the house.

Out on the porch he took a deep breath of night air. It was a breath intended to calm him, but there was no time for another. He ran for the privy. He moved blindly across the yard, flinching at the sharp sprigs that pricked his pink feet.

He could hear in the distance the nightjars churring in the woods. He stumbled on the uneven ground. The moles had been busy and there were many dips and mounds from their burrowing work that were nearly impossible to navigate in the dark. Anton made it to the privy. He retched and retched as the flimsy door swung back and forth, squeaking at its hinges.

His wife had heard him, and she ran out to see what was wrong. She stood behind Anton as he vomited, asking him again and again what was the matter. He emerged from the privy ashen and shaking, sharp pains still knifing his abdomen, but finally able to address his wife.

"Esther Szabó invited me in for a glass of wine on my way home today, and I must have gotten sick from it."

Mrs. Bartal stepped back on her heel. She clasped her hand over her mouth. If Anton could have seen her eyes in the darkness, he would have been afraid of the alarm he found there.

The old couple clutched one another as they inched their way back toward the house in the pitch black of night. Neither had taken time to grab a lantern before coming outside. There was not a single source of light, not from a star, not from a stern little candle glowing in a window, and the pair moved along in short, unsure steps. When they arrived at the porch, Anton eased down onto the step to rest himself. Mrs. Bartal stayed standing, swaying back and forth on her feet, her arms crossed under her bosom, holding herself. My god, what had Esther done? Had it really come to this? Mrs. Bartal raced along the narrow road of her memory, frantically trying to piece together the last weeks.

My husband drinks too much.

I'm fed up with Anton's drinking.

I'm so tired of my husband's drinking.

Mrs. Bartal had said all of this. Had she said more?

Esther and Mrs. Bartal were in the same sewing circle, and Mrs. Bartal had taken great comfort in the group in the years since Anton's retirement. It was a place she could unburden herself about the number of bottles her husband emptied each week, and how that number was growing, and how she dreaded seeing him come home, knowing he would be so completely drunk.

She wasn't the only wife complaining. There were others sharing the same grievances about their own husbands. But it was not two weeks ago that Esther had come to her. Why she had chosen that time and not another, Mrs. Bartal didn't know. She had been complaining about Anton's drinking habit ever since she had joined the group, though it was true she had been more vocal recently. The coming of spring and Anton's obsession over the new batches of brandy—he enjoyed plenty of that, as well—always put Mrs. Bartal more on edge.

Then Esther said something. Mrs. Bartal wasn't sure if Esther was joking, or if she had sought out any of the other women and made such a strange offer, but Mrs. Bartal had been so unsettled by it, she had skipped the last few sewing circles.

Mrs. Bartal shivered in the darkness. She hugged herself tighter. She gathered her courage to speak.

"I complained to Esther about your drinking. Then she asked me why I was bothering with you." Her voice quivered, the taut filaments of her life unraveling. "She told me she had something that could fix my problem."

Early in their marriage, they had often talked to one another in the dark, when the lamplight had gone out and they still had more to say. Now, Anton struggled to make out the shape of his wife, to give vessel to her voice.

"She said I should poison you and be done with it."

MRS. BARTAL HITCHED up the wagon and lit the lanterns at the sides before bringing the horse around to the front. Anton slid in and slumped in a corner. He held his head over the side as Mrs. Bartal drove, spewing a trail of vomit as they sped to Dr. Szegedy's in Cibakháza.

From the time he had heard the frantic banging at the door, it took Dr. Szegedy just a matter of seconds to hurry to his office and open it up. As he washed his hands from the pitcher of water he kept on the table, he instructed Mrs. Bartal to seat Anton in the retractable chair in the center of the examination room. Then Dr. Szegedy hastily secured a rubber bib around his patient's neck.

He strode to the sideboard and leaned down to the bottom cupboard where he kept the stomach pump. It was stored in a fanciful wooden box. Carefully, he pulled it out and set it on the table. He unfastened the latch and opened it. He had rarely had the opportunity to use the instrument, and the box hinges were stiff. The interior of the case was lined with bright, golden velvet.

He pulled the pieces of the pump out from the box. He attached the long tube to the lower tap of the pump and affixed a second, shorter hose to a side tap. He wet the end of the long tube, which would soon enter Anton's throat, with the fresh water that he had asked Mrs. Bartal to fetch. The water would help ease the tube down Anton's throat. He placed the mouth gag, a wooden bite plate, inside Anton's mouth and slid the tube in behind it. He told Anton to swallow. He snaked the tube down into the pharynx and told Anton to keep swallowing. He slid the tube farther, farther, down into Anton until finally it reached his stomach. Deep breaths, he told Anton.

He pressed the lever, watching as the pump filled with everything Anton had consumed in the last few hours that had not yet been vomited out. Mrs. Bartal stood back from the process, listening to the gurgling sounds that filled the room.

When the pump was full, the frothy, wine-soaked contents were emptied into a pan. The room immediately filled with its sour smell. The procedure was repeated several more times until Anton's stomach had been entirely, undoubtedly voided.

It was still night when the Bartals returned home. Anton slept until daybreak, but he was still suffering fatigue. The gendarmes had heard it in the hoarse tremor that had invaded his strong singer's voice.

By the time Bartók and Fricska set out for Esther Szabó's house, it was already late morning. The main road was buzzing with mules and oxen pulling hefty carts filled with milk, hay, or wheat, or even crates full of geese. The old farmers liked to make their deliveries in the morning so they could spend the afternoon tending their vineyards. The women usually ate breakfast with their children around ten o'clock, after the morning chores were finished, and the scent of warm bread and bacon wafted around the gendarmes as they walked. The crier was in step behind them with his drum.

The gate was ajar when they arrived, and there was a narrow view up the steps to the interior of the little cottage, as the front door was also partially open. Esther was in her yard. Her back was to the gate and she was shouting to her children, who seemed to still be inside the house. The crier hadn't even had time to remove his drumsticks from the sleeve before the officers stormed into the yard and seized her. One gendarme trapped her in his arms, while the other slapped a leather cuff on her wrist. It all happened very quickly, before she could run or scream, and by the time she understood what was going on, the gendarmes were dragging her like a heavy branch back through the gate and over the ditch. Esther cried out to her two young children to stay in the house.

A few mongrels scrambled up from the spot where they had been lounging in the morning sun. They set off toward the gendarmes, heads high, funneling their barks into the air. The crier turned around and poked his drumsticks at their muzzles, forcing the hounds back, though they pressed on with their woofs from a safer distance. Chickens near the ditch hurried to get out of the way. Thrushes that had been rustling and chirping in the hedges grew quiet as the gendarmes marched past, tightly gripping their charge.

The sun had warmed both men quickly, and their woolen uniforms had begun to itch in the heat. Their festooned helmets slid forward, coming to rest at the eyebrow. Sweat trickled down their foreheads, and each man had a dapple of sweat at his mustache and rivulets streaming down at his ears.

They had moved from the grass along the ditch to the dirt road that ran alongside it. On fine days, many villagers had their gates open to make it easy to pass between yards. Some had already noticed the gendarmes and were eyeing the spectacle through the wide wooden slats of their fences. The crier kept pace behind them.

"OH GOD! OH GOD! OH GOD!"

Bartók jerked to look back. He passed a look to Fricska, who nodded. The scream had come from the yard they had just passed.

"THE GENDARMES ARE HERE! WE'RE DONE FOR!"

It was high-pitched and shrill. It pierced the morning air like a bullet. Fricska put a hand over Esther's mouth in case she had a mind to shout, too. He could feel her hot breath on his hand. His clammy palm warmed even more.

The pack of dogs had been following them at a distance, but the scream startled them so much that they fanned out through a thicket of trees and raced up to the main road to get away. Bartók dropped his grip on Esther and bolted to the gate. He swung one leg over the ditch, a hand to his bayonet to keep it from slipping, and kicked his boot hard against the gate to pop it all the way open. The force was much stronger than it needed to be, and the gate rebounded back, causing a tremor up the line. Bartók sprinted through. He saw Mrs. Madarász standing in her yard, halfway between the porch and the gate. Her front door was standing wide open.

Bartók knew Mrs. Madarász by sight, just as he knew Esther Szabó by sight. He had made it his business when he had first come to Tiszakürt to know the essential facts about everyone who lived there: names, names of children, common disputes they had with one another. He couldn't recall any trouble he'd ever had with her.

Mrs. Madarász had a soft mane of dark hair, pulled back from her face by a thin black scarf. Her dress was clean and pressed, but it seemed cut too big for her. She looked like a child in it.

She put her hand up to Bartók as he rushed toward her.

"Don't touch me. Don't touch me." Her voice was grave now. "I will tell you everything, but please don't touch me."

WHEN THE FIVE got back to the gendarmerie, the crier was sent off again to round up two village judges to witness both interrogations, although it was unclear what, exactly, Mrs. Madarász had even done. And once everyone was gathered back at the gendarmerie, the village clerk also came over from the village hall. The crier was given orders again, this time to guard Mrs. Madarász in the main chamber, while the officers went with Esther Szabó into a smaller room for questioning. They were followed in by the two judge-witnesses and the village clerk.

The questioning room was small. A narrow table was fitted inside. A few mismatched chairs were set around it, donated by the village hall and the reading circle long ago. An unlit lamp hung low from a wire.

The chairs were pulled out and Esther was dropped hard into one. The plunge into it was clumsy, as if she had toppled down off a high shelf and the chair had broken her fall. Ever so gently, she righted herself. She inched her feet together. She pulled lightly at her skirt to free it from a twist. Each movement was minimal, passive even. She had learned already not to ignite gendarme ire.

The march from her house had been her first brutal lesson. Her shins still throbbed where she had been kicked repeatedly with the hard, blunt toes of their boots, the penalty for not keeping pace. Her arms had been yanked so hard and pulled so far in front of her, she had expected to hear the snap of a break. The men loomed over her now. Esther hung her head down, a practiced peasant bow. She smoothed at her dress, making a little nest in her lap for her hands.

WHAT DID YOU PUT IN MR. BARTAL'S DRINK?!

Esther lurched back from Bartók. She pressed herself so hard against the chair rails, she could feel a shot of pain travel up her spine. Bartók came down in front of her face. His foul breath lingered in the air in front of her.

WHAT DID YOU PUT IN MR. BARTAL'S DRINK?!

Esther flinched, then slumped forward, dropping her head low over her knees. The little rock of knowledge Bartók had just thrown at her was settling in Esther, anchoring her. She hadn't known until now that Anton Bartal was the reason for her arrest.

WHAT DID YOU PUT IN MR. BARTAL'S DRINK?!

She made a study of her hands. Dry weather had parched her skin, etching a pattern of thin lines, penciled gray by the powdery earth of her garden. She stared at her fingernails, which were raw and jagged.

That old drunkard? There's no telling what he ingested.

Esther began to probe the dark fibers of her dress. She pinched the fabric, rolling it between her fingers.

That old fool would drink anything.

Bartók's hand was so swift she didn't even see it. There was just a sudden blur of wool as his arm swung past her like an ax. He slammed his fist hard onto the table. There was such a jarring, earsplitting crack that Esther jolted in her seat. Fricska kicked one of the table legs, and the whole table shuddered.

WHAT DID YOU PUT IN MR. BARTAL'S DRINK?!

MRS. MADARÁSZ'S NERVES hadn't calmed at all while she waited out in the main room, and when she saw the gendarmes and the other men file out from the questioning room, she felt nearly sick with dread. She had been fearing this day for years.

Mrs. Madarász stayed seated as the gendarmes came toward her.

The village clerk and the witnesses completed the circle. They were a forest of men standing over her. Slow coils of smoke rose from the tips of their cigarettes. The crier left to go guard Esther Szabó.

The sun had gotten brighter as noon approached. The warmth, which earlier had felt comforting to her, now stifled the young wife.

During the long minutes she had waited with the crier, she had heard the gendarmes shouting at Esther and the other rough noises in the room, which was just a few yards from where she sat.

But Bartók's voice was steady as he leaned down to face her.

Tell us what you know about Anton Bartal.

It was only now that Mrs. Madarász got her first real look at the gendarmes. She had seen them on patrol from time to time, but their helmets always blocked out so much. With Bartók's face squared in front of her own, she could see the thick, coarse hairs of his mustache. His eyes, Magyar blue.

Well, he was the organist for a long time.

Both gendarmes leaned down into her. She felt them like a wall around her.

You said you would tell us everything. Now tell us.

Mrs. Madarász was unsure how to respond.

She clasped her hands tightly together, as if her secret would hop out if she loosened her grip. Her palms filled with sweat. Her throat was horribly dry and she pushed back the cough that rose up against it. She looked again at the gendarmes, then at the other men, searching for clues.

I don't know anything about Mr. Bartal. I'm here to tell you about my husband.

The heat she had begun to feel boiled up in her now. The men lurching over her grew somehow distant, faraway and small, and this opened a space for her history to be told.

She had been just a slip of a woman when her husband had married her, bones as light as leaves, a body as slender as a whisper. Even now, she had hardly put on ten pounds since the children had been born, but back then he could have carried her on his back without even knowing it. She hardly weighed more than a pillow.

Their first months with each other had been like living in a cozy den. They fed one another. Sang songs together. Took Sunday strolls. Traveled a time or two to Szolnok and Kecskemét. Mrs. Madarász remembered it only hazily now, for when her father-in-law moved in with them, her home became a den of torment.

Her husband had moved him into their house to save his sickly mother from the troublesome beast. He had thought his wife would be above the old man's clutches. She was slight but she was strong, much stronger than his mother, who was also deaf and mute.

But day upon day, the senior Madarász would prey on her. He'd grab her from behind and plant his soiled fingers on her breast, groping for her nipple. He would snatch a fistful of her hair and yank it back to lick her neck. He would describe his lewd thoughts to her. He would strip off his clothes and expose himself.

Her husband suggested she move back to her mother's house, but she refused to surrender her home.

"One day I came home from Esther's and told my husband that Esther had offered us a kind of poison, with which we could get rid of my father-in-law without anyone knowing what he had died of."

Weeks passed. And then the old man came to her when she was in the stable. He shoved her until she fell back against the wall. She slid down to the floor, where she cowered. He threw himself down on her and pawed at her dress, but she gripped it fiercely, holding it to her like a shield. The simple black dress was the only guard standing between her and the rapist, and she cinched it as tight as she could.

If her husband hadn't walked in, hadn't seen her father pressing himself onto her, reaching his hand up under her dress . . .

For a small amount of money and fifty bundles of locust twigs, her husband purchased the poison, arsenic, from Esther Szabó. He fed the arsenic to his father in everything from wine to goulash, until the old man was dead.

The men in her midst were silent. She could hear Esther in the questioning room, trying to have a conversation with the crier. And she could hear a few voices out on the square.

"Do you know where Esther Szabó got the arsenic?" asked Bartók.
"From the midwife, Kristina Csordás."

NAGYRÉV

The news of the Madarász arrest in Tiszakürt quickly made its way to Nagyrév. By the time the crier had announced it, nearly everyone had already heard about it. The young farmers all knew Joe Madarász. They knew his fields, his crops. When he didn't show up, word spread fast.

Did you hear about Joe?

I heard his wife talked him into it.

Isn't it a shock about Joe and his wife?

Mrs. Madarász did it. Joe's just taking the fall.

I knew the old man. Doesn't surprise me.

I never would've guessed Joe had it in him.

Poor Joe. Up the river in Szolnok.

Auntie Suzy had tried to get as much information as she could about the Madarász case. She sent her sons out to get copies of the weekly newspapers and they scanned them for stories about the arrest. The news briefs were little more than short police items, but Auntie Suzy listened closely as the articles were read to her. A few pieces she asked to have read to her more than once. She was looking for footprints, for traces.

Thanks to Dr. Szegedy, whose loose lips couldn't help but repeat the events of the evening he had spent pumping Bartal's stomach, the news had also spread fast that Esther Szabó was being held. But the stories about her began to vary. Some talked exclusively about the organist, who they claimed was just an old drunk who did nothing but guzzle wine and brandy all day, and that the only thing he'd been poisoned with was alcohol itself. They asked why Esther Szabó would want him dead. To them, it served her no purpose to do the old man's long-suffering wife a favor. But others in Tiszakürt sat on the opposite shore of the river of suspicion. They posited that Mrs. Esther Szabó had been erasing anyone she pleased.

A CASE FOR KRONBERG

Kronberg always took his midday break at home, and his dog always accompanied him back to the courthouse in the afternoon. Dandy, a beagle-retriever mix, liked to pad along by Kronberg's side, head up, tail ticking back and forth like a metronome.

The pair walked along Baross Street, through Kossuth Square, until they arrived at the courthouse steps. Small puffs of dust blew around at Kronberg's feet. The cuffs of his trousers were speckled with the fine mist. The road had been paved years earlier, but the swirl of dirt was still a constant pest. When Dandy shook, the powdery dirt cascaded off him onto his master, an unforgivable offense for all but the spirited dog.

Kronberg leaned down and gently placed a basket around Dandy's neck. He reached into his pocket and pulled out a note his wife had jotted down. He tucked it into the dog's collar. He patted Dandy on his side, which sent the dog bounding back the way they had come. Kronberg watched his hound racing down the dusty road, the basket swinging side to side. The dog was off to the butcher, who would read the note tucked in his collar and fill the family's order. Dandy knew a treat waited for him at home if he didn't touch the meats the butcher placed in the basket resting only inches from his nose.

In his office, Kronberg slid out of his suit jacket and hung it near the door. He eased off his hat and placed it next to his jacket. A large window let in the bright morning sun, and the scents of warmed leather and warmed wood already softened the air. Kronberg seated himself at his desk. It was cluttered with papers and files, including a new file on the Tiszakürt murder case, to which Kronberg had recently been assigned.

His friend Barny Szabó,[*] a reporter known affectionately around town as "Editor," was with him. Kronberg and Barny met every weekday morning in Kronberg's office. Barny read the news to the prosecutor, selecting articles from a variety of newspapers, both regional and national. Kronberg would be still as Barny read, making a pyramid of his hands and resting his chin atop it, often closing his eyes to see better what Barny was saying. Sometimes Kronberg would stop him, like a maestro with an unseen wand, and the two men would pause to discuss the story. Kronberg had a habit of drawing diagrams and scenes and numerals in the air. Both men would stare for a moment at the space where Kronberg had drawn, the invisible drawings seen by both men.

As soon as the Tiszakürt case had come to him, Kronberg had asked Barny what he knew about the area. Barny had been a cub reporter for a regional weekly in the Tisza region when he was younger, so he was able to inform Kronberg about the Tisza villages, at least in a general sense.

Kronberg sat back and opened the Tiszakürt folder. It wasn't a large file, but there was a surprising accumulation of tidbits. The news of the Madarász murder had already reached some news journals on the opposite side of the Plains. Kronberg had always been dismayed at how fast a news item could appear, and where it could show up. Newsmen were as hungry as rats and as greedy as kings. He had learned this early. He had known to pick one among the pack and to keep that one close. In Szolnok, his man was Barny.

The Madarász couple had essentially repeated the same confession once they had been transferred to Szolnok, although they added more details. They claimed Joseph's mother had tried to kill her husband several times by putting rust in his soup before they had stepped in. The old woman was no longer alive to defend herself.

The Tiszakürt gendarmes were still hard at work trying to wrangle

---

*No relation to Esther.

confessions out of Esther Szabó and Kristina Csordás, the midwife, for their alleged role in the Madarász case. Old Mr. Bartal, meanwhile, had recovered well.

Kronberg closed the file and set it to one side. He picked up another item that had been left for him, a memorandum from the high sheriff's office, which was attached to a handwritten note.

The memorandum was brief: *This note was forwarded to us from the village clerk in Nagyrév in April. He doesn't know who wrote it. Worth checking into? Tiszakürt isn't far from Nagyrév.*

Kronberg examined the note. It looked to be written in a woman's hand:

> This is Nagyrév's open secret, and many women are involved. Men continue to die and the authorities are doing nothing. The poisoners are carrying on their work undisturbed. This is my last attempt. If this fails, there is no justice.

"NAGYRÉV IS THE HORNET'S NEST"

NAGYRÉV
Saturday, June 29, 1929

There was hardly a single villager who had not been down at the square since dawn preparing for the feast. Tables had been dragged all the way down from the pub the night before. Chairs and benches had been scavenged from the church and the cottages that were in arm's reach of the square.

The blacksmith had brought out workbenches and placed boards over them, and this was where most of the pots and pitchers and demijohns had been placed. There was enough food to feed the village for the entire summer, and not the everyday food of lebbencs soup and goulash, but all manner of meat: goose (the geese had been nicely fattened by the goose girls), duck, pig, and a variety of vegetables and fruits, especially watermelon, which was growing beautifully in the dry weather. There were all kinds of breads, including the baker's enormous ten-pound loaves, and for dessert, there were cakes and gingerbread. The aromas floated in the air like slow-moving clouds. Auntie Suzy lifted her nose, sniffing at them.

She had squeezed herself onto a bench next to her daughter. Her empty baskets were at her heel. She had carried flowers in them. Bouquets of her flowers now adorned her table, as well as several others nearby. It pleased her to look at them. She had cultivated fine blooms over the spring. She could see that now, even more than she had when they were growing in her garden.

Her dress was uncomfortably stiff. The collar was much higher than the collar on her everyday frock, and it was embroidered with white flowers set on dark blue needlework, hallmark colors of the Plains folks' dress. The skirt was shimmering blue and bell-shaped, pleated like a fan from waistline to hem. She had no apron pockets to shove her hands into. She had on a white bonnet, and her white hair was tucked into a bun. As she sat, she had wiggled her feet partway out of her shoes, and they had quickly swollen in the freer space.

Before she left her house, she had tucked her corncob pipe up the inside of her sleeve, leaving the bowl of it poking out at her wrist. It looked like a little yellow-hatted detective hiding under her hand. The sleeve was so tight-fitting with the pipe stuffed in there, it had begun to irritate her arm.

The first time she had worn the costume was at her wedding to her gadjo husband, and she wore it always on this day. The Feast of Saints Peter and Paul was the biggest festival day of the year.

Nearly everyone had taken part in the morning parade led by Pastor Toth. The long procession had ended after a solemn circle had been completed around the church and Pastor Toth had blessed their crowns and crosses, handmade and dangling from wooden poles. Now the poles and crowns and crosses were scattered about, and when curious dogs poked their noses at them, one of the festivalgoers would smack their hands together and hiss at the mongrels to shoo them away.

The midwife had sampled each variety of meat and nearly all the breads. The wine and the sun had relaxed her, and as she looked around the table, sated, she had the thought that Ébner would not have passed up a bite. Eight months had passed since he had died. His wife had also died, but the midwife had never cared for her.

Auntie Suzy and her clan took up nearly three tables. Sitting near her were Lidia and her family, which now included, at least through wild marriage, Rose Holyba. Days after the gendarmes had closed the case on Charles Holyba's suspicious death in '24, Rose had moved in with Lidia's son. They soon had two babies.

Auntie Suzy reached up her sleeve and jiggled her pipe loose. She hadn't smoked since early that morning and the pipe was cool and dry. She had tucked a small pouch of tobacco just beyond the pipe, and now

she snaked a fat finger farther up her sleeve to inch the pouch forward. She plucked some tobacco from it and dropped it into her pipe
bowl. She leaned toward her son. She hadn't room for her matches,
and he reliably carried them with an assortment of other loose items
in his pockets. He lit her pipe for her and she sat upright again, sucking
in a long draw.

She blew out a thin trail of smoke and through its cloud observed
Rose's children. The youngest was not yet walking and the older one
was still small enough to stand up under the table. The little ones
looked like a mix of their parents. Auntie Suzy saw traces of Lidia in
them as well. As for Rose's oldest son, he had not been seen in Nagyrév since his father's death. Rose never spoke of Desi.

The midwife grew bored pondering the children and looked around
at the other tables, until her eyes fell on Petra. She had been tracking
Petra's actions most of the morning, the way she always eyed Petra
when she had the chance. She stared at her now, watching as Petra
picked at her food and took small sips of wine from the glass in front of
her. Auntie Suzy took another draw from her pipe and blew the smoke
hard out her nose.

She had seen Judge among the crowd earlier, but he had disappeared. She had also spotted Kristina Csabai. Kristina and her son
and daughter had gone down to the church lawn for a picnic. The Cser
children had also been down there with them most of the morning.

Anna was running around like she always was, a scattered and
breathless little mouse. Lewis was so drunk he couldn't stand up.
Auntie Suzy wished someone would stick him in a cart and haul him
home.

Henry Miskolczi and his trio had set up near the well earlier in the
morning, when the villagers were busy with the procession. They had
played soft tunes for an hour or two before taking a break to enjoy
the feast. Now that their break was over, Miskolczi stood up from his
stool and stretched. He pulled back his shoulders and pounded a small
burp out of his chest before leaning down to pick up his viola. He had
enjoyed all the meat, but the goose was especially good and, as ever,

he had eaten too much of it. He tucked the viola at his neck, let another burp slip from him, then cocked his head, fixing his instrument in place.

THE DOORS OF the village hall were bolted shut. The count had been inside all morning. He let in Judge and the crier when they arrived and locked the doors behind them again. The crier had fetched Judge from the festivities at the square. Judge had quietly slipped away unnoticed and gone with the crier back to the hall.

Judge stood back from the windows, where pools of heat had formed from the beating sun. He could only faintly hear the festivities. The clock mounted above him ticked soberly, filling him inexplicably with dread.

MISKOLCZI NODDED TO his bandmates. He tapped his foot and on the fourth beat struck his bow to his viola, which drew the crowds to their feet to dance.

Miskolczi and his trio played at the Feast of Saints Peter and Paul every year, and he always looked forward to it. Rarely did he have a chance to play in the open air. Usually, he was crammed into the pub for the Sunday afternoon dance. The atmosphere was so high-spirited, he could close his eyes and imagine he was playing to throngs much larger than he actually was.

Maria had been waiting for just this moment. She sprang up from her bench. She brushed her hands across her blue skirt and hastily patted at her white bonnet, tugging the strings to make sure it was well-fastened. She pulled Franklin to his feet. She brushed her "son's" shoulders with the flat of her palm and wet a finger to tuck a stray lock behind his ear.

The tempo was slow at first and Maria sashayed with it. As it quickened, she flushed. A group of women behind her had linked arms and were dancing in a circle, but Maria kept to her spot in front of the band, facing Franklin. Faster, faster the music played, and she twirled and twirled, snapping her fingers above her head, keeping her eye on Franklin, who kicked and leapt and clapped in one of the fastest-moving csárdás he had ever danced.

Auntie Suzy turned to watch Maria. Her stiff bonnet dug into the back of her neck as she craned her head to see over the heads in front of her. She pulled her pipe from her lips. She lowered her head and spat on the ground, issuing a curse on Maria. She swung back around to her plate. She thrust her pipe back into her mouth and clamped her lips around it.

A swath of heavy sweat had formed on Miskolczi's forehead. It streaked down his face. Sweat pooled in his hands. He kept a firm grip on the neck of his viola to keep it from slipping.

The melody lifted into the open air. He felt completely unboxed by the sweeping nature of the sound. It was his favorite time of year for playing. He was so caught up in the music he was making that he didn't see the crier until he was standing three feet in front of him.

The crier made a motion for him to stop. Miskolczi obeyed. He gave a nod to his bandmates to quiet their instruments. Miskolczi stepped aside, and the crier took a place in front of the whipping bench.

The crier was flanked on one side by Judge and on the other by the count. He slid the drumsticks out of his sleeve and began to beat his drum. The crier rarely had an audience, and he felt a slight nausea as he realized the crowd's attention was fixed on him.

He trilled the drum, then put his hand to the drumhead to quell the sound.

He stepped forward.

I hereby announce that three additional suspects have been charged in connection with the death of Joseph Madarász Sr., in our sister village, Tiszakürt: Lawrence Szabó, his wife, Esther, and the midwife Kristina Csordás. They have been remanded into custody in the Szolnok County prison this morning, where they join Mr. and Mrs. Madarász Jr.

The crier paused to take a breath.

Midwife Csordás and the Szabós have also been charged in the death of our own Stephen Szabó.

Silence followed.

Stephen Szabó, Lawrence's uncle, had passed in '23. He was fifty-one years old, dropped unaccountably into an early grave.

An anguished gasp broke the hush. There were short cries, and a loose rattle of *Oh my!* and *Dear God!*

Auntie Suzy's pipe fell from her mouth.

TISZAKÜRT

Bartók thought the old lady would be the one to crack first. He had known right away how tough Esther was going to be, and her husband was hardly worth bothering with. Did whatever his wife told him to do. He was scared to death of her. But the midwife Csordás had seemed to him . . . not soft, but breakable.

She was so old. Closer to seventy than sixty. At times she had seemed ill in the questioning room, clutching her hand to her heart, kneading her hands. She claimed a weak bladder and kept asking to be excused to the toilet. He had told her off on that. Shouted at the old bitch.

"I'll leave you sitting in your own piss till Christmas!"

But the hag never cried. She didn't produce a single tear.

So it was Esther who had finally talked. She admitted to trying to poison Bartal, and to giving poison to the Madarász family. After that, it took no time at all for her husband to fall. Only then did Csordás begin to open up.

He and Fricska had been at them for weeks and gotten nowhere. It was like pounding a heavy spike into a wall, pounding and pounding, when suddenly the wall shatters to reveal a whole room beyond. But this new twist in the case was just as unexpected as Mrs. Madarász's volunteered confession about murdering her father-in-law. Bartók never would have imagined the Szabós would offer up the killing of Stephen Szabó, who was their uncle, but something else that was said during the confessions had dropped on him like a stone when he heard it:

Nagyrév is the hornet's nest.

THE MIDWIFE LOOKED around her yard, her ear out for odd or unfamiliar sounds. She was seated on the big upturned log that she usually kept near the porch. There were heavy scuff marks in the ground where she had dragged it over to the firepit. She had tried to pat at the marks with her bare feet to erase them, but it was not an earnest effort and there were still some visible scrapes left.

Not yet an hour had passed since she had fled the square. She was still in her traditional dress. It was covered in road dust. The back hem was soiled where her boot heel had caught it several times in her haste to get home. Once in the kitchen, she had tossed her bonnet on the table. A line of grime under her chin traced where her bonnet strings had been.

The log was directly on the spot where her old dog used to lie. If he were still alive, Auntie Suzy knew he'd be pacing and whimpering. He had always been so easily upset by the midwife's moods.

Auntie Suzy had known nearly from the first day that her cousin had been called in to the gendarmes. She had been like a ship's captain, peering with binoculars at a far-off vessel. Watching, waiting to see what it would do.

The fire in the pit burned strong. It had caught easily in the dry June air.

At her feet were her bundles of fly strips. She had cleared every one of them from the sideboard drawer, and she had gone through the pantry and grabbed what vials were there. Everything was all weighted down in her lap now, including the vial she normally kept in her apron pocket.

Auntie Suzy picked up one of the vials and pulled out the wooden stopper. She leaned forward and flung the solution into the fire, then stood back as the blue flames licked the air. She took a wad of her dirty hem and pushed it inside the emptied vial, twisting it around inside the glass until it squeaked. She repeated this procedure until all the vials had been emptied into the fire and dried. When she was finished, she tossed the fly strips into the flames.

She didn't have time to dig up the vials she had buried in her yard. The best she could do was to bury the empty ones she had in her hand.

THE SQUARE HAD emptied quickly after the crier's announcement. The band had packed up their instruments and slipped away. Dishes and pots had been hastily washed and taken home. Men carted the tables away.

After everyone had gone, the mongrels had unfettered access to a feast of fallen foods. They scrambled to eat every last morsel that had dropped on the ground. Now the dogs lazed in the shade of the church lawn, under bushes and low trees, sleeping off full bellies.

Little could be heard from folks once they got back to their cottages. Árpád Street was barren, as most of the shops had all closed for the festival, anyway. The street was as still as a painting, except for the swirling dust, which skipped down the road, pushed along by the winds that had picked up after midday. The only place that was open was the barbershop. Daniel was open every Wednesday and Saturday like clockwork.

The village hall had stayed locked all day, and even as the dinner hour approached it was still so. Judge had returned there after the crier's announcement, without so much as a nod or a whisper to his wife about what was going on. He hardly knew himself what to say about any of it, nor was he sure why he had been summoned, except to serve as a guiding presence for Count Molnar. So far, there had been little for either man to do except wait by the telephone for a call from the gendarmes in Tiszakürt or the prosecutor's office in Szolnok, which was now calling the shots.

When Judge got tired of sitting, he stood. When he got tired of standing, he sat. He had walked the length of the room countless times in the last hours. His pace was a quiet amble, and a leveling force to the count, who strode around the hall as if on patrol. Judge had never met a man as high-strung as Count Molnar, or as persnickety as he was, either. He was a man as different from Ébner as a frog was from an elephant. Judge had thought about that often this day. He wandered over to the window. He leaned against the large windowpane and looked up toward the sun. It was high in the western sky.

THE FIRST THING Daniel heard that seemed out of the ordinary was the dogs yelping in the street. They sounded so shrill, so worried, and their sudden silence as they scampered from the road felt even more foreboding.

The vibration of pounding hooves rose through his shop floor. Daniel rushed to the doorway. He still had his shaving brush in his hand. He watched the gendarmes race past him up Árpád Street and blaze around the corner at Orphan, heading straight for Auntie Suzy's house.

He stepped back into his shop. He blinked back the dust whipped up by the galloping horses.

CUCUMBER SEASON, NO MORE

On the same day as the Saints Peter and Paul Feast, the vice president of the Royal Court of Szolnok ordered a full investigation based on what was revealed during the confessions in Tiszakürt. Auntie Suzy had been the first person in Nagyrév to be taken into custody—she had been fingered as the originating source of Kristina and Esther's arsenic—but hers wasn't the only name given to the gendarmes. Two weeks had passed since Auntie Suzy's festival day arrest, during which time twelve additional suspects had been questioned by Bartók and Fricska, all female, nearly all from Nagyrév.

All this time, Bartók and Fricska had been carrying the load alone. They had set up interrogations in the village hall, as they had done before with the Holyba case, and before that with the midwife and her abortion investigation. Now, a full squadron had been assigned to the inquiry by the headquarters in Tiszaföldvár, which made a total of fourteen officers, including Bartók and Fricska. All descended on Nagyrév. They billeted with local gentry.

Bartók and Fricska had made little headway with the twelve they had already nabbed. They would question the women for a few hours, send them home, and call them back the next day. So far, no one had confessed. By Bartók's calculation, the number of men who had died under suspicious circumstances was now past fifteen. And every day the gendarmes were getting tips about more women.

The gendarme squadron moved the operation from the village hall over to the crier's cottage. Interrogations would now go on around the clock. The crier had moved back into his storeroom at the village hall, just as he had done during the Spanish flu outbreak in '18.

Auntie Suzy was the only suspect in Nagyrév so far who had been taken to Szolnok to be questioned. She had been conveyed by rowboat, arriving before nightfall at the port on the far side of town. The gendarmes led her on foot across town to the prison, where the warden was waiting for them.

As a prosecutor, Kronberg was responsible for the criminal probe. He had brought in two additional investigators to help him. He had sent them directly to Nagyrév.

A forensics team had also been assembled. Dr. Henry Orsos, chief of staff at the Szolnok County Hospital, would be assisted by Dr. Isador Kanitz. The two doctors would be conducting autopsies on site. They were under orders to send samples of any suspicious remains to the National Hungarian Royal Judicial Chemical Institute in Budapest. Their work would begin shortly.

Dr. Gabriel Popp owned a private sanitorium in Szolnok and had a background in research. He had been selected to compare the chemical institute's results (and autopsy results) with statements the suspects were giving about illnesses the deceased had suffered. Finally, all findings were to be double-checked by an independent expert, Dr. Andre Kelemen, an instructor at the University of Pécs.

Local gravediggers had been hired to exhume graves in Nagyrév, Tiszakürt, Tiszaföldvár, and Cibakháza.

Kronberg was feeling the pressure. Some were accusing the court of dereliction of duty in regard to the Charles Holyba case five years earlier. The decision at that time had been to deny the request for an autopsy because of lack of funds. Holyba had been ill enough throughout his life that it was plausible he had died of natural causes, the court had argued. What would the court do if taxpayers learned their money had been spent to determine why a sick person had died? The country's finances had been in shambles back then. The courthouse itself, as Kronberg well remembered, had also been in chaos. Reconstruction had been halted. There weren't even funds to put back what had been torn out.

But a new light was being cast on Holyba's death, and an uneasy consensus was forming that the case had been botched. Now memorandums were being drafted, meetings called, reports written. It was the high sheriff's office that had issued the ruling on Holyba. And it was the high sheriff's office that was being accused of ignoring Count Molnar's warning back in spring about trouble in the village. And it was the high sheriff's office now leaning on Kronberg to right its wrongs.

Kronberg had pulled out everything on the 1924 Holyba death. The files on the Fazekas conviction in 1920 had also been pulled out. While the former case stood out to him for what the court didn't do, the latter case stood out for what Auntie Suzy did to the court. Kronberg had only arrived in Szolnok the summer before, yet he remembered the case well. The arrest of a woman was always something to remember. And that an illiterate Romany peasant woman had hired the city's best defense attorney was always worth remembering. Her acquittal at the higher court in Budapest had deeply embarrassed the royal court, and it could afford only one outcome now when it came to Suzy Fazekas: to convict her and to have that conviction stick.

Kronberg could see that the midwife had been convicted back in 1920 based solely on her confessions to the gendarmes. Kronberg was convinced that if she confessed to him and his team of investigators, it would be harder for her to deny in court, and therefore harder for a higher court to overturn. It's why he had called for her personally.

But after days of fruitless questioning, he and his investigators had gotten nowhere with the midwife. She was as tight as a drum. She had spoken hardly at all, and when she did, it was to ask for a drink or to use the restroom. Nothing spilled from her lips this time.

He called a meeting with Officer Danielovitz, the chief gendarme in charge of the squadron now billeted in Nagyrév. Regarding the Holyba case, he requested Rose Holyba and Lidia Sebestyen be questioned by the gendarmes again. As for the midwife, he crafted a honeypot of a plan, with a central role for Bartók.

BARNY SZABÓ SPENT most afternoons at the Café National, where he had a table permanently reserved. It was close enough to the door so he could see who was coming and going from the hotel, and close enough to the window so he could see who was coming and going from the street. The table itself was small and round and had a marble top.

His notebook was stuffed with loose papers and calling cards, which were constantly escaping. They often floated toward the ground like leaves when he flipped it open, and he would scramble to catch them. The pages of his notebook were crammed with notes and sketches he had made of the various stories he was chasing.

He had piled on the floor a selection of regional and city newspapers he had pulled from the rack of journals the café kept for its customers. On the table were his coffee and a small glass of water.

Barny drew on his cigarette, his lips kissing the cardboard holder he had fastened to the tip. His trousers were rumpled. His shirt was wrinkled. His clothes hung loosely on his slender frame. He liked to comb his fingers through his wavy brown hair, leaving it tousled. No one might have been able to guess where he had spent the previous night, or where he might spend the following one. He sometimes slept curled up on an iron bench at the train station after a night out, or gratefully on a sofa in the living room of a friend. Barny had lived in about as many apartments as years he was old, which was thirty-seven. Every now and then he headed over to the Café National well after midnight for a bowl of "hangover soup," which would inevitably be put on his tab. The headwaiter had a long list of debtors, and Barny's name was high among them.

Sometimes Barny entered the café through the back of the hotel, slipping in past the picture palace and weaving across the line of moviegoers standing under the marquee. A popular summer feature was Fatty Arbuckle in *The Woman Haters,* and several times he had seen Kronberg's children—he had two sons—in line with friends to see the moving picture a second, third, and fourth time.

Barny scanned the room. Groups of men were huddled at tables near him, ensconced in games of dominoes or tarok. Two of his friends were engrossed in a game of chess. He eyed the table where he himself had played chess with the world master, the American Frank Marshall, months earlier. Alone at a table sat a charwoman on her break. She had put on her spectacles and was quietly reading her Bible. Outside some members of a Romany band were pacing back and forth. They wouldn't play until the evening, but they always began to gather out front by three o'clock.

Newsmen liked to call summer the "cucumber season," when nothing much happened that was newsworthy. Many reporters took vacations, slowed down to work on their books, or turned their eyes to long, flowery critiques of theater shows.

Barny was at work on the Tiszakürt case, as he still called it, but he had not yet journeyed out to either village—Tiszakürt or Nagyrév—to see the situation for himself. Kronberg had so far convinced him there was nothing much to see. He had nowhere yet to place the article, anyway. The *Szolnok Gazette,* where Barny had served as coeditor, had been shuttered for nearly a year on what many believed were made-up charges of tax evasion. In a matter of minutes, desks and chairs had been seized, typewriting machines had been confiscated, files strewn on the floor. The government in power, overseen by former naval officer Admiral Horthy—now Regent Horthy—regularly cracked down on newspapers it deemed hostile to its administration.

The regionals had picked up his articles about murder on the Plains, but Barny was aiming for the Budapest papers. So far, none had shown interest.

NAGYRÉV

Every morning since the day of the festival, Judge had woken up and gone directly to the village hall. He spent most of each day in the cramped storeroom serving as witness for the gendarmes as they interrogated suspects. When he wasn't in there, he was out in the vestibule monitoring the women who were waiting their turn, or assisting Count Molnar in the rising number of tasks associated with the inquiry. Now that the interrogations had moved down to the crier's cottage, he jumped back and forth between there and the village hall.

The crier's cottage was the single sentient nerve in a paralyzed body. Nagyrév had all but stopped operating, but for the investigation. The post and telegraph office was still open, but mail was being monitored. The village hall was now being used as a command center for the Szolnok investigators. The smithy had been commandeered to construct metal coffins, the only kind suitable to transport bodies to Budapest. Patrols had been placed at all borders to prevent any escapes.

The tension reminded Judge of the days of Romanian occupation, though who was an enemy and who wasn't was unclear this time.

At night when Judge went to bed, he often stayed awake thinking about what Michael would have thought of it all.

JUST BEFORE 10:00 P.M., two gendarmes escorted a woman named Julianna Petyus back to her cottage after a long afternoon and evening of questioning down at the crier's cottage. Mrs. Petyus had been widowed for several years, and had lived her life quietly in the village since her husband's passing. But an anonymous tip now made her a suspect in her husband's murder. The officers watched her as she made her way up her walk and left after she closed herself into her home.

AN AIR OF GUILT

The count stepped from the crier's cottage out onto the porch. He walked gingerly on its weathered, sagging boards. He stood for a moment under the shade of the pitched roof, which sagged, too, and moaned every time a wind blew by or a bird touched down upon it. The whole cottage seemed to be frowning, disappointed with the hand it had been dealt.

When the investigator joined him out there, the men headed together back to the village hall. Mr. Fölbach was one of two men Kronberg had personally assigned to the case, and he and the count had been side by side since Fölbach's arrival in Nagyrév.

Several dogs jetted about in front of them. The pack seemed to have taken ownership of the area around Shoreditch Road. The count moved past them in a fluster. He waved his hands about, as if trying to erase the sight of them. He issued a scolding to the dogs, his voice squeaking with tension, but they refused to scatter and instead seemed emboldened. The mongrels were just one of many facts of village life that disagreed with him.

The two men rounded the corner onto Árpád Street, which echoed with the incessant clanging coming from the blacksmith's forge. No crows had been seen on the square for weeks, and dust blew around the empty space. As the men moved farther up the road, past the post and telegraph office, and as they neared the village hall, they realized they were being followed.

Fölbach was the first to notice. He had sensed a presence and he had looked behind him to find an old woman several yards back from him, shuffling along in wooden shoes. She stopped when he spotted her. He continued on with the count. They had been discussing their business at the village hall, which was to check in on Dr. Szegedy. The doctor had volunteered to help comb through the death records.

The count and Fölbach were nearing the doors of the hall when they both heard or saw something that made them turn on their heels. The old woman was no longer behind them. The walkway was empty now. The entire street was empty, except for men out on patrol. Fölbach had hardly seen a villager out and about since he'd arrived. It was as if the roads had been cleared of them. They'd all been swept into the crier's cottage or into their tight little homes. But he had a hawk's eye, and he used it to spot the tip of a wooden shoe peeking out from behind a locust tree.

He raced toward the tree. The count was right behind him, but before either man could catch her, the old woman sprang past both of them and darted into the road. Fölbach chased her and caught her quickly, as he was faster in his shoes than she was in her wooden ones. He dragged her back across the road and pressed her up against the wall of the hall. Count Molnar stood back with his arms crossed.

Why are you following us?!

Are you guilty of something?!

Is there something you need to confess?!

Fölbach grabbed the old woman's arm and hoisted her forward, sliding his hand down until he locked onto her wrist. He reached for the other wrist. They were so thin, he could clasp them both in one hand. He held them so tightly, the old woman gasped with pain.

The count struggled to keep up with all that was unfolding. He recognized the woman, but not by name. Mrs. Pápai? Mrs. Simon? Maybe he didn't know her after all. They all looked the same in their black dresses and black scarves and sun-wrinkled faces.

Just then, a gendarme turned the corner onto Árpád Street. The count held his hand up and shouted to the officer.

"Arrest this woman! We think she poisoned someone, as well!"

UP IN THE LOFT

The two gendarmes who had brought Mrs. Petyus to her house late the previous evening had gone back to their billet afterward. So far, no women were being held overnight. The gendarmes were working in twelve-hour shifts, so their first duty on this day was to fetch her again.

The officers stepped over the ditch and banged on Mrs. Petyus's gate. Mrs. Petyus kept one pig each year, which she would fatten and slaughter in winter, and they could hear it now, snorting and squealing.

Again, they banged on the gate. One gendarme put his eye to the gap between the fence slats to eye the yard. The front door was closed. Chickens were pacing around in a frenzy.

They lifted the latch and let themselves through. As they made their way up the path, the throng of chickens gathered around them. The men pushed open the front door and dashed in, followed by several chickens who scrambled in after them. The men made a quick search of the kitchen, the pantry, and the living room.

Julianna Petyus! Come out right now! Where are you, Mrs. Petyus? Come out now!

One officer went into the bedroom. He threw back the covers. He pulled open the wardrobe doors. He checked each corner of the small room.

In the kitchen, the gendarmes hurried to the loft. One stayed back, while the other clambered up the narrow ladder. When he poked his head through the opening, he could see right away several large baskets near him. They were filled with lentils and beans. He could imagine how convenient it would be to pop up the ladder and ladle a scoop of beans needed for supper and then head back down. He had witnessed his mother and grandmother do it thousands of times.

He could hear the pig snorting even up there. He looked across at the rafters. A substantial slab of pork was slung over the rafter nearest him. The slab was so large it very nearly blocked the officer's view of the rope that was hanging beside it, and from which Mrs. Petyus's body dangled. Her face had paled to white. Her lips were blue and there was a faint line of dried spittle on her chin. Her mouth was open, revealing her tongue, which had blackened. Mrs. Petyus's eyes were open wide, in a fixed pose of horror.

I found her!

The gendarme pulled his bayonet from the strap at his waist and with one quick swipe of the blade sliced the thick rope from the rafter. Mrs. Petyus's body fell to the loft floor with a thump.

THE GREAT HONEYPOT

After midday, rain had begun to fall, and by the time Auntie Suzy stepped out from the prison, the rain was steady. She eased herself down the slick steps. She ducked her head low to shield her face from the downpour. She grabbed hold of her son's arm. About a dozen of her family members had been waiting there for her when she was released. They followed behind her now, as if in a cortège. Together, they headed to the rail station.

The time the midwife had spent in the prison was a horror revisited for her. She was afflicted with the same maddening sleeplessness as before. She was crawled upon by the same family of roaches that had crawled upon her all those years earlier, the descendants every bit as filthy as their forebears. She was tortured with delirium from too many hours alone, from walls inching closer and closer to her, from hauntings of vengeful mullo, the departed souls often the only company she had for days. The moment she set foot outside the cell, she made an urgent promise, to herself and to all those who could hear her cry, never to set foot in a prison again.

Once she had settled onto the train, it was a different kind of horror that began to paralyze her. A fear so familiar and so fatal to peace. Her bail had been set at one thousand pengo, a significant amount. It took Count Molnar nearly four months to earn that much money, and he was the highest-paid administrator in the village. That amount of money in itself had been relatively easy for her to come by. She had only to empty one or two buried jars to come up with a thousand pengo. She once again had dozens of jars stuffed with cash concealed on the grounds of her property. She had bills sewn into every hem and every pillow-case. She had the reserve of cash stashed behind her stove. She had some stashed in her loft. Auntie Suzy had come back quite well from the scarcity after her trials. She had worked until her coffers overflowed, and she had built a clientele that extended nearly to the Austrian bor-der. But a lawyer—only attorney Kovacs would do—would take every penny her house was storing for her, and most certainly far more.

What quelled her panic was a plan.

BARTÓK SLIPPED HIS arms through the shirtsleeves and pulled his shoulders forward, as the shirt billowed down his back. The fabric was light and cool against his skin. It felt like a cloud. He was so used to his uniform, the only thing he had worn since the whole affair had be-gun weeks earlier, that he had forgotten what ordinary clothes felt like.

He buttoned up the shirt and slipped on the trousers. They too felt pleasingly light. Both were a fairly good fit, a stroke of luck given how little time he'd had to procure the clothes. Bartók didn't have any civilian clothes with him, just his uniform and the nightshirt that he slept in. He had borrowed the clothes from a councilman.

THE FERRY FROM the Újbög rail station was running on a patchy schedule on account of the rain, and by the time the midwife disem-barked at Nagyrév, she was soaked through to her skin. But for her, the rain felt baptismal. Each raindrop washed away the scent of her prison cell and renewed her resolve never to return.

Auntie Suzy scrambled with her clan across the wide, wet bank. The whole bankside and the meadow above it were pocked with mud holes, which the midwife struggled to avoid. She zigged and zagged in the wet grass, furiously scurrying up toward the road.

As she arrived at Shoreditch Road, she stood upright and stomped her boots. A little spray of mud splashed the hem of her dress. She marched ahead, around the bend toward the square, never laying an eye on the crier's cottage.

Once at home, she felt a wave of warmth. Every time Auntie Suzy had to leave her house for long stretches, she returned with a great sense of sentimentality toward it. Her house was where she felt most safe, and it was the place she most enjoyed. It was where she brewed up her tinctures. Where she made her jams. Where she hummed her ditties and grew her grand flowers. The house abided her in every way, and she took in a deep breath of appreciation before plopping onto the bench and yanking off her sodden boots.

In the bedroom, she peeled off her wet clothes. She put on a fresh dress and climbed under her eiderdown covers. She fumbled for her putsi and uttered several incantations before falling, completely exhausted, into a deep afternoon nap.

ALONG WITH THE clothes, Bartók had also borrowed a summer overcoat from the councilman. He kept it pulled over his head to shield himself from the rain.

He had been under the walnut tree opposite the midwife's house for more than an hour. He had known which train she would be on. He had watched her struggle up the riverbank from the crier's cottage after she disembarked from the ferry. He had rounded onto Árpád just yards behind her and followed her home from a safe distance. He knew she was in her house. But he had not expected to wait this long for her to come out.

Every now and then a walnut struck him. The rain and wind were unburdening the smaller branches and the walnuts were falling from them as if leaping to the ground. It was all Bartók could do not to cry out in pain every time he was hit by one.

There were no low-lying branches to sit upon, so he leaned against the trunk, his arms folded, his head low. Nodding, dozing. There was little to keep him awake. He had made his peace with the weather, and the patter of the rain lulled him. He had gone over in his mind all the events of the morning that had led him here. It was like a checklist. The rush to find some plainclothes to wear. The wait for the ferry to arrive. The quick drumming in his heart when he saw her. He had never done anything like this before, but the interminable wait had drained the thrill and he was ready for it to begin.

Bartók slid his hand into his pocket and pulled out his watch. He rubbed his thumb on the watch face to clear away the rain, and when he looked up he saw a figure emerging from 1 Orphan Street. He dropped the watch back into his pocket. He eyed her. She had a heavy coat with her—likely the only coat she owned—and she had pulled it up over her head, similar to how he had fashioned his own borrowed coat. She had a single basket swinging from her arm. Kronberg had been right. The old wise woman wasn't going to let them down after all.

He watched the midwife waddle up the road, pass by a few houses, then enter the gate of Mrs. Pápai. He knew the house because he had questioned Mrs. Pápai on two occasions already. He scanned for a good hiding spot near Mrs. Pápai's house but couldn't find one. He hurried toward the gate. He thrust himself into the ditch, which he regretted immediately. It was like a bathing tub of mud and slugs.

He could hear Auntie Suzy rapping hard on Mrs. Pápai's window. Bartók was nearly certain Mrs. Pápai was home. No woman was daring to leave her home. But Mrs. Pápai wasn't answering. He listened to the midwife pounding on the window.

I know you're in there! Come out this minute, Mrs. Pápai!

There were several more knuckle raps on the window before Bartók heard the gate latch lift. He lowered his head. He'd take a breath and dive under the ditchwater if he had to.

The gate slammed shut with a forceful bang that sent a tremor down the fence. Bartók could feel it move through him like a bolt. He lifted his head and peered up over the ditch wall. His eyes were level with the midwife's boots. He could see the lines of wet grass at the heels and the small clods of mud all around. With his snake-eye view, he watched her waddle in the sodden grass over to the next house and lift the latch of that gate. This was Mrs. Gyõzõ's house. Bartók couldn't hear much because of the rain, but he could hear the midwife's sharp rap at Mrs. Gyõzõ's window.

The rain-soaked midwife waddled up and down road after road, rapping at window after window, while Bartók crept behind her unnoticed. He hadn't anticipated the number of houses she would call at. He tried to remember each one so he would know where to come back—the one with petunias growing out front, the one with the broken fence slat, the one with a stork nest on the roof, the one across from the row of bushes—but there were so many. He wished he were armed with a pen and paper to make notes on them all. But the fact was, no one came to answer Auntie Suzy's rap at the window.

After she had finished making her way up and down the higgledy-piggledy side roads, she doubled back down Orphan. She moved along quicker than she had all afternoon, nearly hurtling herself along the road, while her basket swayed wildly at her side. Each stomp of her boot sent a spray of rainwater splashing back up at her. Bartók hurried to keep up, dashing from tree to tree, bush to bush, as she stomped straight past her own house, not giving it so much as a nod or a pause, and made a turn, disappearing onto Árpád Street.

Bartók dashed to the end of the road. He teetered at the crossroad, looking one direction, then the other. He was breathing hard. He was soaked through. He glanced across the way toward the Cser pub. Árpád seemed empty, except now he could see the lone figure hustling along in an incongruous winter coat pulled over her head. The midwife had covered quite a bit of distance already, but Bartók managed to close in on her. After she let herself into the gate at 65 Árpád Street, he hurried close and crouched against the fence.

The midwife had been saving Maria's house for last, partly because she was determined to end her day at the Cser pub (as a public demonstration of her will, if nothing else), and partly because she wanted to show up at Maria's place with her jars stuffed with all the cash she had collected.

In her witch's mind, she wasn't begging, she was only recovering what had long been due to her. Every window she had rapped on had a woman behind it who owed her, for secrets she had kept, crises she had calmed, deeds she had done. She had helped them in their times of need—whether they had asked her or not, whether they had known or not—and the time had come for them to pay up.

Yet her jars were still empty. They had been rolling back and forth in her basket, clinking and dinging as they knocked against each other. Every spurn she had felt at every unanswered door began to simmer in her.

She reached her hand up and rapped hard on Maria's window.

MARIA! COME OUT RIGHT NOW!

She rubbed at her knuckles. The skin around them was taut. Nearly all of her joints, her knuckles, her knees, her ankles, were swollen with arthritis. She'd not been able to apply any of her tinctures while she was in jail, and the ache was nearly unbearable now.

She knocked at the window again.

MARIA SZENDI! I DEMAND YOU COME OUT!

After a beat, Auntie Suzy stepped down off the porch, as heavily as an old bear, and waddled into the yard. There were a few sprigs of grass here and there, but most of the ground was dirt, and there were pits where the chickens had taken plenty of dust baths.

She looked around to the side of the house. A new stall—built for the exquisite, two-horse carriage Maria had bought after Michael had died—had been squeezed into the side yard. Auntie Suzy had never seen the carriage up close, but she had been forced to hear about it from others. It was all anyone had talked about for weeks after Maria made the purchase. The stall doors were closed. The carriage must be inside. So Maria was surely at home. Maria was one of the few women in the village who had walked freely about Nagyrév in defiance of the gendarmes, but in recent days she too had holed up in her house.

Auntie Suzy shuffled back across the yard and heaved herself onto the porch again. She rapped once more at the window. She leaned in and peered through the pane, but saw only her reflection, distorted by the pattern of raindrops latticed across the glass.

She drew herself up. She looked around. The sky, which had been dark all day, was beginning to lighten. The rain had turned to a mist.

MARIA SZENDI! COME OUT NOW!

The midwife stood back on her heels. She rocked to and fro, clutching her elbows, considering what to do next.

She cupped her body forward, like a bull. She pulled her arms in. She thrust the heel of her boot as hard as she could into the porch boards until she heard a loud crack, then watched a tiny line inch out from under her foot and zig across the wood as it splintered. She would break all the bones of Maria's porch, if she had to.

The door opened a sliver. Maria's face appeared in the small space. She had a tight grip on the handle, ready to snap the door shut if it came to that.

What are you doing here?! Go away this instant!

Auntie Suzy took a small, staggering step back. Nothing about her afternoon had gone the way she had thought it would. Not a single neighbor had come to the door. After all her barking for Maria to come out, she was rattled to see Maria in front of her.

She stepped forward a few paces.

"Give me fifty pengo!"

The moment the words sprang from her mouth, she wished she'd demanded more. One hundred pengo. One hundred fifty.

"No! What do you need money for, anyway?" Maria pushed her head a tad farther out the small opening and looked around, searching her yard. She landed her eyes back on her old foe again.

"I have no reason to help you now. I don't need anything from you anymore."

The mist that had replaced the rain was now bringing on an oppressive warmth. The sun beat down hard. The midwife was sweating under her layers of wet clothes, which moments before had been making her chilly. Her coat now lay over her arm. She felt a panic rise. She dropped her basket to the ground. She tried to fling off her coat, but it clung to the wet sleeve of her dress. She cursed and spat at the old coat, until finally it peeled away and dropped from her with a limp thud. She kicked it several times, knowing everything was falling away from her. She pounded her fists at the air. She stomped her boots.

"Give me the money, Maria! Right now! If you don't, I will shake Nagyrév like a tablecloth and the whole village will come undone!"

Maria withdrew her head back into her house. She slammed her door shut. It made such a clatter, Bartók flinched.

Auntie Suzy stepped down off the porch. She stormed through the gate and slammed it shut behind her. She looked across to the Cser pub. She was too tired, too weary for the pub. Home was the only place she wanted to be.

BARTÓK STOPPED AT the village hall to report his findings to Count Molnar before heading back to his billet. He had to change into his uniform so he could go back out with the crier for the roundup.

Without delay, Count Molnar placed a call to the prosecutor to relay the results of Bartók's surveillance.

VIGIL

Small flecks of rust glistened on the midwife's palm. A deep red mark had also appeared there. The wire handle of the lantern always made such an imprint when the midwife's grip was especially tight, as it was now. She opened her hands and inspected them in the moonlight. The lantern hung from her open palm. It squeaked at its hinges, where bits of rust had collected. When the old lantern swayed, by the wind or by her anxious hand, a powder of rust was released, speckling the air around her.

For hours, she had heard the crier calling at the gates of various villagers.

She had heard her sister howling in the road as she was dragged away. She had peered between the fence slats and watched Lidia struggle against the grip of the gendarmes. Rose, too. Afterward, she had crawled on her hands and knees to the back of the house, where she hid for hours.

What she knew was what she had always known. There was no way out. The village borders were closed. They were guarded by the night watchman and others. An escape into the forest was a night spent among reed wolves. The gendarmes had laid their trap. She was a queen bee and her hive had been taken from her. When would the officers come for her? It was a punishing wait and she knew their game.

When they came, she would be ready. She lit her lantern with shaky fingers and scurried out to the roadway to stand as a sentry in defense of her own fate.

Throughout the night, she patrolled at the corner of Green and Orphan, pacing back and forth between the two streets, her eye out for gendarmes who, mysteriously, would never come for her. A lone loon's tremolo sang in the sky above her.

GOOSE GIRLS AND
OPEN GRAVES

Three weeks later . . .

BUDAPEST

MacCormac had been on a reporting expedition for weeks with his fellow foreign correspondent M. W. "Mike" Fodor, a native of Hungary. As soon as the two newsmen arrived in Budapest, MacCormac hired Fodor's sister, Elizabeth, as his local assistant. She was a reporter for her family's newspaper in Budapest, spoke fluent English, and had first-rate contacts.

One of the first things MacCormac had observed in Hungary was that reporters there went about their business very much like reporters in Vienna went about theirs. A few correspondents worked directly out of the pressroom at the post and telegraph office, but most set up operations from a café with an exceedingly accommodating headwaiter, just like Gustav at the Café Louvre in Vienna. In Budapest, it was the Café New York the reporters worked from. The only difference being that Budapest, unlike Vienna, was not a hub for foreign correspondents. The reporters who were based out of the café were usually freelancers or reporters from the regional newspapers. But the Nagyrév case had brought in scores of foreign correspondents from across the globe. Hordes of reporters now milled about the café as if it were a trading floor.

The story was easier to cover from Budapest—or, more accurately, nearly impossible to cover from Nagyrév. To get to Nagyrév took an additional day at best, and once there, it wasn't feasible to file stories except by mail, and the mail could take weeks to get to America. Further, the post and telegraph office in the village wasn't equipped to handle the type of wireless transmissions the American news outlets required. Everything coming out of the European bureaus went by telephone to Paris, and from there was dispatched by cable or radio to the United States. There were only a couple of phones in the village, and the connection was too poor for such a long-distance telephone call.

In Nagyrév, there was no place for a newsman to sleep, no place for him to eat (neither the Cser pub or the other, less frequented pub was open for business anymore), and no way for him to get his stories into print. Working the breaking story from Budapest was the only viable option for the foreign press.

MacCormac felt lucky to have Elizabeth on his team. She had been on the lookout for any further news out of Nagyrév and Tiszakürt since the initial item had appeared in the regional weekly newspaper out of Kunszentmárton back in the early days of July, but there had hardly been more than scraps to be found.

The news drought had been orchestrated, MacCormac could see that now. Someone had been controlling the flow of information. But it was now moving wildly fast, and it was hard to guess where the story might turn next. There were suicides, runaways, vandalized graves, stolen coffins, even gendarmes capturing suspects as if kidnapping them. Gravediggers were finding glass vials of arsenic hidden inside the coffins of alleged victims.

And there was a steady barrage of anonymous notes, in which neighbors were fingering neighbors as murderers. The tight lips of the Plains peasant had been pried open, and reporters' pens were scrambling to keep up. The latest count: More than thirty arrests had been made. More than fifty suspects were being held in the crier's cottage in the village and at the prison in Szolnok.

MacCormac knew he was better positioned than his Vienna counterparts. He had full use of the newsroom of the *Pesti Napló*, the paper the Fodor family owned, and the family was very well connected in Szolnok. It was a leg up that MacCormac was putting to good use.

As for local reporters, they had turned Kronberg into an idol. "The Hungarian press has never written so much about a prosecutor, and has never held one in such high esteem," wrote a reporter in *Kis Hírlap,* a newspaper based in Budapest. "For Kronberg, the trials will be a victory lap, a reward rather than an exam, after such hard work."

Still, it was only Barny who had direct access to Kronberg, and in that sense, access to the case at all. What the press got was what Kronberg wanted them to get. It had been, at least up until now, a tightly controlled operation. But the arrival of the foreign press in Budapest was a great concern to the prosecutor. He knew it meant Regent Horthy's scrutiny of him was growing.

NAGYRÉV

A pile of braided ropes lay on the ground in the shade of an old wheelbarrow. Some of them were wildly frayed at the ends and had been crudely woven back together by a gravedigger's thick hands. Another pile had been tossed nearby. There were ropes strewn across the whole of the graveyard. Every time a gravedigger picked one up—there were scores of gravediggers now at work—a burst of powdery dirt clouded the air.

The stench of rotting pine was eased by a light wind. Scraps of decaying wood littered the ground. Nearly forty coffins had been dug up. Some had been buried for more than a decade. When diggers pried open the lids, they gave way with a soft, crumbling crack.

In well-shined shoes, with his trouser cuffs kissing the laces, Kronberg moved gingerly through the labyrinth of deep holes and unearthed coffins, carefully avoiding ropes, ducking under tree branches, stepping over mounds of rusty tools, while keeping a keen eye out for diggers, who unpredictably cast shovels and flung dirt in all the directions Mother Earth offered.

He stopped and stood upright, a hand to his lower back. He pitched his other hand to his forehead, a roof of shade for his eyes so he could see better.

He surveyed the army of diggers as they skulked back and forth across the graveyard. They were local recruits. The money was good and any man without a steady job had come forward for it. In bare feet, with pant legs rolled up past their ankles and wide-brimmed hats hugging their heads, they looked to Kronberg like wandering scarecrows. For days they had been digging up their fathers, their grandfathers, their uncles, their cousins. They shouted to one another in a dialect incomprehensible to Kronberg. Their orders volleyed past him like balls. They also tended to drop their tools right where they were standing. Kronberg had learned quickly to listen for the whirr of a hatchet being thrust down. And they loped around Dr. Orsos and his large table as if it were completely ordinary to have a doctor in a white coat standing in a graveyard in front of a bowl of human organs.

Dr. Orsos had set up directly outside the cemetery caretaker's adobe hut, a bright dollop of white at the far end of the graveyard. Dr. Orsos was performing the Reinsch test on organ samples, and Dr. Kanitz was inside the hut, where there was only room enough for one, doing the same thing.

The Reinsch test was a rudimentary procedure wherein a strip of clean copper foil was heated in an acid solution, along with a sample cut from the organ. If the copper turned black or even a shade of gray, it was proof enough for the doctors that arsenic might be in the organs, and the suspect samples were sent to the chemical institute in Budapest. There, the Marsh test was conducted, which was a much more comprehensive arsenic-detecting tool.

A few cases would soon be disproved, including Ébner and Auntie Suzy's estranged husband, who had both died around the same time the previous year. Neither body would be found to have arsenic in them. The same would be true for Alexander Kovacs Sr.'s body. He had died shortly after Maria had returned to Nagyrév, but his corpse would show no discernible traces of arsenic. The same was not true of Alex Junior.

As soon as his coffin was opened and Dr. Orsos observed the corpse, he was immediately suspicious. Arsenic had a way of preserving a body. He had to note the date, still readable on the side of the coffin, to be sure he was dealing with a man dead ten years. He made copious notes, which to Kronberg read like literature.

> The whole body is, surprisingly, so well mummified that it remained in one piece, stiff and dried out. The surface of the corpse, especially the face, the head, and the upper part of the chest, is covered with a thick layer of yellowish-golden-brown-white mold. On the left side, even the eyelid has remained intact. The hair is rather thick, long and slightly yellow-gray. The neck muscles and organs are so perfectly preserved that the color of the muscles remains brownish-gray. The head is light, barely weighing one kilo. The skull's skin resembles leather; it has preserved all its layers. The temple muscles are dried and of a faded brownish color. . . . The brain is receded into the back part of the skull and covered with 8 or 9 mm long and 1 mm wide, short-winged brown corpse-bugs. They emit an acid and foul odor. . . . The skin of the chest and stomach has the same color as bacon skin. Underneath the skin, the fat layer is yellow and exudes a stale stench. . . . [W]e see that the heart is of medium size and its shape and location are well recognizable. The heart is a light reddish-brown color. The chambers are still in place. . . . We took 100 grams from the heart and placed it in glass No. III.

The doctors had found Michael Kardos's remains in a similar state of preservation. Samples from both corpses had already been sent to the chemical institute.

Built into the hut was a long, narrow, thin-paned window, which many gales had blown through and many storms had bullied. Animals had pecked and clawed it until there were several scratches in the glass. Now a group of peasants had sprouted up around it like flowers. They gaped into the window at Dr. Kanitz. Kronberg was sure they were from neighboring villages. He had seen several carts with plates from Abony and other places outside Nagyrév as he had entered the graveyard. Dr. Kanitz held the remains up to the window, where there was better light, but he kept them there for a moment or two longer than was necessary.

Kronberg heard a light rustling near him, the sound of a snake, or perhaps a rabbit or squirrel. He looked down at his feet. The ground was sandy and pitted with small stones. Many of the grave markers were wooden, but some were stone, like the one near him. He leaned over it and peered down to see a woman, clad in the color of the darkest night, crouching against the headstone. She gripped it with both hands for support and peered over it, trying to get a look at what Dr. Orsos was doing.

He heard another rustling behind him and turned to look. The sun was too bright to make out the white ribbons dotted low in the sky, but the geese waddling along in the dirt looked to Kronberg like puffs of fallen clouds.

The goose girls had come up from the oxbow, which had proven too wet from a recent rain to feed their charges. The girls walked a crooked path between the graves, carrying their wooden sticks with the flowing white ribbons high, like flags for the goslings, who followed obediently, stopping from time to time to eat the grass.

OLD MAN CSER

Lewis had fallen. He was facedown on the ground with chickens peck-ing around him. He had swallowed some dirt.

He rolled over on his back but found it too hard to lift himself. He rolled back over on his stomach. He grasped for something to hold on to, anything for leverage. He wasn't quite sure where he was. Inside his yard? Outside it?

He pushed himself up with his palms and grabbed hold of a nearby bush. There was a row of bushes outside his pub, he remembered, and this helped orient him. Lewis took hold of the bush as if he were climbing a ladder, one hand over the other, until he was more or less standing upright. He let go. His head swam with drink. He nearly pitched forward into the bush until he swung backward, his arms spinning like cart wheels in search of a simple balance that eluded him. But before spiraling out again, he regained his footing, and at this point he was able to summon once again where he was headed and why he was angry.

Lewis had managed to get through most of the summer without any direct involvement in the gendarmes' business down at the crier's place. He had not been around to see them come for his wife the first few times she was brought in for questioning, and he was only mini-mally aware that their neighbor Mrs. Kiss had been taken in, too. He hadn't given much thought as to what was wanted with either of them. He only barely took notice of the suited men from Szolnok who now swarmed the village. And he cared not more than a grumble that his business had died off almost completely as a result of the investigation. The bedlam in Nagyrév had not dislodged him from his bar in any way. It had moved around him like the hands of a clock, while he slumped with his bottle in the middle of it all.

That dirty bitch.

The quicker he moved, the steadier he felt, so he began to lurch down Árpád Street, reeling into the locust trees that trimmed the road, and whirling back out onto his path again like a top. The news was a horsewhip upon him, driving him to Anna.

Earlier, the pub door had flung open. The sudden shaft of light had lit the place like a flare. Lewis had been alone—there hadn't been a customer in weeks—and he turned to see who was there.

One of his neighbors, a man he had grown up with, stood in the doorway in stark silhouette, like a dark stain on the sun.

Lewis, did you hear? Anna just confessed that she killed your dad.

AN UNBURDENING

Two benches had been squeezed into the crier's kitchen, and there were ten crows seated on them. The crows had their backs to the crier's bedroom, where the interrogations were taking place, and their faces to the yellowed wall. There was enough room in front of them, though just barely, for the gendarmes to pass by. Several more benches were currently stacked on the grounds outside. The ebb and flow of suspects was like a tide washing in and out.

Maria Szendi was seated on the bench behind Anna, and near Maria was Kristina Csabai. Mrs. Kiss was on the opposite end and Mari Fazekas was wedged right up next to Anna, so close it was as if their arms had been knitted together. The heft of Mari's thigh pushed against Anna's rawboned leg. Every time Mari took a breath, it was a balloon expanding, and Anna was pressed even tighter, pressed as flat as a flea.

Anna was uncomfortable, yet she was unmoved by the devil's daughter sitting beside her.

There was one smudged window, and sunlight poured through it as if the room were a bucket it was filling with its glory. The faded old tapestry in the small main room had been vivified by the light, and the few items the crier had out—his fishing pole in the front room and a couple of ceramic pots in the kitchen—looked nearly dainty. The row of black dresses was like a line of dark seeds laid out, ready for planting. For Anna, the stark rays caused a twinge to her eye, which was so swollen it looked as if it had been sewn shut with needle and thread. A thin line of red was traced across her lids. Her brow was inflamed, too, and was inked with the deep purple of a dark night, a stain that mapped the color of her truth from the bridge of her nose all the way down to her cheekbone.

Not quite a day had passed since Lewis had put it there. He had lurched through the open door of the cottage and gotten one swift punch to her face before the gendarmes could restrain him and push him back out. Her eye was still exquisitely sore. Sudden moves, or even lowering her head, brought on throbbing pain.

Anna hadn't confessed to killing Lewis's father. She had, however, confessed to not stopping Mrs. Kiss from killing him.

The old man used to shit all over the house. His shit would drop straight to the floor in unformed stools that pooled at his feet. Old Mr. Cser would tread through it and leave a trail of feces through the cottage, which Anna would have to clean up after she cleaned him. He pissed where he sat and she'd have to clean that, too. He was also blind. Sometimes she'd find him standing in a corner as if he were boxed in. When Lewis Junior was born, Anna constantly worried that the old man would harm him. Not on purpose, of course. But trip over him or piss on him or something. Lewis slept wherever he fell down, but the old man slept in the living room with her and the baby. After a while, she stopped sleeping. She'd be awake all night taking care of him or the baby. She withered down to nothing.

Mrs. Kiss suggested she do something about it, but she didn't have the nerve. "My husband would beat me to death," she kept telling Mrs. Kiss.

But she didn't stop Mrs. Kiss from putting arsenic-laced fly stone in the old man's soup. He died three weeks before her son's second birthday.

No one would have been the wiser about old Mr. Cser had it not been for mistaken assumptions by both Mrs. Kiss and the gendarmes. They brought Mrs. Kiss in on the notion she might know something about the deaths of Anna's babies. But as soon as she got in front of them, she started talking about Mr. Cser.

That was happening a lot to the gendarmes, women confessing to crimes no one had even known had been committed. And just as often, widows were begging for their husbands' remains to be dug up, just to prove, should anyone ever want to know, that the man had died of natural causes.

The bench was hard, like a church pew, and sitting on it hour after hour had inserted splintering pain into the ossein parts of Anna.

The suspects had started spending their nights at the inn, a large house located near the edge of the village, where some of the gendarmes were also now lodging. Under normal circumstances, the inn was seldom full, and often empty. Sometimes peddlers stayed there if they couldn't find a villager to take them in for the evening, but it was usually used by hunters when their party was too big for a local squire's hunting lodge. The crows bunked together in one room. They slept on straw mats and piled blankets, and the innkeeper's wife prepared breakfast for everyone in the morning.

It was midday before Anna was called once again into the crier's bedroom. Out on the porch, people were bringing lunch to family members who were detained. They crowded at the open door with kettles and pots, trying to see past the councilman who stood guard at the entrance. As Anna passed by, she caught whiffs of lentils and lebbencs soup and mutton. Her mind took a quick turn to her son and daughter, with dread that they might be out there now and would be there when she got out.

Once she was inside the crier's bedroom, it was clear to Anna the gendarmes were no longer interested in hearing about Mr. Cser. They had learned everything they needed about the old man, enough to charge Mrs. Kiss with murder and Anna as a coconspirator. This time, they wanted to know about the babies.

Anna told them.

She told them about her daughter with the rosebud lips and her son born at midnight. She told them about her empty breasts and her empty cupboards. She told them about her rush to save her son's soul with a last-minute christening, and about the terrible eternity in purgatory to which she had condemned his dead sister. She told them about the question the midwife had asked her, which had ended with poison in her infant's body, and about the question the midwife's daughter had posed seven years later. She told them about the hemor-

rhaging, and about babies born half-alive and dying without any special solution applied to their lips. She told them she had always known
she could never outrun God.

Her confession was breathless and tearless. When she finished, she
shuffled out of the crier's bedroom and took her seat on the bench
again.

She set her feet squarely on the floor. Her boots were a size too
large, but sweat and all the idleness had swelled her feet to fit them.
She slouched forward. She snaked a finger under the scarf knotted at
her chin and wiggled it looser. She settled her hands back in her lap,
and no sooner had she done so than she felt them in the hot grasp of
Mari's hands.

If she had been wedged next to Mari before, now she could barely
breathe for the lack of room. Mari's portly frame had been like an
ungirded sack in the freer space, and Anna was forced to make herself
even smaller to fit on the smaller patch she had been left.

Mari's hands were as hot as an oven, but Anna shivered anyway.

Mari cupped her palms like a roof over Anna's hands, which were
as small as a child's. Mari brought them to her chest and cupped them
there. She raised her head up, stretching her neck over Anna for a
clearer view to the front room, where all the gendarmes had gathered.
She could see them hovering around the food, which had been brought
in from the porch. Mari leaned in close to Anna, putting her lips at
Anna's ear.

"Dear Mrs. Cser," she whispered. "I *beg* you, to the great God
above, please take back your confession."

It was easy for Mari to figure out that Anna had confessed. No one
had to announce it to her. She could see it in the gendarmes. When
they weren't lured away by lunch, the officers took turns guarding the
women. They would edge through the narrow passage in front of them,
kicking feet instead of stepping over them. They'd lean down and shove
their hand into a shoulder. They'd lean lower, into their faces.

Whore.

Bitch.

I hope you're sitting in piss.

I can smell the rope they're going to hang you with.

When they circled around the other side, they'd poke the tip of a bayonet into a crow's back, pulling away just before the fabric of the dress was torn.

But once a crow had confessed, she was ignored, skipped over like bad fruit, and Mari had noticed that not a single officer had so much as looked at Anna after she left the crier's bedroom.

"Please, let's say it was my mother who did this."

A heat began to coil in Anna, a slender snake of rage that had never made its home in her before. She snatched her hands back from Mari's grip. She jerked her head away and closed her one good eye as if drawing a curtain down on the scene.

Mari whispered again. "You and I have never fought. We've always been on good terms."

Anna snapped her head back around to Mari.

"Get away from me!!"

In the front room, the gendarmes had begun to eat freely from the pots of food meant for the women. The councilmen who were present had begun dishing some into bowls to feed the suspects. Later, the women would be escorted to the privy, but for now no one was watching them.

Mari leaned forward over her lap. She plunged one hand deep into her boot, stretching her fingers down toward her ankle until she fished out her straight razor. She had stashed it there the day the gendarmes had come for her mother. It was from her ex-husband's collection. It had a German label with a covering made of dark bone. Daniel had left several of his barber instruments when he had fled the household. She had gathered them and stored them all these years.

She flipped open the cover.

"I will never confess. Not even to God."

Mari drew the blade swiftly across her wrist in one clean slice.

A RESCUE, AND RESOLVE

Kronberg had walked from the graveyard to the riverfront in shoes meant for walking on town streets, cobblestones, or smooth, unpitted paths. Nagyrév's walkways were utterly untamed by comparison. Now that he had tramped through the upturned soil at the graveyard and the boggy grasses on the bank, his shoes were as dirty as a schoolboy's, scuffed and muddied. But the mile between his two points of call had been a sobering one. The earth at the graveyard was unclean in so many dark ways and he had been unable to clear his mind of it. Kronberg could feel the weight of the murders on him.

But for his shoes and his mood, he looked like a man who had just stepped off of a steamboat for a holiday. His suit jacket was squared on his shoulders. His bow tie was snug at his collar. The temperature had topped at ninety degrees, and from time to time he removed his hat to wipe his brow with a handkerchief he kept in his trouser pocket. The river breeze also helped cool him.

He edged farther down the bank to where a large rowboat was moored. It was painted the brown of dark tree bark, though years of sun had dulled the color. Patches of it had turned dark gray. Painted in white block letters along the side was GENDARMERIE. The paint was tired, chipped and curling at the tip of each letter.

He listened to the hollow knock of the boat against its mooring, and watched as a deep shadow fell across it, cast by a tugboat coming to the dock. The mooring for the larger vessels—the vehicle ferry, for example, and the boat the Schneider goosery in Kecskemét used—

docked several yards farther upriver. Kronberg could hear the deck-hands hollering to one another.

A dog lay on the grass near the shore, contentedly nursing her pups. The heat of the sun had relaxed her. Kronberg's own dear dog, Dandy, liked to bask in the sun in the courtyard at home, and he thought of him now. Downriver, a couple of boys fished from atop a boulder that jutted out sharply from the banks. The bright sun gave them inky, slender silhou-ettes, and they moved around the tips of their rock like shadow puppets. Farther down were the reedy marshes where the black storks preyed, and even farther down, near the city of Szeged, was Witches Canyon, named for a midwife called Anna and a dozen others who were accused of witch-craft and burned at the stake in July 1729, two hundred years earlier.

Kronberg could hear the rustling behind him and he turned to look. It was the reason he had come.

He had spent no time at the crier's cottage during his visits to Nagyrév. He had left that business to his investigators and the local councilmen, and of course the gendarmes and their superintendent. But he had been summoned to witness a grim parade. He couldn't yet know it would seed an important idea.

He eyed the snake of black-clad women marching from the crier's cottage through the damp meadow. They kept their chins pressed to their chests and their hands clasped in front of them. They were as silent as praying nuns, with only the swish of their dresses to announce them.

Among the ten women were five he was quite familiar with: Kris-tina Csabai, Rosa Kiss, Anna Cser, Maria Szendi, and Mari Fazekas. Mari's wrist was bandaged, and he noted she held it in a way that made it easy for him to spot. He surveyed Mari for traces of Auntie Suzy. She had the same battle-ready mien of her mother.

Kronberg stepped aside to allow them to pass. He saw in the dis-tance the two deckhands from the tugboat.

Neither Kristina, charged as an accomplice in the murder of her husband in 1923, nor Mari, charged with various counts of illegal abortion and infanticide, had confessed. Kristina had vehemently de-nied wrongdoing. Mari had been more evasive in her answers. Maria Szendi had confessed to killing her husband and her only son. She had no choice but to confess. There had been enough arsenic in each man to kill ten men. Kronberg surveyed her now for signs of remorse.

A gendarme hurried ahead to pull the boat close. He held it steady as the women wobbled aboard. Many had never been in such a craft, and the gentle ripples of the tide that rocked the boat startled them. Kronberg observed them as they grabbed on to one another or gripped the plank they were seated on. Once all the women were settled, two gendarmes stepped in and took their seats, one at the bow and one at the stern. They pushed back from the bank with an oar, then set their course north to Szolnok. It was the first of many such transports from the crier's cottage to the prison. The journey up the Tisza would take four hours. It disappointed Kronberg to think that Suzy Fazekas would never be on that boat.

KRONBERG TURNED TO head back up the bank. The gendarmes' boat was now out of sight, and he was vaguely aware that the deckhands had begun to trail up the bankside behind him. He could hear their banter, but like the gravediggers at the cemetery, their dialect was thick and unintelligible to his ear. He quickened his pace. He had all manner of business waiting for him at the village hall, including a briefing from Count Molnar. The count and Dr. Szegedy had completed their review of the death records and had discovered several more suspicious deaths they wanted to discuss with him. There was also the matter of the progress of the investigations in the other villages. More bodies had been disinterred in Cibakháza, Tiszaföldvár, and elsewhere, and four arrests had been made in Cibakháza. Kronberg had sent a letter to Governor Almásy requesting permission to examine coroner reports in every village in the region going back twenty years.

Behind him, the deckhands' banter dropped off. Their voices had become suddenly lyrical and luring, yet touched with menace. Kronberg turned back around just as the two men were closing in on the dog. They looked like boxers circling around her.

The dog lay on her side. Her pups were still suckling. She lifted her head but an inch and growled at the deckhands. *Stay away.*

The men closed in, tightening like a belt around her. She growled again, this time baring her teeth. Delighted by the challenge, the deckhands laughed. One began to bark and howl. The other got down on his haunches and bared his own broken and stained teeth back at her.

The dog lifted herself further now, snarling wildly at her bullies. The deckhand who had been squatting hurried to his feet. He backed away but not for long, as he was not a man to be outdone by a beast. He took a giant step toward the dog and kicked her in the ribs.

She sprang up. Her puppies dashed in all directions in a run for cover, but an unlucky one scrambled across the man's path.

The little one caught his eye, and he lunged forward and kicked it, too. A pop sounded when his boot hit the pup. It was the sound of air forced from its lungs. The newborn sailed in a high arc over the bank and the spiral of its tender body brought silence to the riverbank. The next sound Kronberg heard was a splash as the puppy smacked the water before sinking fast into the river's depths. The deckhands howled with laughter.

The bitch charged toward the river. Her legs were the swiftest Kronberg had ever seen. She moved faster than it seemed her body was aware it could move. She plunged into the water and disappeared beneath its surface.

Kronberg raced after her. He ripped off his suit jacket as he ran. He got tangled in the tall grass. The ground was uneven, and he dodged the holes and rocks in his path. His legs felt thick and clumsy, unwilling to give him the speed he needed. As he arrived at the river's edge, he came to a sudden halt to watch breathless as the bitch's head broke through the river's glassy surface. He stepped back as she thrust her head side to side, sending a spray of water cascading out from her thick coat, and it was only then that he could see the pup dangling from her mouth. It squirmed in her grip. He watched as she swam with it to shore. She sloped up the small hill and gently placed her whelp on the grass. She began to lick the shivering, shocked little creature.

Kronberg sank down into the sand. He laid his jacket across his lap. His breath was still catching in his throat and his heart was still racing. He lowered his head to his knees.

How could a mother kill her son?

A POPULACE SEETHES,
A PROSECUTOR SCHEMES

The investigation had stirred up all of Hungary. There was not a café, a church, a town square, a reading circle, a living room in all of the country that wasn't buzzing with speculation about the murderers. Newspapers with scandalous headlines like the one blazoned across the front page of the *Kunszentmárton Journal* were flying off the stands: COME VISIT NAGYRÉV, THE VILLAGE OF DEATH. Newsboys had begun to load up with two newspaper-stuffed satchels strapped across their shoulders.

Presses seemed to be on a constant run. The *Szolnok Gazette* had been shuttered for nearly a year by the Horthy regime, but even it had suddenly been granted permission to start publishing again. Literary legends like Zsigmond Móricz and Lajos Kassák had also taken an interest in the case. So far, Móricz had examined much, interviewed many, but written little. Kassák, on the other hand, had not delved into the case the same way, but felt free to express his opinion, which represented the opinion of nearly every middle-class Magyar.

"A woman remains a woman, no matter what," he wrote. "She wants not only bread, but also beautiful dresses to draw men's attention to her irresistible sexuality. Every woman, even if she lives in the greatest squalor, wants to conquer. Women create their own laws . . . valid only for the members of their circle. They are generally narrow-minded and have no sense of responsibility. On the other hand, they can be overbearing because they want to get everything they fancy. Cultured women, in some respect, have risen beyond this, but women in [the Tisza region] have remained at such a low level that, could we gauge their desires and deeds by general social laws, we should rightly call them beasts."

The nation's midwives, however, were fighting back against the press's portrayal of them. *Kis Hírlap* printed a letter to the public signed by a group of midwives incensed by the attack on their profession in the wake of the Nagyrév scandal. Midwifery was not, the women stated, the primitive practice the reporters were making it out to be. It was instead a vocation at the vanguard of village life, offering top-notch care for women and healing methods for all that were as yet ummatched by medical doctors.

To MacCormac, the situation had all the makings of a medieval drama. In Vienna and the Balkans, he was chasing fascists and Reds, but in Hungary, he was chasing poison-peddling women who had apparently revived a dark tradition on the Continent. They reminded him of the aristocratic Spanish-Italian family of the Middle Ages who used arsenic, among other means, to kill the unwanted in their path. MacCormac concluded that the women of the Hungarian Plains were poor, illiterate, backwater Borgias, and he was as intrigued by them as he was by any Balkan spy or Romanian prince vying for his attention.

In recent days, he and Mike Fodor had indulged in long discussions about how the people of a place so seemingly simple and bucolic could become so murder-minded. Fodor had been born in Budapest, but his family had village roots and he knew how a wayward midwife could turn a village on its head. Fodor had tutored MacCormac on some of the wild and twisting grapevine tales he had heard growing up, in which certain wise women of the earlier ages had a mysterious history of "lopping off dead branches of family trees." The stories had been told with an indiscernible glint, and MacCormac was not sure whether Fodor believed them, or if he simply relished the mystery.

What MacCormac knew for certain was that the situation on the Plains was turning out to be one of the largest murder rings in history.

SZOLNOK

The man was elegantly attired and held a silver platter on the palm of his gloved hand. The platter was covered with a grand silver lid shaped like a dome, and had a slim handle wide enough to fit one finger through. The silver had been polished to a mirror sheen and reflected back to him in waves the black shine of his dinner jacket.

He stood under the dimmed lamps of the entrance. He was flanked by lively tables of aristocrats enveloped in cigar and pipe smoke, and the grinning pride of their own clever words. The maître d' opened the casino doors, and the waiter slipped through them to the outdoors. He blinked back the sudden flood of daylight, then moved gracefully, swiftly down the red-carpeted stairs onto the dust and gravel of Gorove Street.

The challenge of his new daily duty had become much greater for him in the last few days. Much of Kossuth Square was under a marquee, with scores of booths and stands that spilled out into unclaimed spaces near the street and along the walkways. The largest international trade fair in Central Europe had come to town and sellers had come in from all over the continent: Athens, Sarajevo, Sofia, Munich. They had even come in from London.

All of the first district, and most of the second and third, had been cordoned off for the fair. As many vendors were crammed into passageways and courtyards as were on the open squares. There were Beidermeier drawing rooms set up. Spaces were filled with stunning mirrors on display, gilt tubs, perfumes, rums. There were toys of all manner and people were test-driving the Modrá motorcycles on display at the Franz Joseph Promenade over near the city's famed artist colony. A person couldn't walk ten yards without running into a goldsmith or a silversmith. Even the National Hungarian Milk Cooperative had a booth. To the waiter, all the noise and clutter and cheer normally contained by the casino walls seemed to have manifested itself outside.

Across from Kossuth Square, directly in front of the county hall, three stately motorcars were standing, as beautifully black and shimmering as the waiter's own dinner jacket. A driver sat behind the wheel of each, either reading a stack of newspapers or resting his eyes.

The stamp of tradesmen was everywhere on Kossuth, and only a narrow perimeter had been demarcated around the courthouse and prison. Despite the crowds, the waiter had come to enjoy this daily sprint.

But as he glided toward the street, he found his way blocked by a bus, cherry red and rumbling, which had stopped to pick up passengers. He paused to think about his next move. He could feel the heat of the platter warming his hand. A trace of moisture had formed at the lip of the lid. He stepped back from the passengers and hurried onto the street behind the bus. He eased in front of a light roar of motorcars and carriages and stuck out his hand to command a halt. He stepped briskly across Gorove Street, the rattle of the platter at his ear.

From his office window, Kronberg surveyed the man. He watched the waiter navigate behind and around kiosks and past pushcarts, occasionally lifting the platter high over his head to avoid a collision. He saw him step into the cordoned-off area that marked the courthouse and stride farther along until he disappeared inside the prison. For nearly two weeks, the waiter had been making daily deliveries to the prison to fulfill an order placed by Petra Joljart Varga.

When the prison was finally rebuilt—the League of Nations loans had finally come through—its capacity was increased from thirty inmates to seventy, largely by the addition of a second floor. The kitchen had likewise expanded. But there had rarely been more than a dozen convicts incarcerated at one time, so most of the new facility had gone unused.

Now the inmate population was nearly double what the jail was equipped to handle. There were one hundred women being detained in the Nagyrév case alone. And one of the problems the sudden overcrowding had created was a shortage of food for the detainees. The dingy café inside the Hotel Hungarian King on the square had begun catering for the prison kitchen at the beginning of the month, as had a handful of other nearby restaurants, including the one on Garden Street and the one inside the county hall. But only Petra was having her meals served every day directly from the National Casino, as fine a dining spot as could be found in all of Szolnok. She was paying for it herself.

Kronberg had been judicious about who he was housing together in cells. Mari Fazekas was in with two women, one from Nagyrév and the other from another Plains village, an artist named Priscilla, who was being tried for a fraud case. Priscilla had already reported to Kronberg's team what Mari had revealed in their long, chatty talks together. Mari had given the artist various versions of what had happened at little Stephen's birth. In one account, Mari hadn't been there at all during the delivery, but instead had been at a hospital in Budapest recovering from a leg injury. In another of her accounts, she was present during Stephen's birth, but only as an assistant. In yet a third, she admitted she had delivered the baby, but he had been stillborn. In that version, she told her cellmate that Anna had darkly instructed her, "Get that carcass out of here!"

While most women were kept two to a cell, and some, like Mari, were in a group of three, Kronberg kept certain inmates isolated, including Petra and Kristina Csabai. Neither woman had yet admitted they had killed their husbands, and Kronberg knew from experience that time spent in solitary confinement could do a lot to change a person's mind about confessing.

But he also knew other gambits could work. Petra's husband had been blinded during the war, but it was only after his remains were brought to Budapest that it was discovered he was the first Hungarian soldier to lose his sight in battle. Kronberg knew how the public would react to this. He had wasted no time in leaking the information to Barny, and soon it would be blasted across every front page in every newspaper in every region of the country.

The prosecutor's office had also hired a local psychoanalyst, Dr. Feldmann, to conduct psychological exams. Feldmann was a follower of the groundbreaking work Sigmund Freud was carrying out in Vienna, and had himself begun to explore the dreams the women were having. They had such poor sleeping conditions that many were not dreaming at all, or were having the kinds of shattered dreams that exhaustion brings. But soon Dr. Feldmann learned that two women, quartered in separate cells, were each having the same recurring dream. One of the women was Rose Holyba.

In their dreams, each woman found herself walking on the bank of the Tisza, where the soil was soft under her feet. In Rose's dream, she was always carrying a brick in her hand, which she intended to use to build a new house. Suddenly, the ground would start to churn and the soil would turn to quicksand. Each woman would sink, struggling to get out of the ground's grasp, dogged by a choking feeling. The women would awaken struggling to get their breath.

Kronberg wasn't sure what to make of the dreams. He would leave that to Dr. Feldmann. Their souls and their psyches weren't his domain. His own sleep was undisturbed, except for his increasing unease about Anna.

Every Tuesday and Friday was visiting day at the jail. It would swell with people. Many would be forced to wait outside until they were cleared to come in, and Kronberg could often see a long line of them trailing up from the direction of the train station, loaded with baskets of food and clean dresses and undergarments. Franklin made the trip faithfully every Tuesday and every Friday. He would usually drive his carriage up the evening before and stay in a hotel nearby.

The only reasonable way to accommodate so many people was to have the inmates gather with their guests in the prison yard. There had been some trouble with the visitors passing flasks of alcohol to the prisoners, and more concerning problems of prisoners smuggling out notes, directives for alibis written with large chunks of rust peeled from the pipes that ran along the cell walls. But more guards had been put on duty to quash the trouble.

A simple coincidence had brought the ungodly acts of Lewis Cser to Kronberg's attention. The prosecutor had begun stopping in at the prison at the start of his midday break to check in with the warden, and on visiting day, this often meant the warden could be found in the yard. He would stand at the threshold, and Kronberg would join him there for a minute or two.

Whenever Lewis spoke, he gave as much volume to his words as possible. His voice seemed to come from somewhere inside a barrel. It was difficult not to hear him, even in a large crowd.

"How the fuck do I get out of here?!"

Kronberg looked to see who had said it. He saw Anna crouching, Lewis looming.

"You idiot whore. You don't even know where the goddamn door is!"

No one would know until later, until Anna had formally requested bail, that the only reason Lewis had come that day was to demand Anna come home to take care of the children.

Kronberg had Lewis removed from the building, with orders that he never be allowed to return.

Weeks later, on a brisk autumn day, Anna, alone momentarily in her cell, tied her headscarf around her neck and attached it to the radiator. She crossed her hands under her armpits and slid down, down, down, dangling for a minute, two minutes, her breath nearly gone from her body, before a guard entered and rushed to untie her.

WHEN KRONBERG SAW the motorcade finally pull away from the county hall, it was nearing the end of the day. The meeting was at a much higher level than his rank, yet had everything to do with him. He had briefed the president of the royal court for hours in preparation for the tête-à-tête with Governor Almásy and Regent Horthy, as the court's president, not Kronberg, would be the one making the court's argument for allowing the Nagyrév case to stay with the Szolnok prosecutor's office.

This day was, without question, the most critical since the investigation had gotten underway. For the first time in Kronberg's life, his career was hanging in the balance.

He had gone over every action he had taken since the first murder came to light. He had created a mental timeline of events. Had he made any missteps? Had he left any room for cracks to form? Could a case be made that a prosecutor in Budapest could try these women better than he? The royal court was still trying to tamp down the rumblings about the failure in the Holyba case. Budapest was hungry to take over the Nagyrév investigation. The president of the court was over there fighting to keep it.

Earlier in the day, Kronberg had fought hard for it in his own cunning way.

Early that morning

Barny stood at the top of the riverbank, where the ground was level and a path was etched along the edge of an unpaved, stony lane. He had spent much of the morning slouched against a tree, his notebook in his hand and his hat pulled low over his head to give shade to his eyes.

He made scribbles about the scene and sketched in the margins when he got bored, filling them with the trees and the scrub he could see. He made a sketch of the view to the larger port farther down and its ship station. The mongers were offloading their goods there. The west of the city was where the plants and the mills were situated, spread out around the station like a small kingdom: the sugar factory, the brick factory, the vinegar factory, the ice factory, the railway parts factory, the Remington typewriter factory, the textile mills, the timber mills, the paper mills. Barny doodled the plumes of smoke feathering out of the smokestacks.

Barny couldn't help but take note of the boys from the Tabán district, who had been at work for hours hauling stones up the steeper part of the bank. The Tabán was one of the poorest parts of Szolnok, and the young people earned money getting the heavy stones off the large ships and up to the road. Barny could see them now, a half mile from where he stood near the old, shabby dock. Their feet were as fast as flight on their runs back to the ship for another haul, their voices soft and light, like songbirds.

Barney reached into his vest pocket. It was littered with loose tobacco and small scraps of paper. He fished out his beaten-up pocket watch. The back was scuffed and the face bore a tiny fracture in the glass. He cupped his hand over it to lessen the glare. It was only a few minutes past ten o'clock.

Kronberg had tipped him off, as ever. Barny had arrived quite early, as was his habit. He was sure he'd gotten the time right, yet there was no boat. But no sooner had Barny dropped his watch back into his pocket than he saw the boat appear from around a bend.

It drifted quietly toward the old pier. Barny could hear the ripple of the light wake. He watched the gendarme at the bow lean forward and toss a line over the bollard like a noose. The boat drifted closer and made a hollow knock against the dock, and a gendarme jumped out to moor it more firmly.

The women emerged slowly from the boat. Charcoal figures sketched at the bottom of a blue sky. They peered up at the bank, blinking into the sun. The two gendarmes reached back into the boat to retrieve their plumed helmets and bayonets.

There had been many transports such as this in recent weeks, but none had conveyed Auntie Suzy.

Barny watched as the women scrambled up the dodgy bank, hoisting themselves from rock to rock and grabbing low branches, which they used to propel themselves upward or to save themselves from slipping back. The dock had been meant for hobby fishermen, barefoot with fishing rods, not middle-aged women in long dresses and hobnailed boots.

Barny heard some racket behind him. He looked toward it. A pack of newsmen was rushing in his direction, apparently headed to the large port. He squatted down as low to the ground as he could get. He pressed up against the tree trunk, trying not to be seen. He gripped his notepad to his chest. He heard their footsteps grow louder and louder, and it sounded to him like a small stampede. To a man, they dashed by the battered old fishing dock without seeing it or him. Barny laughed to himself.

Up until now, Kronberg had fed the press everything he wanted them to know through Barny. Everything written about Nagyrév had been written by Barny first. But the prosecutor changed tack. On this day, Kronberg wanted all of the news buzzards circling and he wanted the crows on full display.

It amused Barny that the pack of them had gone to the wrong

dock. They had expected the women to come into the larger port. He watched as they realized their error and doubled back.

The crows were still struggling to get ashore when the newsmen began descending the bank. They skidded and stumbled down the hill, shouting throaty, wind-choked questions at them. To Barny, they looked like schoolboys in a race.

As the pack neared, the gendarmes charged back at the reporters. The officers plunged forward, each with one hand on a helmet, the other on the rifle strapped to his side.

Silence! There will be no questions!!

They commanded a retreat, and the newsmen hastily obeyed.

When the prisoners had finally climbed up the bank and reached the lane, the gendarmes arranged them single file, then each officer took a wing position on either side. The trail of reporters followed behind the line of women like a disorderly kite tail.

The route Kronberg had instructed the gendarmes to take was not at all a direct one. That would have been to follow along the river and cut over to the prison at or near Garden Street. But they were to wind through the center of the city.

The tread on Barny's old shoes had almost worn through, and he could feel the rocks as if he were in his stocking feet. He had noted the scruffy boots the women wore, the dried-out leather, the tattered laces, the repatched soles, and they reminded him of his own.

For a long while he could hear nothing but the crunch of stones. It sounded to him like death was walking. Death, he thought to himself, had woken up to take a morning stroll.

He looked behind him. The kite tail had grown longer. A loose band of adolescents had joined the procession behind the last of the newsmen.

As the women trudged along, onlookers began to pepper the route. A washerwoman creaked open a window and leaned out for a better view. A priest out for a walk with his dog hushed the mutt, which had picked up the scent of drama and was barking. A delivery boy stopped his bicycle to stare.

Nearly every doorway began to fill with a merchant, a barber, a chef, a banker, a jeweler, a printmaker, a lawyer, who watched the grim parade with mouths agape. When the crows passed a corner café, the patrons seated outside began to hiss and boo. A charwoman pitched her broom like an arrow at the crows. One of the gendarmes reached down and threw it back to her.

When the gendarmes arrived with their charges at the boundary of the trade fair, they stopped briefly to discuss how to proceed. They decided to snake the line of crows behind a row of tarpaulins and around a series of wooden kiosks, then march them directly down a center aisle of the fair. The fairgoers glared hard at the women. Some of them screamed and hissed.

They emerged at Baross Street. The kite tail of reporters was still attached to the line of women, and had gained more stragglers, who were determined to see the walk to its end. Some at the back could not even see the women. They followed the grandly plumed helmets of the gendarmes as if they were feathered beacons.

Barny occupied a coveted spot right behind the last crow in the line. He had studied her shambling gait, the round arc of her shoulders. Through the slight movements of her head, he had come to know what obscenity could make her steal a glance, and what she could stoically soldier past.

The pace was slow and exaggerated, and he figured they had covered far less than a mile in what seemed to be far more than an hour. The gendarmes had halted the procession once to answer questions posed by the mayor, who had taken a position along the route for just the occasion.

On Baross Street, a different gaggle of reporters was in a huddle near a fruit drink stand, covering another event. One of the shorter reporters, who was on the outskirts of the huddle, was standing on tiptoe and waving his hand, begging for the little sea to part so he too could get a look.

Just then, it did.

Barny had long been a friend of Tibor Pólya. There was no place in Szolnok and few places in the country Pólya could go and not be recognized. He was one of the most noted artists in Central Europe, a man

Barny had featured in many of his articles, and someone Kronberg had gotten to know quite well through the Szolnok artist colony, which attracted well-known artists from all across Europe. Kronberg was an amateur artist himself and was frequently a guest of the colony. Barny was not at all surprised to see Pólya there. To the contrary, he had been expecting it. Now that the huddle of reporters had parted, Barny could see the artist sampling a pineapple syrup with Regent Horthy, who was flanked by the governor and the high sheriff. The scene had been staged by Pólya and Kronberg.

The gendarmes led their charges slowly, deliberately, past the regent. The jeers directed at the crows grew louder, and could still be heard when they reached the prison doors.

Within days, Kronberg would release nearly half of the women now being held. He had proved his point to Horthy.

His great regret, of course, was not being able to try Auntie Suzy. But he had, by this time, nearly all the other suspects he needed in custody to begin his case, not least among them the midwife's sister, Lidia, and her counterpart, Rose Holyba.

That might never have happened if it hadn't been for his man in Nagyrév, Officer Bartók, who, it turned out, had a few tricks of his own.

UNDERCOVER, UNDER BED

Five weeks earlier . . .

Saturday, July 20, 1929

The crier's bed was fairly low to the ground. The space between the floor and the supporting lattice of ropes that held the mattress couldn't have been more than fifteen inches. Bartók had forgotten to tighten the ropes before he crawled underneath, and now they sagged down in front of him. He could see the coarse fibers and the fine hairs where they had frayed. He felt caged by them.

The old straw-stuffed mattress needed desperately to be aired. Bartók could barely breathe because of the musty, choking smell. He had pushed himself back against the wall where a lot of dust had gathered, and that too made him struggle for a clear breath.

His arms were pulled close to his chest in a boxer's pose. He had drawn his knees in. The crier kept winter blankets under the bed, and Bartók had shoved them down near his feet to get them out of the way.

He had a harshly curtailed view of the room. There was a jagged crack in the wall. Part of the rug, woven together from rags, was visible, as was part of a table leg. The door was not plumb with the floor, and in the gap, he could see the sharp shadow of a shoe, which he took to be Fricska's. Directly in front of him, he could see a pair of black boots. The bootlaces draped down the sides. He could only see the heels and the ankles, which were considerably wide. Lidia had thick arthritic ankles, like her sister.

He could feel her heft on the mattress. Rose Holyba was sitting next to Lidia.

A puddle of perspiration had formed in front of him. Sweat was dripping from his forehead. His shirt was also drenched in sweat. The wetness he felt against the cool wall offered some relief. He had been under the bed for at least twenty minutes. He had gotten into position as soon as the suspects had been taken out to the privy for their toilet break. They always went as a group, and Fricska had helped him get settled before they all came back, and before Lidia and Rose had been ushered into the crier's bedroom for their interrogation.

The two crows had sat wordlessly for a while, expecting the gendarmes to enter. The normal procedure, as they had become familiar with it, was that the gendarmes and the witness came into the room with the suspect. The witness usually sat on the bed while the gendarmes stood. They had been interrogated multiple times, although never at the same time. This arrangement was new to them. They were alone together, with no one else around. Even at the inn at night, they had a gendarme or a councilman guarding them.

Lidia spoke first.

"We must admit everything. They won't leave us in peace until we do."

"What should I say?"

"Tell them you bought the poison in a shop."

Lidia's voice was similar enough to Auntie Suzy's that hearing it was jarring to Bartók. What had taken place the previous day was still fresh in his mind, and it seemed for a moment it was Auntie Suzy sitting there on the bed.

"I don't want to do that! I'd rather say I got it from Auntie Suzy."

"Don't say that, because then you'll get me in trouble."

Bartók could hear his partner Fricska pressing against the door. He could hear the crack and push of the wood. He knew Fricska like a brother, and he knew he was trying to be very still.

As was he. Every muscle was clenched, tightened like a spring. The only thing demanding to move were his lungs.

"Look. Confess everything here and deny it in court. If it worked for our Suzy at her abortion trials, it'll work now," Lidia advised Rose.

Bartók had to remind himself that this was practically her daughter-in-law she was talking to, the mother of her two young grandchildren.

"I have good friends at the court. They'll help you. But leave me out of it. If you do decide to confess now, I promise to raise the children."

Was Fricska hearing all of this? Bartók wasn't sure.

He had a feeling like he was back in the war. Hiding in a muddy trench. Stock-still. Ready to charge.

Rose brought the subject around to the soup, the last tainted victual that Charles had consumed, and which Lidia had brought to him. She suggested they tell the gendarmes there must have been something in the soup. Lidia didn't like this one bit.

"Why would you say that?! Why would you tell them he ate from the soup that I cooked?!"

Bartók knew it was time. He had everything he needed.

Ready. Aim. Fire.

Bartók thrust his arms out from under the bed. He grabbed Lidia's fat ankle with both hands. His feet had gotten tangled in the stack of blankets and he kicked violently at them to free himself. He held on to her ankles like a man needing to be saved.

Lidia shrieked. Then Rose did.

"You're under arrest! You're under arrest!" Bartók shouted from under the bed. "You're both under arrest!"

Lidia struggled to pull her leg free, but Bartók held tight. He pulled himself out from under the bed still hanging on to her ankle. His head was facedown and he hugged her boot as if he were kissing it.

Fricska had already bolted in. Judge and Count Molnar came rushing in behind him.

Rose sprang up from the bed. She stood shaking in the farthest corner of the room, wishing for her high branch.

ONE MAD DASH

The Day Before . . .

Friday, July 19, 1929

The wire had cut a groove into the midwife's palm. It had all but buried itself in the thick of her flesh. When the handle was new, it had made a perfect loop, a metal halo, that arced nicely over the lantern. But now the wire was bent and hardened and rusting. When she opened her hand and flexed it back, she could see the red mark of her grip. Tiny specks of rust from the aging wire glistened on her skin.

She brought the lantern up to her face. She squinted through the sooty grime on the glass to examine the flame. It was just a small nub now. Not even a flicker. And not worth relighting. She lowered the lamp back down to her side and looked out to the point where the dawn was forming.

The night had been still. At some point, she had begun to feel a mastery over it. There hadn't been a bootstep in hours, and even then, the last ones she had heard had only been a farmer heading to his stable. The night watchman hadn't been around, either. He had been reposted to the edge of the village to help watch for women trying to leave. And she hadn't heard the crier's drum all night.

Her head had felt tight and brittle when she started her vigil. Her thoughts were like tiny pellets zipping and pinging against the bones of her skull, and there was a hail of them: Her sister in the crier's cottage. Rose's fickle mouth. Maria. Unanswered doors. The crier's drum. The crier's drum. The crier's drum. They had all brought her to a place beyond worry, and she had nearly paced new potholes into the road because of it.

There had come a point when the scratchy noise of fear was smoothed in some measure by the calm night. Exhaustion bled the rest of it from her. They had not come for her. Why had they not come for her?

The slim, pink line of day began to grow, which caused Auntie Suzy to abandon her post and take up her vigil indoors.

SINCE THE INVESTIGATION began, the count had been arriving at the hall earlier than usual each morning. He normally started his workday around eight o'clock, which was far earlier than Ébner ever had, but now he was likely to turn up as early as six, and even then he found there was never enough time to manage all the work that was mounting. Dr. Szegedy sometimes arrived soon after him, but he had moved on to research the death records in another village, Tiszaföldvár or Tiszakürt, the count couldn't remember which one.

The early hours in the hall had become nearly sacrosanct to him, a time to restore an iota of order to a situation stamped with disorder, without being interrupted by investigators, gendarmes, or councilmen.

The councilmen had been his biggest bane since he had taken office, and had it not been for the investigation, the count felt certain that a move would have been afoot to oust him. He thought, with more than a little self-satisfaction, that without his persistence and his constant call for order, the women's deeds might have gone unnoticed for another twenty years.

Before arriving at the hall, he had stopped in at the crier's cottage to take a look. It was the first chance the count had to see for himself what Auntie Suzy's outing the previous day had produced. He was unnerved by it. Women sat shoulder to shoulder on benches borrowed from the chapel. Some were young, not older than twenty-five, and some were old, about seventy. Their heads were bowed and many were keening. It looked to the count like some peculiar rite being performed.

In his office, he kept the candlestick telephone in the top right corner of his desk. He reached for it now, sliding it across the desk until it was squarely in front of him. He removed the receiver and brought it to his ear. The final result of the roundup had not yet been reported to Kronberg. He leaned into the transmitter. He dialed 24, the direct line to the prosecutor's office.

AUNTIE SUZY HAD always liked how the morning light dappled her kitchen. It poured through the weave of her lace curtains, where it patterned her walls and sideboard. Each bright morning of her life in that house had been marbled with sunshine.

She had seated herself in the stream of the light. Her fingers were wrapped around a warm bowl of coffee, which she steered carefully to her lips, then thrust down in a leaping gulp. She always drank coffee as if she were putting out small fires in her throat, and she always preferred to drink it from a bowl, as her parents and grandparents had done. Even the gadjo used to drink it that way. The midwife was loath to break the tradition.

Somewhere, she could hear a lamb bleating. It was probably Mr. Tuba's. She had midwifed that lamb in the spring. Behind the bleat was the beating drum, which she could not yet hear.

The house slept and woke like she did. It felt like a companion to her. Both were missing Mari. Her daughter had always begun talking first thing upon rising and carried on through the day, and the silence since she had moved out felt like a cutting loss. Auntie Suzy had wondered about her often overnight. She guessed she too had been taken in.

Gendarme bastards. The devil will eat their souls.

Flowers she had picked weeks earlier were still out in jars on the sill. The jar water was cloudy, with beige swirls of scum at the surface. It had a putrid odor. The petals were brown and curled.

The midwife had hardly spent a night at home since the Saints Peter and Paul Feast and nearly everything was as she had left it that day. She reached for a petal, crumbling it in her hand like ash and dropping it onto the table in front of her. She felt emptied of every physical and mental resource.

Except for the nap she had taken the previous afternoon when she returned from Szolnok, she hadn't slept in some forty-eight hours. She had also exhausted herself walking in the rain for hours, and she had been plying her brain all night with impossible puzzles of escape while she was out on her watch. She dropped her hand into her apron pocket and pulled out a kerchief she had put there. She balled it in her hand and wiped it across her forehead and neck before stuffing it back in her pocket.

She reached for another petal, and as she did, she spotted through the curtain the tops of the feathered helmets that showed over her fence.

Auntie Suzy shoved back the bench. She slammed her bowl onto the table. The coffee sloshed, spraying her hands and apron. She hoisted herself up. The bench fell backward onto the floor with a tremendous clunk.

Suzannah Fazeeeeekas! Come out, pleeeease!

She could hear the drumbeat now.

Fuck the devils!

Auntie Suzy dropped down to her knees and crept to her door. She reached up for the handle and gently pressed it down. The crier called her name again.

Susaaaannaahhh Fazeeeekas! Come out, pleeease!

The door creaked partway open. Auntie Suzy paused in the middle like an undecided dog, her palms on the porch, her knees still on the floor inside. She could smell the odor of her body. Bands of her hair were fixed to her face with sweat. Her mouth hung open. She was breathing hard.

A loud bang at the gate caused her to lurch back.

Suzy Fazekas! COME OUT RIGHT NOW!

This time a gendarme was shouting.

COME OUT NOW, SUZY, OR WE'RE COMING IN!

She leaned back on her haunches. She looked behind her, back into the house. She looked toward the gate, then eyed the distance to her stable. Any move seemed fatally flawed.

She watched as her gate wobbled back and forth. It cracked and rattled with violent shakes. Both gendarmes were shouting now. Auntie

Suzy eyed the gate latch, and the triple-knotted rope looped around it. She had secured the gate after she had come in from her patrol. Her skin still bore light scratches from its battle with the rough twine.

She could see through the gaps in the fence that a small crowd was gathering. Their voices began to blend into one cacophonous call.

The gate cracked again, a clean split of wood. Auntie Suzy scrambled off the ground as fast as her age and her heft allowed. Once she was on her feet, she spun around, as confused as a child in a game. Another loud crack and the gate came crashing down.

Nearly everyone who had been at home on Green Street, and nearly everyone who had been at home on Orphan Street, and anyone who had seen or heard the ruckus from Jókai or Kossuth or even Árpád, had come to watch the gendarmes arrest the midwife. Some spilled in after them, while the rest crowded into the open space where the gate had just stood.

Under the eave was the large log the midwife often sat on. She picked it up and heaved it at the gendarmes.

She ran toward her well. She grabbed the wooden bucket and flung it in their path.

"Menj a fenébe!"

When she reached her stable, she went straight for the iron pot under the workbench. She hadn't time to shut the door, but by the time the gendarmes rushed in, she had gulped down four or five swallows of what sloshed around in the bottom of the pot.

Among the neighbors now in her yard were several very young children. They had come with their mothers. They watched everything through a dense crowd of legs.

Danielovitz and Császár were the arresting officers this time, and both had been hindered in the pursuit by their heavy helmets and bayonets. They thrust them off now. Császár's helmet bounced under the workbench, where Auntie Suzy had crawled. He leaned down into her wild, grimacing face.

He fell to his knees. He ducked his head to clear the bench and reached for the midwife. She was curled into a ball with her legs pulled up at her chest. Her sweat-soaked dress smelled foul. He made a move for her arm, but the midwife was quicker. She uncoiled her legs like a spring and shoved him in the chest. He fell sprawling back to the ground.

He scrambled to right himself. She had shoved him a few feet back, and he scurried to get under the workbench again and have another go. Danielovitz crouched on the other side. Each gendarme grabbed an arm and pulled.

The open door let in a large shaft of light, but it was partially blocked by the neighbors. Where before they had stood gaping at the fence, now they stood gaping at the stable door.

Császár knew immediately what poison Auntie Suzy had poured down her throat. He had potash sitting in a pot in his own stable at home. It was a concoction that had been leached from vegetables, and he used it to make soap and bleach and fertilizer, like everyone else he knew.

The gendarmes had managed to get Auntie Suzy out from under the workbench. The sunlight coming in from the doorway was sharp on her face, hardening her mien even more. Her eyes were partially hidden behind a curtain of stringy hair, but Császár could still see them. They darted around frantically. She began gurgling and breathing openmouthed. Császár had thrown his body over hers, restraining her hands with his own. Her feet kicked at the air. She looked like a rabid cow.

"Who here has a cart? We need to get her to a doctor."

No one answered.

"Who has a cart? Who here has a cart? Or we could just use an ox! We could prop her up on an ox, or just a mule, or whatever someone's got and get her there!"

No one spoke.

The midwife had a bucket of milk sitting atop the workbench. When old Mr. Ambrose was alive, he had kept her well supplied with milk, and after he died she had a harder time getting such a steady, ample supply. But since she had been living alone, one bucket had been plenty for her.

Danielovitz seized the bucket and dropped it to the floor next to Császár. Milk sloshed onto the floor.

Auntie Suzy's back suddenly arched. Császár pressed his chest into hers, trying to restrain her. Her neck slowly elongated. Her hands grew rigid in his.

Danielovitz cupped his hands and plunged them into the cold bucket of milk. Getting milk down her was the only hope he had of neutralizing her poisoned blood. He thrust the milk that he had pooled in his palms onto the midwife's face.

The neighbors stayed in the doorway, gasping and craning for a better look. The children who had started to cry had been carried off.

Danielovitz tried to pry her mouth open, but her jaw was locked in place. He reached for the bucket. He brought the edge of it to her lips. He tilted it forward, steadily pouring the milk out onto her face, where it dripped down her neck and settled in a puddle on the floor. Not a drop landed in her clenched mouth.

Császár had felt her body stiffen and now he felt the rattle. It was like trying to hold back a train barreling beneath him. The midwife shuddered with an electric force that frightened him. Her torso bucked and bucked. Her head hammered the floor and he could see a growing mat of blood in her hair. He pressed into her more, still trying to get her to be still.

Within a minute, the old midwife was dead.

"FORGIVE THE SINS OF THOSE
WHO OBEYED SATAN"

Sunday, September 1, 1929

The heat inside the chapel was sweltering. The doors had been propped open to let some of it escape, and to let the people outside hear the sermon. Dozens were gathered on the steps near the entrance, though a few had gone around to the sides to listen near a window.

One hundred twenty parishioners were crammed into the pews. They shared hymnals, as there weren't enough to go around. They fanned their faces with their hands. Most had come from other villages, Abony, Nagykőrös, Szentes, and even from as far away as Debrecen, a city nearly a hundred miles from Nagyrév.

Sometime over the summer, the local bishop had moved swiftly to suppress the charges that the lack of spiritual leadership had caused the women to succumb to evil. The office of the Calvinist episcopate had been inundated with letters and telegrams blaming the church for the murders and urging that something be done.

Pastor Toth had also gotten angry letters. "Sir, the murderers' sins are your fault," wrote one citizen. "If a pastor doesn't know the people in his parish are committing sins, he is an accomplice. We demand you be held accountable. You will be held responsible." The writer ended with a threat. "We will meet." It had been printed on a postcard, sent from the Szolnok railway station, which offered little clue to the sender's identity.

The bishop went on a firing spree in the region, removing scores of teachers and clergy, and appointing "proved" men in their place.

Pastor Toth was the first to go. He was replaced by a new pastor, who had brimstone in his collar.

It was the fiery preacher's first service in Nagyrév. He had spent days preparing the homily. He had practiced it several times in front of his wife. When he arrived at the chapel in the morning, he had dodged a group of reporters shouting questions to him.

He preached for hours. He strode up and down the aisle.

"God, forgive the sins of those who obeyed Satan and now await justice," he bellowed. "I know those women who committed crimes have regretted it, and now they will dig out the murdered persons from the graves with their own hands."

He swept his hand upward, and the congregation rose. The organist began to play a familiar hymn.

While the churchgoers sang, out in the graveyard, more bodies were being exhumed. Twenty-nine bodies had been raised out of the ground by this time. Seventeen of them had been examined. Arsenic was found in each.

Over in the crier's cottage, six more suspects were waiting to be questioned.

Sparks flew from the smithy, as the blacksmith forged more metal coffins.

CODA

Top Hats and Gowns, and to the
Gallows She Goes

Tuesday, January 13, 1931

Maria was fully dressed by the time Franklin appeared. She had put on a gray dress and black stockings. She wore a pair of simple black shoes. Her graying hair was pulled back off her shoulders.

She had called for the minister moments before Franklin arrived, and the two men stood alongside one another near the door.

Reverend Loos had been the last person she had seen the evening before. She had eaten a hearty meal of goulash as she waited for him to get to her. The warden had promised he would stay with her so she wouldn't be alone, and he sat beside her at the low wooden table that had been squeezed into her cell. The goulash was seasoned with roasted cress, her favorite, and came with a side dish of rice pudding, also her favorite.

The evening was spent with the reverend reading Bible passages to her. They had been interrupted once, by the prison doctor, who was let in to offer Maria a sedative, which she declined. At midnight, she asked Reverend Loos to leave, and when he was gone, she took out what remained of her rice pudding and ate it. Afterward, she lay down on the prison cot to sleep.

She was seated now on the low cot. She gripped the edge with both hands. She rocked forward and back, forward and back.

She stared at the floor as she addressed Franklin.

"Your sister couldn't bother herself to come? I made her my daughter, but where has she been? Not with me."

It was true, Marcella had not visited Maria in prison. Maria had not seen or heard from her since Maria had first been hauled to the crier's cottage.

Franklin was wrapped in his heavy szür, the one that had belonged to Alex Junior, who had received it as an heirloom from his father. It was as heavy as several blankets, and Franklin felt nearly crushed under it. Underneath his szür, he had donned formal wear, as was required, for which Maria had paid a handsome sum.

He had not slept or eaten in days.

He reached into his pocket and pulled out a flask of brandy. He removed the cap and handed the flask, which had also belonged to Alex Junior, to Maria. She took it from him and knocked back several swallows.

Just after 7:00 A.M., Prosecutor Kronberg entered the prison yard, preceded by other members of the court. It was Maria's turn to enter the yard. She was flanked on either side by a prison guard. She had refused a coat. Her hair was still pulled back, although some strands had loosened. She smelled of sweat and brandy. Her legs were too wobbly for her to stand on her own, and she collapsed in the doorway. The two guards cupped her elbows in their hands and lifted her through the snowy yard. The invitees, dressed in finery—a grim custom— stood back to make way.

The hangman stepped forward. He had come earlier in the week from Budapest with his crew to erect the gallows and prepare the noose. The previous afternoon, he had measured the convict's height and weight, to determine the width and length of rope he would need, as well as the precise size of the stool.

Maria screamed out into the yard, her long wail mixed with prayer. The crowd that had gathered on the rooftop across the street could hear her well, despite the noise from the thousands who were in the square. They looked down onto the scene, as if from balcony seats onto a stage.

The judge rose.

"I hereby confirm that Maria Szendi Kardos has been condemned to death, and that the sentence has been upheld by Admiral Horthy, the regent of the Kingdom of Hungary, for the murder of her son and her husband."

He motioned the other members of the court to rise.

"I now give the prisoner to the royal prosecutor."

Kronberg stepped toward the gallows. He squared himself in front of the hangman, who was outfitted in top hat and tails, like him. The racket on the square was loud and Kronberg had to shout to be heard.

"State Executioner, fulfill your duty."

The hangman strode to the scaffold. The prison guards held Maria's arms as the hangman's two henchmen grabbed her legs and bound them with rope. Together, they steadied her on the stool, pressing her feet down onto the wood. The hangman moved behind her and lightly placed a noose around her neck. She faced out to the gathering in the prison yard.

"Cover my face!" Maria shouted. The hangman complied, placing his hand over Maria's face.

He probed her neck with his thumb.

"God have mercy on me!" she screamed. "God have mercy on me!"

The hangman placed a black cotton cloth over her head. Maria screamed. The hangman nodded to one of his henchman, who leaned over and yanked the stool away, causing the noose to jerk tight around Maria's neck. Swiftly, he grabbed Maria's feet and jerked them hard.

Maria's body thrashed violently. The henchman kept tugging her feet. The second henchman joined him.

The two men continued to hold Maria's feet. Her body flailed.

After eight minutes, the struggling ceased. The henchmen released their grip. They stepped back as the hangman stepped forward.

Maria's body swayed now gently in the cold January air. The hangman approached it. He placed his ear to the chest and listened. He waved the prison doctors over. Each took a turn listening for a heartbeat.

The hangman walked solemnly over to Kronberg, who stood.

"I am reporting to the mighty king's attorney that I have carried out my duty."

Franklin, the sole mourner among the gathered, let out a piercing shriek.

By 9:00 A.M., the crowds on the square had dispersed. The Hotel Hungarian King had opened. The apothecary had opened. The post and telegraph office had opened. The bus had started its route again.

In the prison yard, Maria's body still hung from the gallows as snow began to fall.

THE AFTERMATH

By mid-September 1929, Kronberg would order an additional fifty bodies to be disinterred. By the end of the year, 162 bodies would be exhumed.

Kronberg's petition to have the death records of the previous twenty years examined was denied. He believed there were hundreds more victims.

The Royal Court of Szolnok would deem eighty-two deaths suspicious.

Indictments were brought against sixty-six women and seven men (as accomplices) from Nagyrév, Tiszakürt, and Cibakháza. Twenty-nine women and two men went to trial for the murder of forty-two men.

Sixteen women were convicted.

Both men who stood trial, Lawrence Szabó, for participating in the murder of his uncle, Stephen Szabó, and Joseph Madarász Jr., for the death of his father, Joseph Senior, were also convicted. They were sentenced to life.

Anna Cser was convicted of aggravated murder for her involvement in the death of her father-in-law and sentenced to fifteen years. Her sentence was reduced to eight years by a higher court. She was forty-five years old when she entered prison. Lewis died in 1936, two years before she was released.

Mari Fazekas was sentenced to ten years for the death of three-day-old Stephen Cser. Kronberg had asked for the death penalty. After serving two years in prison, her sentence was overturned by Hungary's Supreme Court. Fazekas returned to Nagyrév in 1932. She was officially dismissed as the village midwife in July of the same year. She fought the dismissal and filed a claim of compensation for lost work, which was denied. She lost her battle to be reinstated in 1935.

Kristina Csabai was convicted of the murder of her husband, Julius, and sentenced to fifteen years. Her sentence was upheld by higher courts. Although she confessed once, after a long period of solitary confinement, she otherwise maintained her innocence. She died in custody.

Mrs. Madarász received a sentence of eight years for conspiring to murder her father-in-law, Joseph Senior.

Petra Joljart Varga was convicted of the murder of her husband, Stephen Joljart, and sentenced to life. The decision was overturned by a higher court the following year, and she was acquitted of the charge.

Lidia Sebestyen was found guilty as accomplice to murder in the death of Charles Holyba, and sentenced to life in prison. The Supreme Court reduced her sentence to fifteen years.

Rose Holyba received a life sentence for the murder of Charles Holyba, which was upheld by the Supreme Court.

Esther Szabó was sentenced to death for the murder of Stephen Szabó. By the time she went to the gallows, she had given birth to a baby girl while in prison. The child was eleven months old when her mother was hanged. Esther was allowed to keep her child with her until an hour before her death and was reported to have maintained her composure until nearly the end. When she saw the scaffold, she fainted and had to be carried to the gallows.

Kristina Csordás was sentenced to death for the murder of Stephen Szabo.

Maria Szendi was the first woman to be hanged in Hungary in eighty years. She was buried in a public cemetery in Szolnok. The day before her execution, she dictated her will to Kronberg. She left everything to Franklin.

Along with Auntie Suzy and her neighbor, Julianna Petyus, two other women committed suicide, including one while in captivity in Szolnok the night before her trial began, and one whose lawyer arrived at her house in time to see her body being carried out. He had come to deliver the news that she was innocent, as no arsenic had been found in her dead husband's remains. Another woman was declared mentally unfit to stand trial and was committed to a psychiatric hospital.

Mari's estranged husband, Daniel, was never charged with a crime, and aided the gendarmes in their investigation.

Except for the abortions, Auntie Suzy was never formally charged with any crime.

In the early 1930s, unknown villagers set fire to Count Molnar's property. After this and other forms of intimidation, he left the village.

In 1935, Kronberg was made provisional president of the Royal Court of Szolnok, and in 1937 his appointment became official. In June 1945, he was appointed vice president of the Budapest prosecutor's office, and two years later he became president at large. He retired in 1953, and died in 1955 at the age of sixty-nine. His son, John Junior, followed in his footsteps and became a prosecutor in Szolnok.

Barny Szabó was captured by Nazis and, with other Jews of Szolnok, first kept in the yard of the synagogue, located near the home of his close friend Kronberg. He was then transported to a concentration camp that had been set up inside the sugar factory and kept there in squalid conditions. On June 29, 1944, he was among Szolnok's 2,038 Jews who were sent to Auschwitz. He did not survive.

Jack MacCormac left Vienna in 1931 and returned briefly to his native Canada before being assigned to cover Washington, D.C. At the outbreak of World War II, MacCormac—already a veteran of the Great War—was embedded with the Ninth Army. He was reassigned to the Vienna bureau after the war and continued there until his death of a massive heart attack while salmon fishing in Norway in 1956. He was sixty-eight years old.

Some would argue that Nagyrév today is as desolate as it was one hundred years ago. It saw relative prosperity under communism, when collective farms offered job security and everyone was guaranteed a pension, albeit a small one. During the early 1990s, the local economy was hard hit by the shift to a free market, and many residents abandoned the village and moved to larger towns and cities. In the latter part of the decade, a few of Budapest's young "new rich" pinned their hopes on an economic boom and bought cottages there, intending to use them as vacation homes. They never moved in. For a while, Auntie Suzy's house was owned by a priest. In the early aughts, her great-niece was the village librarian.

There is still no police force in the village.

POSTSCRIPT

Around one o'clock in the morning on Sunday, February 16, 1986, Tamara Chapman picked up a drink a customer had left for her. The protocol at Christos II Tavern, where nineteen-year-old Tamara had recently begun working, was for the bartender to put all the drinks that customers purchased for the waitstaff onto a drinks tray on a shelf behind the bar. After closing, the staff could consume them if they still wanted them.

As Tamara went to take a sip of the drink, an Irish whiskey concoction known as a B-52, she was overcome with the smell of ammonia even before she got the glass to her lips. It appeared to be wafting off the drink itself. The odor was horrific, and Tamara quickly slammed the drink back down onto the table. Who, she asked the barkeep, had left the B-52 for her? The bartender that evening was Marsha Veercamp, who told Tamara that a petite brunette dressed in an overcoat and a dark-colored beret had come in about forty minutes earlier and ordered the B-52, then shortly afterward gave the drink back to Marsha and told her to "make sure Tammy gets this," which was when Marsha put it on the drinks tray. When Tamara heard this, she knew exactly who had just tried to kill her.

It was the second attempt on her life that week.

Two days earlier, Tamara had been summoned to Joe Kool's, a new eatery on Richmond Street, by a woman named Diane. Tamara knew the woman. Diane was her boyfriend's previous girlfriend, and Diane had been trying all kinds of schemes to lure him back, including a fake pregnancy. When Tamara got Diane's message on her answering machine telling her to meet at Joe Kool's, she didn't know what to think. Diane had said Ken, the boyfriend, would be there and that the two of them had something they wanted to tell her. But Tamara knew Ken was out of town all week, in Windsor. Or at least that's where he was supposed to be. The last time she had spoken with him, he had given no indication that anything was wrong between them. And she expected to hear from him the following day, Valentine's Day. She hoped for flowers from him.

When Tamara entered the restaurant, she spotted Diane sitting alone at a booth. "Ken's going to be late," Diane said as Tamara approached the table. "He told us to wait for him at his apartment."

Unsure what to think, Tamara let Diane drive her to the apartment on Piccadilly Street. The two women entered the main door of the building, and Tamara watched as Diane fished a key from underneath a stairwell and opened Ken's apartment door with it.

Inside, Diane went straight into the kitchen. "Let me get you something to drink," Diane said, but Tamara refused. Diane began talking about Ken. "He doesn't love you. He loves me. It's time for you to end this," she said. Tamara resisted Diane's words. Suddenly, as if out of nowhere, an Irish whiskey was on the counter. Tamara wondered where it had come from, as Ken was more of a beer guy. She didn't even know he had Irish whiskey at his place. "Drink this. It will relax you."

Tamara felt pressured to take a sip. As soon as she did, her lips went numb. She could smell ammonia in the drink. Diane was watching her. Tamara calmly put the glass down, went over to the sink, and poured herself a glass of water. She was terrified.

"On second thought, I really shouldn't drink anything," she said to Diane. "I need to get to work."

The day following the incident with the second drink, Tamara and Ken, now back from Windsor, took the bar drink to the police station. There, it was determined that the B-52 had been laced with enough cyanide to kill Tamara six times over.

Sergeants Dave King and Mike Overdulve were assigned to the case. King's penchant for detective work served him well in his private life, where he was well-known among his family and friends as being a pretty adept historian, and someone who particularly indulged himself by poring over crimes long since lost to history.

The more Sergeant King learned about Diane, the more convinced he became about who she really was. On his days off, he began traveling to Ottawa, a six-hour drive from London, to further investigate her background, spending hours scrolling through microfiche.

"Poison is an invisible weapon used against a defenseless victim," said Assistant Crown Attorney David Arntfield at Diane's trial. She was convicted of attempted murder and sentenced to seven years in prison. When the verdict was read, Diane's father, Julius Fazekas, sobbed openly from the gallery.

By that time, King was quite familiar with Julius. Because of his research, he believed Julius to be the grandson of the infamous midwife in Nagyrév, and Diane Fazekas her great-granddaughter. If this is true, Diane had employed the same method her old-world ancestor had used sixty, seventy, eighty years before her, to rid the world of people who stood in her way.

NOTES AND EPHEMERA

ON THE LADIES, THEIR TRIALS, AND WHATNOT . . .

Lidia and Rose were tried together, and their trial was moved from an earlier date to Friday, December 13, 1929. Not only was this Friday the thirteenth, but it was—perhaps not coincidentally—Luca Day, well known regionally as the day of the wicked. Tradition dictated that on this day, men and boys would stand on a chair specially crafted for the day, and from this vantage point could spot all the witches in their midst.

There were two main lawyers the women hired for their trials, Mr. Kovacs and a lawyer named Julius (Gyula) Virag. Virag seemed to have modeled his courtroom style after that of Clarence Darrow, the American attorney who made impassioned pleas to save the lives of his two clients in the infamous Leopold and Loeb trial in 1924. However, Virag was shut down quickly each time he tried to make his own impassioned pleas on behalf of his clients. He also managed to nearly be held in contempt of court for witness tampering, when he went to Nagyrév to interview potential witnesses.

Before her trial, and presumably again before her execution, Maria Szendi wrote desperate appeals to her former connections in Budapest, the members of Parliament and the like who had once plied her with gifts and favors. She begged them to help get her exonerated. None of them responded.

In late September 1930, Mari's daughter, Lidia, paid a visit to the barrel maker Henry Toth, to feel him out as to whether or not he would say anything about when Mari and Auntie Suzy entered his stable on the night of baby Stephen's christening (and ultimately also the night of his death). Meanwhile, Mari wrote letters from prison, using rust peeled from the pipe in her cell, to instruct friends and family on how to testify. Her letters were intercepted by the guards and given to the prosecutor's office. The prosecutor considered both of these acts attempts to influence witnesses.

Petra Joljart Varga filed suit against the royal court after her conviction was overturned. She wanted compensation for lost work, reimbursement for expenses incurred while incarcerated, and damages for pain and suffering. After the court received her petition, Count Molnar called her into the village hall. When she arrived, she noticed a gendarme helmet on the table and a rifle in the corner. She was duly intimidated, and fled the village hall immediately. Molnar had spoken about her lawsuit with the president of the court, Joseph Borsos. His response? "What does this woman want? She should be happy that she is at home and should sit tight on her ass." Her case was ultimately rejected on the premise that she had been acquitted based on a lack of evidence, not innocence.

Four years after Maria was executed, her house was finally sold. Soon after the new owners took possession, they found a stash of arsenic hidden in a secret cabinet. The discovery made headlines in regional newspapers.

On the Village, and Such . . .

Nagyrév means "Big Port." The village was named in 1901.

In addition to the Cser pub, there was also Novak's pub, not far from Anna and Lewis's place. Around town, Mr. Novak was known as "Kiskalap," which means "little hat," because he wore a special type of round-brimmed hat of Tiszaföldvár, where he originally came from. There was also a pub and general store called Sárai's, which was farther from the village center.

In the 1930s, there were just under five hundred houses in the village. There were 329 horses, 414 cows, 1,274 pigs, and 49 sheep. There were four cabinetmakers, one cartwright, one barber, nine cobblers, three blacksmiths, two tailors, one miller, one barrel maker, three grocers, two haberdashers, and two drapers.

The roads in Nagyrév were not named until sometime after the Great War, possibly the 1920s.

Mr. Kodash, the baker, carried the loaves of bread on his back.

Children often made toy animals out of thistles. Boys often flew kites or played skittles, a type of bowling game.

In the 1920s, a movie theater opened up in Tiszakécske, and the kids from Nagyrév used to go there by ferry.

After the Great War, Hungarian peasant men began to wear work pants and dungarees, but until that time, they were usually seen wearing linen shirts and kilts. Their clothing looked like nightdresses, cinched with a belt.

Most Plains peasants, despite their work in the fields, were obsessively hygienic. They bathed even in the iciest water if it was the only means of getting clean.

Clothes were usually washed on Mondays or Tuesdays.

Farmers often slept in their boots, in case one of their animals needed them in the night. Many, even most, slept in the stables with them and had a space set up like a rudimentary bedroom.

The bell ringer rang the small bell 150 times and the large bell another 150 times, for a total of 300 times, to announce the death of a male. To announce the death of a female, each bell was rung 100 times.

Most girls didn't attend school past the second grade, which was enough schooling to learn how to read and write and to perform essential arithmetic. Most boys attended through third grade. Children wrote their lessons in the silty dirt or sand the teacher poured onto the tables. Maria attended school through the fifth grade and was considered well educated.

Babies were usually carried to their baptism wrapped in their mother's wedding shawl. If the family had a well in their yard, the baptismal water was taken from there, put into a jug, and carried to the church. After the baptism, it was traditional for the accompanying midwife or godmother to say: "We took in a little heathen and brought back an angel."

Well water was not always safe to drink, so alcoholic drinks were consumed instead. Alcohol was thought to ward off disease and therefore children were also given small doses. Unfortunately, the wide consumption of alcohol often led to addiction.

In a traditional village burial, after a grave is dug, leafy branches are placed over it to deter evil spirits from getting in before the coffin is lowered. After the coffin is nailed shut, it's carried out of the house feetfirst. Pallbearers knock it three times on the threshold, so the dead won't find their way back.

A pig roast (or "pig sticking") was traditionally held near Christmas or the new year. In some villages, the pig was killed on November 19, St. Elizabeth's Day, but only if it snowed (or "if Elizabeth shakes her petticoat").

Many Nagyrév villagers had their small vineyards in Tiszaföldvár, where the train station was located. Usually it was land they rented, probably from a member of the gentry.

Etc. . . .

Romany are not related to Romanians, although that is a common misconception.

Midwives had long been critical for family planning. Women relied on them to terminate unwanted pregnancies as safely as possible. There were various methods employed, but often herbs were used, and Auntie Suzy would have used herbs for most abortions she performed. Side effects could be severe, even fatal, and it would have been challenging for her to ensure the herbs were taken as prescribed, as in many cases, the dosage itself was tricky. For example, a tincture of 30 drops, 3 to 4 times a day; or 3 teaspoons per cup, 1 quart daily. A slight variation could have dire consequences.

White arsenic, the "poison of poisons," can have a range of effects, and is toxic even in the tiniest doses. Symptoms of poisoning can include a sharp, burning pain in the stomach and esophagus; dry mouth; tightness in the throat; profuse vomiting and diarrhea; intense hiccupping; milky/watery stools or bright green stools; damage to the heart and veins; low blood pressure; decreased circulation, which causes blue skin; cold or clammy hands and feet; and convulsions.

In smaller doses over a period of time, the victim can suffer severe headache, vertigo, muscle cramps, kidney failure, nerve damage, hair loss, muscular atrophy, water on the brain, paralysis, and nausea, vomiting, and diarrhea.

On Hungary...

The Curse of Turan is alleged to have begun in 1000 C.E., when King Stephen declared that Hungary would convert to Christianity. The legend goes that a powerful shaman issued a curse that would last one thousand years as a protest to Christian rule.

After the Red Terror came the backlash White Terror, wherein counterrevolutionaries sought revenge, mostly on innocent Jews and peasants.

In the aftermath of the Great War—and the Red Terror and White Terror that followed—came the question: What should Hungary be? Most Magyars wanted to return the country to a kingdom. But Central Powers made it clear a return of a Habsburg to the throne would not be tolerated. The names of other nobles were bandied about, including Count László Széchenyi, chiefly because he was married to the wealthy American aristocrat Gladys Vanderbilt. The kingdom was reestablished with Admiral Horthy as regent. He was given nearly all the powers of the crown. Under his rule, Hungary became a "kingdom with a king, ruled by an admiral without a fleet in a country without a coastline."

Hyperinflation set in at the start of the 1920s, and between 1922 and 1924, the inflation rate was 98 percent.

Spanish flu hit Hungary in September 1918 and carried on for eighteen months. Half of the population fell ill with the virus, and an estimated one hundred thousand died from it (of a postwar population of less than eight million). Half of those who died were between the ages of twenty-five and forty-five. The mortality of health care workers was extremely high.

It's presumed that all contemporary coroners—what Hungarians called "bell ringers"—are medical examiners, but even today that's not always the case. For example, sixteen hundred American counties employ coroners who have no medical background. They are not allowed to perform autopsies, but can pronounce deaths and sign death certificates. They are usually elected positions and pay minimally.

On Szolnok, and Such . . .

Governor Almásy was a relative of László Almásy, the protagonist in *The English Patient*.

The grandfather of Nicolas Sarkozy, the former prime minister of France, was vice mayor of Szolnok at the time of the trials.

The Hotel National was developed and built by two brothers, who happened to be the father and uncle of Mike (given name "Marcel") Fodor and his sister Elizabeth (Erzsébet in Hungarian, or Erzsi). The Hotel National was later renamed the Hotel Grand and was used as a field hospital during World War II.

The Hotel Tisza was built with post–World War I reconstruction money. It became the place where aristocrats gathered for afternoon teas at 5:00 P.M. In the 1930s, it became a gathering spot for jazz performers, and it is rumored that Louis Armstrong stayed there when he visited the city.

The artist colony in Szolnok, which Kronberg frequented, is arguably the oldest in Hungary. Toward the end of the 1920s, there was a move to establish a coalition with an American art academy. This push was made by well-regarded artist Tibor Pólya, who spent three years in the United States trying to get it off the ground.

In addition to 1924 Olympian Gisella Tary, Szolnok had another fencing Olympian in the 1928 games, Gyula Glykais. Glykais and his team won gold medals in '28 and '32. He practiced in the cellar of the city hall building. It is unclear where Tary practiced.

The arsenic trials were covered by nearly every major European, British, and American newspaper, and were still capturing attention as late as 1937, when the *Oakland Tribune* ran a two-page spread on the murderers. *Ripley's Believe It or Not* ran a feature in 1933. The New York trial of Ruth Snyder, accused of the murder of her husband, drew the same kind of attention in 1927 that Maria's trial drew in 1930 in central Hungary. Both women were tried in front of sellout crowds, and both were horribly disparaged by the press (as were all the women involved in the arsenic trials). The *Daily Mirror* hired a phrenologist, who described Ruth's eyelids and mouth as "hard, unsympathetic, as cracked as a dried lemon." He said she had the character of a "shallow-brained pleasure-seeker, accustomed to unlimited self-indulgence. . . ." For Maria, famous writers hired themselves out to write of her horrid character.

Revered writer Zsigmond Móricz, who had a front-row seat at Maria's trial, described her as "revolting," and said that she looked and behaved like a "corrupt working-class woman . . . she speaks in the worst dialect of the capital, using words either out of place or unexpected from a peasant woman." All of the women on trial were "dissolute bitches, village sluts, perverts," and "prisoners of their sexual desire."

Móricz visited Nagyrév at the time of the trials and was given a tour by Michael Kardos's sister. He later labeled the village "the island of nobody."

June 2 to September 19, 1944, was the "Frantic Attack" on the region by American and British forces. Szolnok was bombed twelve times, causing devastating damage and significant loss of life. The train station was also bombed several times. When Soviet troops entered the city, they found only a couple of thousand residents remaining.

Kronberg's son, John Junior, in a letter to Budapest authorities, describes the family's hardship during and after the Frantic Attack. By this time, John Junior was a prosecutor with the Royal Court of Szolnok. (He does not mention in the letter that John and Irene Kronberg's Szolnok house was eventually ransacked by the Nazis. John Senior's precious art collection was stolen at this time.)

June 2, 1944, was the first bombing of Szolnok by the Americans. I escaped to the [nearby] vineyards with the permission of the president of the court. Later, we moved to Tószeg [7.5 miles south of Szolnok], from where I traveled to the office together with my father by bicycle. My father was already ill with coronary artery problems. It was dangerous for him to ride 22 km a day by bicycle [13.7 miles]. In the late days of September, he could no longer travel to the office.

On October 7, the president of the court declared that soon the city

will be evacuated. I sent a horse carriage to Tószeg for my parents, but
my father had a heart attack, and he was transferred to the hospital.
My mother also stayed in the hospital, as she was sick, too. A military
doctor—who was on holiday and was the father-in-law of one of the
employees of the hospital—gave an injection to my father. They could not
give lunch to my father in the hospital, nor to the other patients, because
there was not enough food. I could buy only a few apples with worms in
the nearby shop. My father could eat only fruits, and could not drink any
fluid. We finally were able to transfer him and my mother to Budapest, to
the Szt. Rókus Hospital. . . . I had to find work to pay for this, so I applied
for a job in the Ministry. In November, finally I got a job in the Budapest
Criminal Court, but I could not start working, because of the "Nyilas"[*]
government. During the bombing of Budapest, we had to hide ourselves.
After that, my wife and I returned to Szolnok by foot [a distance of
sixty-eight miles].

On the Newsmen and -women of the Day . . .

News correspondent Dorothy Thompson arrived in Vienna in 1921
and called it "a scenic little slum." She found the postwar city, once
the epicenter of a mighty empire, now "a city of dread," on the edge of
famine, teeming with refugees, soldiers, welfare commissioners, free-
booters, profiteers, displaced peasants, and an assortment of "gentle
folk starving gracefully in Biedermeier salons."

Much can be found online about Mike Fodor's prolific career and his
extraordinary generosity to fellow journalists. Dan Durning's "Vienna's
Café Louvre in the 1920s and 1930s" offers a fascinating look at the
role cafés played for journalists during that era.

In 1934, Fodor and John Gunther were the first reporters to interview Hitler's relatives and show the relative poverty Hitler had grown
up in. The disclosure infuriated the Nazi Party, and Fodor and Gunther
were placed on a Gestapo "death list." In 1938, Fodor had a harrowing
escape from the Nazis that led him out of Austria after the Anschluss

---

[*] Nyilaskeresztes Party, also known as the Arrow Cross, a far-right party in power
from October 1944 to March 1945. Under its brief rule, up to fifteen thousand ci-
vilians were murdered by the government.

into Czechoslovakia, Belgium, then France, before finally finding refuge in the United States in 1940 for the duration of the war.

Fodor's sister Elizabeth was married to Andor de Pünkösti, a highly decorated soldier in an elite regiment, who in the post–World War I chaos fought against Béla Kun's regime. He became an ardent Horthyist, but when Horthy finally caved to the Hungarian Nazis, or Arrow Cross, he opposed them as well. According to Mike Fodor's son Denis—a career journalist for *Time*—when a team of secret police came to the door of Elizabeth and Andor's house, Andor shot them dead, then killed himself, having vowed never to be taken down by the fascists.

Elizabeth died of a heart attack in 1953. Communists had taken over every room of her house, except her bedroom and the bedroom of her maid.

Jack MacCormac was probably the most uncelebrated foreign correspondent of the "golden age of journalism," and presumably this was his own doing. He was a Canadian, born and raised in Ottawa. He was the second of ten children, although his elder sister died early in life. At twenty-three, he became the youngest member of the Ottawa Parliament press gallery, and in 1916, at twenty-four, he became an officer in the Eighth Canadian Siege Battery. While serving in France, he was awarded the Military Cross for "acts of exemplary gallantry during active operations against the enemy."

(MacCormac's father is credited with saving the parliamentary library on February 3, 1916, when he, a librarian, raced to close the iron doors after a fire broke out in the House of Commons Reading Room. The quick-thinking act preserved the library and its priceless contents, while the rest of Parliament was consumed by the blaze. It also preserved Conny MacCormac's place in Canadian history.)

In 1929, Jack and Molly lived at 8 Rosenbursenstrasse in Vienna, where the *New York Times* bureau was also located. For context, Sigmund Freud lived a couple of miles away at that time.

Jack was recalled from Vienna in 1933 and went back to London and then to Washington, D.C., and finally joined, as a member of the press corps, the march of the U.S. Ninth Army as it advanced toward

Germany in 1944. The following year, he returned to Vienna, which was once again ravaged by war.

A little more than a decade later, he was expelled from Budapest during the 1956 revolt, but not before seeking refuge for two weeks in the U.S. legation there. His time spent covering the crisis affected him deeply. In November 1956, he wrote the following to fellow journalist Simon Bourgin: "For the rest of my life I shall never be able to think of [the Hungarian Revolution] without a lump in my throat. Half the time I had tears in my eyes. I doubt if ever a newspaperman has covered a story which so tore at their emotions. It was terrible to see it fail and know that you were a part of the West that had failed them." Kati Marton writes about Jack's time in Budapest during the revolt in her book *Enemies of the People.*

MacCormac was so revered by his colleagues that his fellow journalist C. L. Sulzberger, whose family owned the *New York Times,* wrote a tribute to him in addition to the obituary that ran in the paper. In it, he praised MacCormac as "one of the most courteous, decent, gallant, honest newspapermen who ever lived." Sulzberger gave evidence of the gallantry: "Only a few years ago . . . he attended a gay Viennese Bal Masque and, when an enthusiastic, somewhat bibulous roughneck attacked a friend of his, dispatched that individual with grace and efficiency, posing thereafter (well lit, with a benign smile and florid costume), with one foot upon the neck of the prostrate victim."

Paul Lendvai, a long-standing and powerful presence in Austrian media, was a protégé of Jack MacCormac, who hired him after Lendvai fled the Soviet crackdown in 1956. Lendvai had this to say of his mentor: He was a "withdrawn, quiet gentleman. He was very distinguished, and so exceedingly helpful. For me, he was a symbol of what is best in journalism."

On Diane Fazekas . . .

Her sentence was reduced to five years. She was released to a halfway house soon afterward, where she served out the rest of her sentence. Tamara and Ken eventually married. Tamara saw Diane only once, by accident at a skating arena, ten years after the conviction.

SELECTED BIBLIOGRAPHY

I list here only the primary sources used in piecing together events, as well as monographs I found useful for understanding village life in the region (known locally as Tiszazug).

This bibliography is by no means a complete record of all the works and sources I have consulted, or interviews I have conducted. It is intended for those who want to further explore the "arsenic trials" and the circumstances under which they occurred.

Bodó, Béla, Ph.D. *Tiszazug: A Social History of a Murder Epidemic,* 1st ed. East European Monographs, 2002.

Durning, Dan, Ph.D. *Vienna's Café Louvre in the 1920s and 1930s: Meeting Place for Foreign Correspondents,* Version 1.0. www.academia.edu. 2012.

Fél, Edit and Tamás Hofer. *Proper Peasants: Traditional Life in a Hungarian Village.* Subscriber's ed. *Viking Fund Publications in Anthropology* 46, 1969.

The Hungarian National Archives, Jász-Nagykun-Szolnok County Archives. All materials related to the arsenic trials—HU-MNL-JNSZML-VII.1.a.-1929.-13, et al.

Kis Hírlap, selected articles. 1929.

Kis Újság, selected articles. 1929, 1930.

Magyar Telegráfiai Hirügynökségmti (Hungarian Telegraphic News Agency). *Texts of Reports Made About the Trials of the Tiszazug Arsenic Women.* 1930.

New York Times, selected articles. 1929, 1930, 1931.

Pesti Napló, selected articles. 1929.

Szolnok Újság, selected articles. 1929, 1930, 1931.

ACKNOWLEDGMENTS

Shortly after I finished the proposal for this book, which is my first, I learned my father was dying. He was actively dying, a term I recently learned. He was very awake and alert, but with only 5 percent of his heart still working, he had just hours left with us. I Skyped into his Jacksonville, Florida, hospital room from my home in Austria for my last words with him. "I want you to know," I said, at some point in the conversation, "I'm dedicating my book to you."

"Oh, wow," he said. He was clearly moved. He eased his head back on his pillow as he took in the news. He paused a beat, then slowly lifted his head back up. "Wait a minute," he said. He'd had a moment to consider my gesture. "Isn't that book about all those ladies who killed all those men?" I could hear the doctors and nurses in his room break out laughing. My father was pleased with himself. I told him he'd have to take it or leave it, as it might be the only book I write. "I'll take it," he said. He was smiling.

I didn't know then how long it would take to birth this book, or that I would have to write it in three different countries and two U.S. states, including, somewhere in there, borrowed space at a church. As the length of time grew, so did the grace of those around me. I owe the deepest debt of gratitude first and foremost to my agent, Joe Veltre, of the Gersh Agency, for standing by me, and for championing this book. My editors, Mauro DiPreta and Andrew Yackira, provided the deft skill and encouragement I needed. A very special thanks to the American Society of Journalists and Authors, for their grant that saved me.

How to thank my extraordinary assistant, the inimitable and aptly named historian, Attila Tokai, who understood from the first minute what I was after? If you have to spend months in a hot, airless, poorly lit room poring over one-hundred-year-old handwritten documents, do it with Attila. With all of my heart, I thank you, Attila.

A profound thank-you to my sister, Jude, for her virtual hand-holding, her many, many selfless journeys, and most of all for reminding me to dance in the sand. To the rest of my siblings—Steve, John, Sarah, and Joellyn—who are remarkable cheerleaders. To my "almost" grandpaw, Worth Kidd, the first real writer I ever knew, who keeps showing up in my dreams. To Mama, for Rosamund and Candy.

To my primary reader, Jon Dathen, for his Romany soul and his ability to talk me back from a ledge. Thank you to my core readers: not only Jon, but Andie Warren, Carolyn McSparren, Janine Latus. Thank you to Jon Krasnoff and Wendi Sugarman, for their love. Thank you to Eric and Robin Turner, for Martha's Vineyard; to Lisa Stillman and Jessie Songco, for Pinkie the Truck and their all around goodness; to Lizzy Schule, for holding space for me when I needed it most.

A heartfelt thanks goes to the people at the Hungarian National Archives in Szolnok, all of whom were patient with me and Attila for months on end, and as accommodating as they could possibly be. I am forever in your debt. Special thanks to Drs. Benedek Varga and László Magyar of the Semmelweis Library for History of Medicine; to the Geographical Museum of Tiszazug; to the Szolnok County Court, specifically prosecutor Árpád Varga; to the people of the Szolnok prison, who let me tour at length; to criminal psychiatrist Dr. Max Friedrich of the University of Vienna; to the Church of Jesus Christ of Latter-Day Saints for its assistance in locating vital records; to my translators, Ildikó Terenyei and Maria Szurmai; to the Kronberg family; to Paul Lendvai, Mollie MacCormac, and Denis Fodor, for letting me in on who Jack MacCormac really was; and to Tamara Chapman and Mike Overdulve for their cooperation. Thank you to all the people of Szolnok and Nagyrév who assisted me in countless ways.

Vielen Dank to my former neighbor in Austria, Harald Leban, who made that first trip to Nagyrév with me, and to Milojka Gindl, for being Milojka. Thank you to my dear Remi, my beloved friend, who showed up in this life as a dog. And last, a most sincere thank-you to Eduardo, the Magician.

ABOUT THE AUTHOR

Patti McCracken was born in Virginia Beach, Virginia, in October 1964. At fifteen, she moved with her family to Clearwater, Florida. After college, she worked for a newsmagazine in Washington, D.C., for a decade before moving to Chicago, where she was an assistant editor at the *Chicago Tribune*. She eventually relocated to Europe, where she was a journalism trainer, free press advocate, and newsroom consultant for the then-emerging democracies of the former Soviet bloc. She was based in an Austrian village, but her work often included long stints in Eastern and Central Europe, the Balkans, the Caucasus, and later North Africa and Southeast Asia. She was twice a Knight International Press Fellow. Over more than twenty years, her articles have appeared in *Chicago Tribune*, *San Francisco Chronicle*, *Wall Street Journal*, *Guardian*, *Smithsonian* magazine, and many more outlets. This is her first book.

After seventeen years abroad, McCracken returned to the United States. She now resides on Martha's Vineyard. For more information, visit the author's website at PattiMcCracken.com.